PostgreSQL Replication

Second Edition

Leverage the power of PostgreSQL replication to make your databases more robust, secure, scalable, and fast

Hans-Jürgen Schönig

BIRMINGHAM - MUMBAI

PostgreSQL Replication
Second Edition

First published: August 2013

Second edition: July 2015

Production reference: 1240715

Published by Packt Publishing Ltd.
Livery Place
35 Livery Street
Birmingham B3 2PB, UK.

ISBN 978-1-78355-060-9

www.packtpub.com

Credits

Author
Hans-Jürgen Schönig

Reviewers
Swathi Kurunji
Jeff Lawson
Maurício Linhares
Shaun M. Thomas
Tomas Vondra

Commissioning Editor
Kartikey Pandey

Acquisition Editor
Larissa Pinto

Content Development Editor
Nikhil Potdukhe

Technical Editor
Manali Gonsalves

Copy Editors
Dipti Mankame
Vikrant Phadke

Project Coordinator
Vijay Kushlani

Proofreader
Safis Editing

Indexer
Priya Sane

Graphics
Sheetal Aute

Production Coordinator
Komal Ramchandani

Cover Work
Komal Ramchandani

About the Author

Hans-Jürgen Schönig has 15 years of experience with PostgreSQL. He is the CEO of a PostgreSQL consulting and support company called Cybertec Schönig & Schönig GmbH (www.postgresql-support.de). It has successfully served countless customers around the globe.

Before founding Cybertec Schönig & Schönig GmbH in 2000, he worked as a database developer at a private research company focusing on the Austrian labor market, where he primarily focused on data mining and forecast models. He has also written several books about PostgreSQL.

This book is dedicated to all the members of the Cybertec family, who have supported me over the years and have proven to be true professionals. Without my fellow technicians here at Cybertec, this book would not have existed. I especially want to thank Ants Aasma for his technical input and Florian Ziegler for helping out with the proofreading and graphical stuff.

Special thanks also go to my girl, Sonja Städtner, who has given me all the personal support. Somehow, she managed to make me go to sleep when I was up late at night working on the initial drafts.

About the Reviewers

Swathi Kurunji is a software engineer at Actian Corporation. She recently completed her PhD in computer science from the University of Massachusetts Lowell (UMass Lowell), USA. She has a keen interest in database systems. Her PhD research involved query optimization, big data analysis, data warehousing, and cloud computing. Swathi has shown excellence in her field of study through research publications at international conferences and in journals. She has received awards and scholarships from UMass Lowell for research and academics.

Swathi also has a master's of science degree in computer science from UMass Lowell and a bachelor's of engineering degree in information science from KVGCE in India. During her studies at UMass Lowell, she worked as a teaching assistant, helping professors in teaching classes and labs, designing projects, and grading exams.

She has worked as a software development intern with IT companies such as EMC and SAP. At EMC, she gained experience on Apache Cassandra data modeling and performance analysis. At SAP, she gained experience on the infrastructure/cluster management components of the Sybase IQ product. She has also worked with Wipro Technologies in India as a project engineer, managing application servers.

She has extensive experience with database systems such as Apache Cassandra, Sybase IQ, Oracle, MySQL, and MS Access. Her interests include software design and development, big data analysis, optimization of databases, and cloud computing. Her LinkedIn profile is `http://www.linkedin.com/pub/swathi-kurunji/49/578/30a/`.

Swathi has previously reviewed two books, *Cassandra Data Modeling and Analysis* and *Mastering Apache Cassandra*, both by Packt Publishing.

I would like to thank my husband and my family for all their support.

Jeff Lawson has been a user and fan of PostgreSQL since he noticed it in 2001. Over the years, he has also developed and deployed applications for IBM DB2, Oracle, MySQL, Microsoft SQL Server, Sybase, and others, but he has always preferred PostgreSQL because of its balance of features and openness. Much of his experience has spanned development for Internet-facing websites and projects that required highly scalable databases with high availability or provisions for disaster recovery.

Jeff currently works as the director of software development at FlightAware, which is an airplane tracking website that uses PostgreSQL and other pieces of open source software to store and analyze the positions of thousands of flights that fly worldwide every day. He has extensive experience in software architecture, data security, and networking protocol design because of his roles as a software engineer at Univa/ United Devices, Microsoft, NASA's Jet Propulsion Laboratory, and WolfeTech. He was a founder of distributed.net, which pioneered distributed computing in the 1990s, and continues to serve as the chief of operations and a member of the board. He earned a BSc in computer science from Harvey Mudd College.

Jeff is fond of cattle, holds an FAA private pilot certificate, and owns an airplane in Houston, Texas.

Maurício Linhares is a technical leader of the parsing and machine learning team at The Neat Company. At Neat, he helps his team scale their solutions on the cloud and deliver fast results to customers. He is the creator and maintainer of async, a Scala-based PostgreSQL database driver (`https://github.com/mauricio/postgresql-async`), and has been a PostgreSQL user and proponent for many years.

Shaun M. Thomas has been working with PostgreSQL since late 2000. He has presented at Postgres open conferences in 2011, 2012, and 2014 on topics such as handling extreme throughput, high availability, server redundancy, failover techniques, and system monitoring. With the recent publication of Packt Publishing's *PostgreSQL 9 High Availability Cookbook*, he hopes to make life easier for DBAs using PostgreSQL in enterprise environments.

Currently, Shaun serves as the database architect at Peak6, an options trading firm with a PostgreSQL constellation of over 100 instances, one of which is over 15 TB in size.

He wants to prove that PostgreSQL is more than ready for major installations.

Tomas Vondra has been working with PostgreSQL since 2003, and although he had worked with various other databases — both open-source and proprietary — he instantly fell in love with PostgreSQL and the community around it.

He is currently working as an engineer at 2ndQuadrant, one of the companies that provide support, training, and other services related to PostgreSQL. Previously, he worked as a PostgreSQL specialist for GoodData, a company that operates a BI cloud platform built on PostgreSQL. He has extensive experience with performance troubleshooting, tuning, and benchmarking.

In his free time, he usually writes PostgreSQL extensions or patches, or he hacks something related to PostgreSQL.

www.PacktPub.com

Support files, eBooks, discount offers, and more

For support files and downloads related to your book, please visit www.PacktPub.com.

Did you know that Packt offers eBook versions of every book published, with PDF and ePub files available? You can upgrade to the eBook version at www.PacktPub.com and as a print book customer, you are entitled to a discount on the eBook copy. Get in touch with us at service@packtpub.com for more details.

At www.PacktPub.com, you can also read a collection of free technical articles, sign up for a range of free newsletters and receive exclusive discounts and offers on Packt books and eBooks.

https://www2.packtpub.com/books/subscription/packtlib

Do you need instant solutions to your IT questions? PacktLib is Packt's online digital book library. Here, you can search, access, and read Packt's entire library of books.

Why subscribe?

- Fully searchable across every book published by Packt
- Copy and paste, print, and bookmark content
- On demand and accessible via a web browser

Free access for Packt account holders

If you have an account with Packt at www.PacktPub.com, you can use this to access PacktLib today and view 9 entirely free books. Simply use your login credentials for immediate access.

Table of Contents

Preface

Since the first edition of *PostgreSQL Replication* many new technologies have emerged or improved. In the PostgreSQL community, countless people around the globe have been working on important techniques and technologies to make PostgreSQL even more useful and more powerful.

To make sure that readers can enjoy all those new features and powerful tools, I have decided to write a second, improved edition of *PostgreSQL Replication*. Due to the success of the first edition, the hope is to make this one even more useful to administrators and developers alike around the globe.

All the important new developments have been covered and most chapters have been reworked to make them easier to understand, more complete and absolutely up to date.

I hope that all of you can enjoy this book and benefit from it.

What this book covers

This book will guide you through a variety of topics related to PostgreSQL replication. We will present all the important facts in 15 practical and easy-to-read chapters:

Chapter 1, Understanding the Concepts of Replication, guides you through fundamental replication concepts such as synchronous, as well as asynchronous, replication. You will learn about the physical limitations of replication, which options you have and what kind of distinctions there are.

Chapter 2, Understanding the PostgreSQL Transaction Log, introduces you to the PostgreSQL internal transaction log machinery and presents concepts essential to many replication techniques.

Chapter 3, Understanding Point-in-time Recovery, is the next logical step and outlines how the PostgreSQL transaction log will help you to utilize Point-in-time Recovery to move your database instance back to a desired point in time.

Chapter 4, Setting Up Asynchronous Replication, describes how to configure asynchronous master-slave replication.

Chapter 5, Setting Up Synchronous Replication, is one step beyond asynchronous replication and offers a way to guarantee zero data loss if a node fails. You will learn about all the aspects of synchronous replication.

Chapter 6, Monitoring Your Setup, covers PostgreSQL monitoring.

Chapter 7, Understanding Linux High Availability, presents a basic introduction to Linux-HA and presents a set of ideas for making your systems more available and more secure. Since the first edition, this chapter has been completely rewritten and made a lot more practical.

Chapter 8, Working with PgBouncer, deals with PgBouncer, which is very often used along with PostgreSQL replication. You will learn how to configure PgBouncer and boost the performance of your PostgreSQL infrastructure.

Chapter 9, Working with pgpool, covers one more tool capable of handling replication and PostgreSQL connection pooling.

Chapter 10, Configuring Slony, contains a practical guide to using Slony and shows how you can use this tool fast and efficiently to replicate sets of tables.

Chapter 11, Using SkyTools, offers you an alternative to Slony and outlines how you can introduce generic queues to PostgreSQL and utilize Londiste replication to dispatch data in a large infrastructure.

Chapter 12, Working with Postgres-XC, offers an introduction to a synchronous multimaster replication solution capable of partitioning a query across many nodes inside your cluster while still providing you with a consistent view of the data.

Chapter 13, Scaling with PL/Proxy, describes how you can break the chains and scale out infinitely across a large server farm.

Chapter 14, Scaling with BDR, describes the basic concepts and workings of the BDR replication system. It shows how BDR can be configured and how it operates as the basis for a modern PostgreSQL cluster.

Chapter 15, Working with Walbouncer, shows how transaction log can be replicated partially using the walbouncer tool. It dissects the PostgreSQL XLOG and makes sure that the transaction log stream can be distributed to many nodes in the cluster.

What you need for this book

This guide is a must for everybody interested in PostgreSQL replication. It is a comprehensive book explaining replication in a comprehensive and detailed way. We offer a theoretical background as well as a practical introduction to replication designed to make your daily life a lot easier and definitely more productive.

Who this book is for

This book has been written primary for system administrators and system architects. However, we have also included aspects that can be highly interesting for software developers as well—especially when it comes to highly critical system designs.

Conventions

In this book, you will find a number of text styles that distinguish between different kinds of information. Here are some examples of these styles and an explanation of their meaning.

Code words in text, database table names, folder names, filenames, file extensions, pathnames, dummy URLs, user input, and Twitter handles are shown as follows: "We can include other contexts through the use of the include directive."

A block of code is set as follows:

```
checkpoint_segments = 3
checkpoint_timeout = 5min
checkpoint_completion_target = 0.5
checkpoint_warning = 30s
```

When we wish to draw your attention to a particular part of a code block, the relevant lines or items are set in bold:

```
checkpoint_segments = 3
checkpoint_timeout = 5min
checkpoint_completion_target = 0.5
checkpoint_warning = 30s
```

Any command-line input or output is written as follows:

```
test=# CREATE TABLE t_test (id int4);
CREATE TABLE
```

New terms and **important words** are shown in bold. Words that you see on the screen, for example, in menus or dialog boxes, appear in the text like this: "Clicking the **Next** button moves you to the next screen."

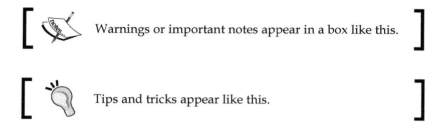

Warnings or important notes appear in a box like this.

Tips and tricks appear like this.

Reader feedback

Feedback from our readers is always welcome. Let us know what you think about this book—what you liked or disliked. Reader feedback is important for us as it helps us develop titles that you will really get the most out of.

To send us general feedback, simply e-mail feedback@packtpub.com, and mention the book's title in the subject of your message.

If there is a topic that you have expertise in and you are interested in either writing or contributing to a book, see our author guide at www.packtpub.com/authors.

Customer support

Now that you are the proud owner of a Packt book, we have a number of things to help you to get the most from your purchase.

Errata

Although we have taken every care to ensure the accuracy of our content, mistakes do happen. If you find a mistake in one of our books—maybe a mistake in the text or the code—we would be grateful if you could report this to us. By doing so, you can save other readers from frustration and help us improve subsequent versions of this book. If you find any errata, please report them by visiting http://www.packtpub.com/submit-errata, selecting your book, clicking on the **Errata Submission Form** link, and entering the details of your errata. Once your errata are verified, your submission will be accepted and the errata will be uploaded to our website or added to any list of existing errata under the Errata section of that title.

To view the previously submitted errata, go to https://www.packtpub.com/books/content/support and enter the name of the book in the search field. The required information will appear under the **Errata** section.

Piracy

Piracy of copyrighted material on the Internet is an ongoing problem across all media. At Packt, we take the protection of our copyright and licenses very seriously. If you come across any illegal copies of our works in any form on the Internet, please provide us with the location address or website name immediately so that we can pursue a remedy.

Please contact us at copyright@packtpub.com with a link to the suspected pirated material.

We appreciate your help in protecting our authors and our ability to bring you valuable content.

Questions

If you have a problem with any aspect of this book, you can contact us at questions@packtpub.com, and we will do our best to address the problem.

1
Understanding the Concepts of Replication

Replication is an important issue and, in order to get started, it is highly important to understand some basic concepts and theoretical ideas related to replication. In this chapter, you will be introduced to various concepts of replication, and learn which kind of replication is most suitable for which kind of practical scenario. By the end of the chapter, you will be able to judge whether a certain concept is feasible under various circumstances or not.

We will cover the following topics in this chapter:

- The CAP theorem and physical limitations of replication
- Different types of replication
- Synchronous and asynchronous replication
- Sharding and data distribution

The goal of this chapter is to give you a lot of insights into the theoretical concepts. This is truly important in order to judge whether a certain customer requirement is actually technically feasible or not. You will be guided through the fundamental ideas and important concepts related to replication.

The CAP theorem and physical limitations of replication

You might wonder why theory is being covered in such a prominent place in a book that is supposed to be highly practical. Well, there is a very simple reason for that: some nice-looking marketing papers of some commercial database vendors might leave you with the impression that everything is possible and easy to do, without any serious limitation. This is not the case; there are physical limitations that every software vendor has to cope with. There is simply no way around the laws of nature, and shiny marketing cannot help overcome nature. The laws of physics and logic are the same for everybody, regardless of the power of someone's marketing department.

In this section, you will be taught the so-called CAP theorem. Understanding the basic ideas of this theorem is essential to avoid some requirements that cannot be turned into reality.

The CAP theorem was first described by Eric Brewer back in the year 2000. It has quickly developed into one of the most fundamental concepts in the database world. Especially with the rise of NoSQL database systems, Brewer's theorem (as the CAP theorem is often called) has become an important cornerstone of every distributed system.

Understanding the CAP theorem

Before we dig into the details, we need to discuss what **CAP** actually means. CAP is an abbreviation for the following three concepts:

- **Consistency**: This term indicates whether all the nodes in a cluster see the same data at the same time or not. A read-only node has to see all previously completed reads at any time.

- **Availability**: Reads and writes have to succeed all the time. In other words a node has to be available for users at any point of time.

- **Partition tolerance**: This means that the system will continue to work even if arbitrary messages are lost on the way. A *network partition* event occurs when a system is no longer accessible (think of a network connection failure). A different way of considering partition tolerance is to think of it as message passing. If an individual system can no longer send or receive messages from other systems, it means that it has been effectively *partitioned* out of the network. The guaranteed properties are maintained even when network failures prevent some machines from communicating with others.

Why are these three concepts relevant to normal users? Well, the bad news is that a replicated (or distributed) system can provide *only* two out of these three features at the same time.

 Keep in mind that only two out of the three promises can be fulfilled.

It is theoretically impossible to offer consistency, availability, and partition tolerance at the same time. As you will see later in this book, this can have a significant impact on system layouts that are safe and feasible to use. There is simply no such thing as *the* solution to all replication-related problems. When you are planning a large-scale system, you might have to come up with different concepts, depending on needs that are specific to your requirements.

 PostgreSQL, Oracle, DB2, and so on will provide you with CAp ("consistent" and "available"), while NoSQL systems, such as MongoDB and Cassandra, will provide you with cAP ("available" and "partition tolerant"). This is why NoSQL is often referred to as eventually consistent.

Consider a financial application. You really want to be consistent and partition tolerant. Keeping balances in sync is the highest priority.

Or consider an application collecting a log of weather data from some remote locations. If the data is a couple of minutes late, it is really no problem. In this case, you might want to go for cAP. Availability and partition tolerance might really be the most important things in this case.

Depending on the use, people have to decide what is really important and which attributes (consistency, availability, or partition tolerance) are crucial and which can be neglected.

Keep in mind there is no system which can fulfill all those wishes at the same time (neither open source nor paid software).

Understanding the limits of physics

The speed of light is not just a theoretical issue; it really does have an impact on your daily life. And more importantly, it has a serious implication when it comes to finding the right solution for your cluster.

We all know that there is some sort of cosmic speed limit called the speed of light. So why care? Well, let's do a simple mental experiment. Let's assume for a second that our database server is running at 3 GHz clock speed.

How far can light travel within one clock cycle of your CPU? If you do the math, you will figure out that light travels around 10 cm per clock cycle (in pure vacuum). We can safely assume that an electric signal inside a CPU will be very slow compared to pure light in vacuum. The core idea is, "10 cm in one clock cycle? Well, this is not much at all."

For the sake of our mental experiment, let's now consider various distances:

- Distance from one end of the CPU to the other
- Distance from your server to some other server next door
- Distance from your server in Central Europe to a server somewhere in China

Considering the size of a CPU core on a die, you can assume that you can send a signal (even if it is not traveling anywhere close to the speed of light) from one part of the CPU to some other part quite fast. It simply won't take 1 million clock cycles to add up two numbers that are already in your first level cache on your CPU.

But what happens if you have to send a signal from one server to some other server and back? You can safely assume that sending a signal from server A to server B next door takes a lot longer because the cable is simply a lot longer. In addition to that, network switches and other network components will add some latency as well.

Let's talk about the *length* of the cable here, and not about its bandwidth.

Sending a message (or a transaction) from Europe to China is, of course, many times more time-consuming than sending some data to a server next door. Again, the important thing here is that the amount of data is not as relevant as the so-called latency, consider the following criteria:

- **Long-distance transmission**: To explain the concept of latency, let's cover a very simple example. Let's assume you are a European and you are sending a letter to China. You will easily accept the fact that the size of your letter is not the limiting factor here. It makes absolutely no difference whether your letter is two or 20 pages long; the time it takes to reach the destination is basically the same. Also, it makes no difference whether you send one, two, or 10 letters at the same time. Given a reasonable numbers of letter, the size of the aircraft required (that is, the **bandwidth**) to ship the stuff to China is usually not the problem. However, the so-called *round trip* might very well be an issue. If you rely on the response to your letter from China to continue your work, you will soon find yourself waiting for a long time.

- **Why latency matters**: Latency is an important issue. If you send a chunk of data from Europe to China, you should avoid waiting for the response. But if you send a chunk of data from your server to a server in the same rack, you might be able to wait for the response, because your electronic signal will simply be fast enough to make it back in time.

 The basic problems of latency described in this section are not PostgreSQL-specific. The very same concepts and physical limitations apply to all types of databases and systems. As mentioned before, this fact is sometimes silently hidden and neglected in shiny commercial marketing papers. Nevertheless, the laws of physics will stand firm. This applies to both commercial and open source software.

The most important point you have to keep in mind here is that bandwidth is not always the magical fix to a performance problem in a replicated environment. In many setups, latency is at least as important as bandwidth.

Different types of replication

Now that you are fully armed with the basic understanding of physical and theoretical limitations, it is time to learn about different types of replication. It is important to have a clear image of these types to make sure that the right choice can be made and the right tool can be chosen. In this section, synchronous as well as asynchronous replication will be covered.

Synchronous versus asynchronous replication

Let's dig into some important concepts now. The first distinction we can make is whether to replicate synchronously or asynchronously.

What does this mean? Let's assume we have two servers and we want to replicate data from one server (the master) to the second server (the slave). The following diagram illustrates the concept of synchronous and asynchronous replication:

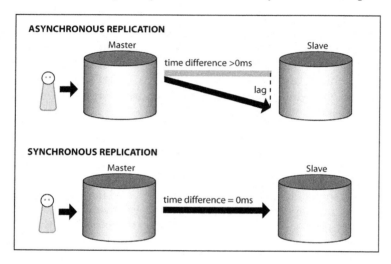

We can use a simple transaction like the one shown in the following:

```
BEGIN;
INSERT INTO foo VALUES ('bar');
COMMIT;
```

In the case of asynchronous replication, the data can be replicated *after* the transaction has been committed on the master. In other words, the slave is never ahead of the master; and in the case of writing, it is usually a little behind the master. This delay is called **lag**.

Synchronous replication enforces higher rules of consistency. If you decide to replicate synchronously (how this is done practically will be discussed in *Chapter 5, Setting Up Synchronous Replication*), the system has to ensure that the data written by the transaction will be at least on two servers at the time the transaction commits. This implies that the slave does not lag behind the master and that the data seen by the end users will be identical on both the servers.

Some systems will also use a **quorum** server to decide. So, it is not always about just two or more servers. If a quorum is used, more than half of the servers must agree on an action inside the cluster.

Considering performance issues

As you have learned earlier in the section about the speed of light and latency, sending unnecessary messages over the network can be expensive and time-consuming. If a transaction is replicated in a synchronous way, PostgreSQL has to make sure that the data reaches the second node, and this will lead to latency issues.

Synchronous replication can be more expensive than asynchronous replication in many ways, and therefore, people should think twice about whether this overhead is really needed and justified. In the case of synchronous replication, confirmations from a remote server are needed. This, of course, causes some additional overhead. A lot has been done in PostgreSQL to reduce this overhead as much as possible. However, it is still there.

 Use synchronous replication only when it is really needed.

Understanding replication and data loss

When a transaction is replicated from a master to a slave, many things have to be taken into consideration, especially when it comes to things such as data loss.

Let's assume that we are replicating data asynchronously in the following manner:

1. A transaction is sent to the master.
2. It commits on the master.
3. The master dies before the commit is sent to the slave.
4. The slave will never get this transaction.

In the case of asynchronous replication, there is a window (lag) during which data can essentially be lost. The size of this window might vary, depending on the type of setup. Its size can be very short (maybe as short as a couple of milliseconds) or long (minutes, hours, or days). The important fact is that data can be lost. A small lag will only make data loss less likely, but any lag larger than zero lag is susceptible to data loss. If data can be lost, we are about to sacrifice the consistency part of CAP (if two servers don't have the same data, they are out of sync).

If you want to make sure that data can never be lost, you have to switch to synchronous replication. As you have already seen in this chapter, a synchronous transaction is synchronous because it will be valid only if it commits to at least two servers.

Single-master versus multimaster replication

A second way to classify various replication setups is to distinguish between single-master and multi-master replication.

"Single-master" means that writes can go to exactly one server, which distributes the data to the slaves inside the setup. Slaves may receive only reads, and no writes.

In contrast to single-master replication, multi-master replication allows writes to all the servers inside a cluster. The following diagram shows how things work at a conceptual level:

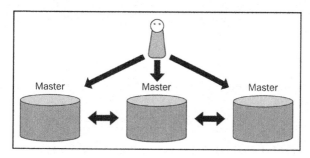

The ability to write to any node inside the cluster sounds like an advantage, but it is not necessarily one. The reason for this is that multimaster replication adds a lot of complexity to the system. In the case of only one master, it is totally clear which data is correct and in which direction data will flow, and there are rarely conflicts during replication. Multimaster replication is quite different, as writes can go to many nodes at the same time, and the cluster has to be perfectly aware of conflicts and handle them gracefully. An alterative would be to use locks to solve the problem, but this approach will also have its own challenges.

 Keep in mind that the need to resolve conflicts will cause network traffic, and this can instantly turn into scalability issues caused by latency.

Logical versus physical replication

One more way of classifying replication is to distinguish between logical and physical replication.

The difference is subtle but highly important:

- Physical replication means that the system will move data *as is* to the remote box. So, if something is inserted, the remote box will get data in binary format, not via SQL.

- Logical replication means that a change, which is equivalent to data coming in, is replicated.

Let's look at an example to fully understand the difference:

```
test=# CREATE TABLE t_test (t date);
CREATE TABLE
test=# INSERT INTO t_test VALUES (now())
RETURNING *;
t
-----------
 2013-02-08
(1 row)

INSERT 0 1
```

We see two transactions going on here. The first transaction creates a table. Once this is done, the second transaction adds a simple date to the table and commits.

In the case of logical replication, the change will be sent to some sort of queue in logical form, so the system does not send plain SQL, but maybe something such as this:

```
test=# INSERT INTO t_test VALUES ('2013-02-08');
INSERT 0 1
```

Note that the function call has been replaced with the real value. It would be a total disaster if the slave were to calculate now() once again, because the date on the remote box might be a totally different one.

 Some systems do use statement-based replication as the core technology. MySQL, for instance, uses a so-called `bin-log` statement to replicate, which is actually not too binary but more like some form of logical replication. Of course, there are also counterparts in the PostgreSQL world, such as pgpool, Londiste, and Bucardo.

Physical replication will work in a totally different way; instead of sending some SQL (or something else) over, which is logically equivalent to the changes made, the system will send binary changes made by PostgreSQL internally.

Here are some of the binary changes our two transactions might have triggered (but by far, this is not a complete list):

1. Added an 8 K block to `pg_class` and put a new record there (to indicate that the table is present).
2. Added rows to `pg_attribute` to store the column names.
3. Performed various changes inside the indexes on those tables.
4. Recorded the commit status, and so on.

The goal of physical replication is to create a copy of your system that is (largely) identical on the physical level. This means that the same data will be in the same place inside your tables on all boxes. In the case of logical replication, the content should be identical, but it makes no difference whether it is in the same place or not.

When to use physical replication

Physical replication is very convenient to use and especially easy to set up. It is widely used when the goal is to have identical replicas of your system (to have a backup or to simply scale up).

In many setups, physical replication is the standard method that exposes the end user to the lowest complexity possible. It is ideal for scaling out the data.

When to use logical replication

Logical replication is usually a little harder to set up, but it offers greater flexibility. It is also especially important when it comes to upgrading an existing database. Physical replication is totally unsuitable for version jumps because you cannot simply rely on the fact that every version of PostgreSQL has the same on-disk layout. The storage format might change over time, and therefore, a binary copy is clearly not feasible for a jump from one version to the next.

Logical replication allows decoupling of the way data is stored from the way it is transported and replicated. Using a neutral protocol, which is not bound to any specific version of PostgreSQL, it is easy to jump from one version to the next.

Since PostgreSQL 9.4, there is something called **Logical Decoding**. It allows users to extract internal changes sent to the XLOG as SQL again. Logical decoding will be needed for a couple of replication techniques outlined in this book.

Using sharding and data distribution

In this section, you will learn about basic scalability techniques, such as database sharding. Sharding is widely used in high-end systems and offers a simple and reliable way to scale out a setup. In recent years, it has become the standard way to scale up professional systems.

Understanding the purpose of sharding

What happens if your setup grows beyond the capacity of a single machine in a single-master setup? What if you want to run so many transactions that one server is simply not able to keep up with them? Let's assume you have millions of users and tens of thousands among them want to perform a certain task at the same time.

Clearly, at some point, you cannot buy servers that are big enough to handle an infinite load anymore. It is simply impossible to run a Facebook- or Google-like application on a single server. At some point, you have to come up with a scalability strategy that serves your needs. This is when sharding comes into play.

The idea of sharding is simple: What if you could split data in a way that it can reside on different nodes?

Designing a sharded system

To demonstrate the basic concept of sharding, let's assume the following scenario: we want to store information about millions of users. Each user has a unique user ID. Let's further assume that we have only two servers. In this case, we can store even user IDs on server 1 and odd user IDs on server 2.

The following diagram shows how this can be done:

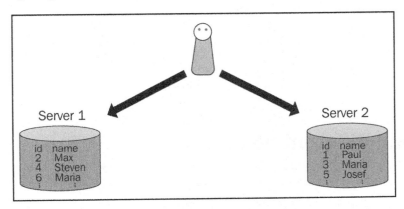

As you can see in our diagram, we have nicely distributed the data. Once this is done, we can send a query to the system, as follows:

```
SELECT * FROM t_user WHERE id = 4;
```

The client can easily figure out where to find the data by inspecting the filter in our query. In our example, the query will be sent to the first node because we are dealing with an even number.

As we have distributed the data based on a key (in this case, the user ID), we can search for any person easily if we know the key. In large systems, referring to users through a key is a common practice, and therefore, this approach is suitable. By using this simple approach, we have also easily doubled the number of machines in our setup.

When designing a system, we can easily come up with an arbitrary number of servers; all we have to do is to invent a nice and clever partitioning function to distribute the data inside our server farm. If we want to split the data between 10 servers (not a problem), how about using `user ID % 10` as a partitioning function? If you are interested in sharding, consider checking out `shard_manager`, which is available on PGXN.

When you are trying to break up data and store it on different hosts, always make sure that you are using a proper partitioning function. It can be very beneficial to split data in such a way that each host has more or less the same amount of data.

Splitting users alphabetically might not be a good idea. The reason for that is that not all the letters are equally likely. We cannot simply assume that the letters from A to M occur as often as the letters from N to Z. This can be a major issue if you want to distribute a dataset to a thousand servers instead of just a handful of machines. As stated before, it is essential to have a proper partitioning function, that produces evenly distributed results.

> In many cases, a hash function will provide you with nicely and evenly distributed data. This can especially be useful when working with character fields (such as names, e-mail addresses, and so on).

Querying different fields

In the previous section, you saw how we can easily query a person using their key. Let's take this a little further and see what happens if the following query is used:

```
SELECT * FROM t_test WHERE name = 'Max';
```

Remember that we have distributed data using the ID. In our query, however, we are searching for the name. The application will have no idea which partition to use because there is no rule telling us what is where.

As a logical consequence, the application has to ask every partition for the name parameter. This might be acceptable if looking for the name was a real corner case; however, we cannot rely on this fact. Requiring to ask many servers instead of one is clearly a serious deoptimization, and therefore, not acceptable.

We have two ways to approach the problem: coming up with a cleverer partitioning function, or storing the data redundantly.

Coming up with a cleverer partitioning function would surely be the best option, but it is rarely possible if you want to query different fields.

This leaves us with the second option, which is storing data redundantly. Storing a set of data twice, or even more often, is not too uncommon, and it's actually a good way to approach the problem. The following diagram shows how this can be done:

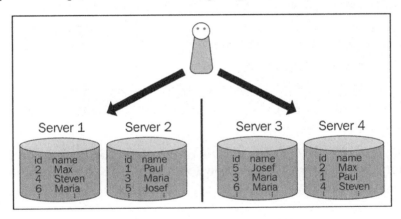

As you can see, we have two clusters in this scenario. When a query comes in, the system has to decide which data can be found on which node. For cases where the name is queried, we have (for the sake of simplicity) simply split the data into half alphabetically. In the first cluster, however, our data is still split by user ID.

Pros and cons of sharding

One important thing to understand is that sharding is not a simple one-way street. If someone decides to use sharding, it is essential to be aware of the upsides as well as the downsides of the technology. As always, there is no Holy Grail that magically solves all the problems of mankind out of the box without them having to think about it.

Each practical use case is different, and there is no replacement for common sense and deep thinking.

First, let's take a look at the pros of sharding:

- It has the ability to scale a system beyond one server
- It is a straightforward approach
- It is widely supported by various frameworks
- It can be combined with various other replication approaches
- It works nicely with PostgreSQL (for example, using PL/Proxy)

Light and shade tend to go together, and therefore sharding also has its downsides:

- Adding servers on the fly can be far from simple (depending on the type of partitioning function)
- Your flexibility might be seriously reduced
- Not all types of queries will be as efficient as they would be on a single server
- There is an increase in overall complexity of the setup (such as failover, resyncing, maintenance and so on)
- Backups need more planning
- You might face redundancy and additional storage requirements
- Application developers need to be aware of sharding to make sure that efficient queries are written

In *Chapter 13, Scaling with PL/Proxy*, we will discuss how you can efficiently use sharding along with PostgreSQL, and how to set up PL/Proxy for maximum performance and scalability.

Choosing between sharding and redundancy

Learning how to shard a table is only the first step to designing a scalable system's architecture. In the example we showed in the previous section, we had only one table, which could be distributed easily using a key. But what if we have more than one table? Let's assume we have two tables:

- A table called t_user for storing the users in our system
- A table called t_language for storing the languages supported by our system

We might be able to partition the `t_user` table nicely and split it in such a way that it can reside on a reasonable number of servers. But what about the `t_language` table? Our system might support as many as 10 languages.

It can make perfect sense to shard and distribute hundreds of millions of users, but splitting up 10 languages? This is clearly useless. In addition to all this, we might need our language table on all the nodes so that we can perform joins.

One solution to the problem is simple: you need a full copy of the language table on all the nodes. This will not cause a storage-consumption-related problem because the table is so small. Of course, there are many different ways to attack the problem.

 Make sure that only large tables are sharded. In the case of small tables, full replicas of the tables might just make much more sense.

Again, every case has to be thought over thoroughly.

Increasing and decreasing the size of a cluster

So far, we have always considered the size of a sharded setup to be constant. We have designed sharding in a way that allowed us to utilize a fixed number of partitions inside our cluster. This limitation might not reflect in everyday requirements. How can you really tell for certain how many nodes will be needed at the time a setup is designed? People might have a rough idea of the hardware requirements, but actually knowing how much load to expect is more art than science.

 To reflect this, you have to design a system in such a way that it can be resized easily.

A commonly made mistake is that people tend to increase the size of their setup in unnecessarily small steps. Somebody might want to move from five to maybe six or seven machines. This can be tricky. Let's assume for a second that we have split data using `user id % 5` as the partitioning function. What if we wanted to move to `user id % 6`? This is not so easy; the problem is that we have to rebalance the data inside our cluster to reflect the new rules.

Remember that we have introduced sharding (that is, partitioning) because we have so much data and so much load that one server cannot handle the requests anymore. Now, if we come up with a strategy that requires rebalancing of data, we are already on the wrong track. You definitely don't want to rebalance 20 TB of data just to add two or three servers to your existing system.

Practically, it is a lot easier to simply double the number of partitions. Doubling your partitions does not require rebalancing of data because you can simply follow the strategy outlined here:

1. Create a replica of each partition
2. Delete half of the data on each partition

If your partitioning function was `user id % 5` before, it should be `user id % 10` afterwards. The advantage of doubling is that data cannot move between partitions. When it comes to doubling, users might argue that the size of your cluster might increase too rapidly. This is true, but if you are running out of capacity, adding 10 percent storage to your resources won't fix the problem of scalability anyway.

Instead of just doubling your cluster (which is fine for most cases), you can also give more thought to writing a more sophisticated partitioning function that leaves the old data in place but handles the more recent data more intelligently. Having time-dependent partitioning functions might cause issues of its own, but it might be worth investigating this path.

> Some NoSQL systems use range partitioning to spread out data. Range partitioning means that each server has a fixed slice of data for a given time frame. This can be beneficial if you want to perform time series analysis or something similar. However, it can be counterproductive if you want to make sure that data is split evenly.

If you expect your cluster to grow, we recommend starting with more partitions than those initially necessary, and packing more than just one partition on a single server. Later on, it will be easy to move single partitions to additional hardware joining the cluster setup. Some cloud services are able to do that, but those aspects are not covered in this book.

To shrink your cluster again, you can simply apply the opposite strategy and move more than just one partition to a single server. This leaves the door for a future increase of servers wide open, and can be done fairly easily.

Consistent hashing is another approach to distributing data. This technique is widely used in NoSQL systems and allows us to extend clusters in a more flexible way. However, the same technique can be used for PostgreSQL, of course.

Let's assume we have three servers (A, B, and C). What happens in consistent hashing is that an array of, say, 1,000 slots can be created. Then each server name is hashed a couple of times and entered in the array. The result might look like this:

```
43 B, 153 A, 190 C, 340 A, 450 C, 650 B, 890 A, 930 C, 980 B
```

Each value shows up multiple times. In the case of insertion, we take the input key and calculate a value. Let's assume hash (some input value) equals 58. The result will go to server A. Why? There is no entry for 58, so the system moves forward in the list, and the first valid entry is 153, which points to A. If the hash value returned 900, the data would end up on C. Again, there is no entry for 900 so the system has to move forward in the list until something is found.

If a new server is added, new values for the server will be added to the array (D might be on 32, 560, 940, or so). The system has to rebalance some data, but of course, not all of the data. It is a major advantage over a simple hashing mechanism, such as a simple `key % server_number` function. Reducing the amount of data to be resharded is highly important.

The main advantage of consistent hashing is that it scales a lot better than simple approaches.

Combining sharding and replication

Once data has been broken down into useful chunks, which can be handled by one server or a partition, we have to think about how to make the entire setup more reliable and fail-safe.

The more servers you have in your setup, the more likely it will be that one of those servers will be down or not available for some other reason.

 Always avoid single points of failure when designing a highly scalable system.

In order to ensure maximum throughput and availability, we can again turn to redundancy. The design approach can be summed up in a simple formula, which should always be in the back of a system architect's mind:

"One is none and two is one."

One server is never enough to provide us with High Availability. Every system needs a backup system that can take over in the event of a serious emergency. By just splitting a set of data, we definitely do not improve availability. This is because we have more servers, which can fail at this point. To fix this problem, we can add replicas to each of our partitions (shards), just as is shown in the following diagram:

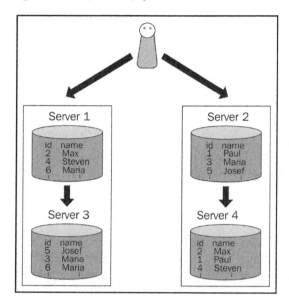

Each partition is a separate PostgreSQL database instance, and each of those instances can have its own replica (or replicas). Essentially, it is the same concept as you will find in a RAID 1+0 setup on the hardware side.

Keep in mind that you can choose from the entire arsenal of features and options discussed in this book (for example, synchronous and asynchronous replication). All the strategies outlined in this book can be combined flexibly. A single technique is usually not enough, so feel free to combine various technologies in different ways to achieve your goals.

Various sharding solutions

In recent years, sharding has emerged as an industry-standard solution to many scalability-related problems. Thus, many programming languages, frameworks, and products are already providing out-of-the-box support for sharding.

When implementing sharding, you can basically choose between two strategies:

- Rely on some framework or middleware
- Rely on PostgreSQL's means to solve the problem

In the following chapters, we will discuss both options briefly. This little overview is not meant to be a comprehensive guide, but rather an overview to get you started with sharding.

PostgreSQL-based sharding

PostgreSQL cannot shard data out of the box, but it has all the interfaces and means required to allow sharding through add-ons. One of these add-ons, which is widely used, is called PL/Proxy. It has been around for many years, and offers superior transparency as well as good scalability. It was originally developed by Skype to scale up their infrastructure.

The idea behind PL/Proxy is basically to use a local virtual table to hide an array of servers making up the table.

PL/Proxy will be discussed in depth in *Chapter 13, Scaling with PL/Proxy*.

Summary

In this chapter, you learned about basic replication-related concepts as well as the physical limitations. We dealt with the theoretical concepts, which are the groundwork for what is still to come in this book.

In the next chapter, you will be guided through the PostgreSQL transaction log, and we will outline all important aspects of this vital component. You will learn what the transaction log is good for and how it can be applied.

2
Understanding the PostgreSQL Transaction Log

In the previous chapter, we dealt with various replication concepts. That was meant to be more of a theoretical overview to sharpen your senses for what is to come, and was supposed to introduce the topic in general.

In this chapter, we will move closer to practical solutions, and you will learn how PostgreSQL works internally and what it means for replication. We will see what the so-called **transaction log** (**XLOG**) does and how it operates. The XLOG is the very backbone of the PostgreSQL onboard replication machinery. It is essential to understand how this part works in order to fully understand replication. You will learn the following topics in this chapter:

- How PostgreSQL writes data
- Which memory and storage parameters are involved
- How writes can be optimized
- How writes are replicated
- How data consistency can be ensured

In this chapter, you will also learn about replication slots and logical decoding. Once you have completed reading this chapter, you will be ready to understand the next chapter, which will teach you how to safely replicate your first database.

How PostgreSQL writes data

PostgreSQL replication is all about writing data. Therefore, the way PostgreSQL writes a chunk of data internally is highly relevant and directly connected to replication and replication concepts. In this section, we will dig into writes.

The PostgreSQL disk layout

One of the first things we want to take a look at in this chapter is the PostgreSQL disk layout. Knowing about the disk layout can be very helpful when inspecting an existing setup, and it can be helpful when designing an efficient, high-performance installation.

In contrast to other database systems, such as Oracle, PostgreSQL will always rely on a filesystem to store data. PostgreSQL does not use raw devices. The idea behind this is that if a filesystem developer has done their job well, there is no need to reimplement the filesystem functionality over and over again.

Looking into the data directory

To understand the filesystem layout used by PostgreSQL, we can take a look at what we can find inside the data directory (created by `initdb` at the time of installation):

```
hs@chantal:/data/db94$ ls -l
total 60
drwx------ 10 hs hs   102 Feb  4 11:40 base
drwx------  2 hs hs  4096 Feb 11 14:29 global
drwx------  2 hs hs    17 Dec  9 10:58 pg_clog
drwx------  2 hs hs     6 Dec  9 10:58 pg_dynshmem
-rw-------  1 hs hs  4450 Dec  9 10:58 pg_hba.conf
-rw-------  1 hs hs  1636 Dec  9 10:58 pg_ident.conf
drwx------  4 hs hs    37 Dec  9 10:58 pg_logical
drwx------  4 hs hs    34 Dec  9 10:58 pg_multixact
drwx------  2 hs hs    17 Feb 11 14:28 pg_notify
drwx------  3 hs hs    22 Feb 11 15:15 pg_replslot
drwx------  2 hs hs     6 Dec  9 10:58 pg_serial
drwx------  2 hs hs     6 Dec  9 10:58 pg_snapshots
drwx------  2 hs hs     6 Feb 11 14:28 pg_stat
drwx------  2 hs hs   108 Feb 12 13:12 pg_stat_tmp
drwx------  2 hs hs    17 Dec  9 10:58 pg_subtrans
drwx------  2 hs hs     6 Dec  9 10:58 pg_tblspc
drwx------  2 hs hs     6 Dec  9 10:58 pg_twophase
-rw-------  1 hs hs     4 Dec  9 10:58 PG_VERSION
drwx------  3 hs hs  4096 Feb  3 11:37 pg_xlog
```

```
-rw-------  1 hs hs    88 Dec  9 10:58 postgresql.auto.conf
-rw-------  1 hs hs 21264 Feb 11 14:28 postgresql.conf
-rw-------  1 hs hs    47 Feb 11 14:28 postmaster.opts
-rw-------  1 hs hs    68 Feb 11 14:28 postmaster.pid
```

You will see a range of files and directories, which are needed to run a database instance. Let's take a look at them in detail.

PG_VERSION – the PostgreSQL version number

The PG_VERSION file will tell the system at startup whether the data directory contains the correct version number. Note that only the major release version is in this file. It is easily possible to replicate between different minor versions of the same major version (for example, inside the 9.3 or 9.4 series):

```
[hs@paulapgdata]$ cat PG_VERSION
9.2
```

The file is plain text readable.

base – the actual data directory

The base directory is one of the most important things in our data directory. It actually contains the real data (that is, tables, indexes, and so on). Inside the base directory, each database will have its own subdirectory:

```
[hs@paula base]$ ls -l
total 24
drwx------ 2 hs hs 8192 Dec  9 10:58 1
drwx------ 2 hs hs 8192 Dec  9 10:58 12180
drwx------ 2 hs hs 8192 Feb 11 14:29 12185
drwx------ 2 hs hs 4096 Feb 11 18:14 16384
```

We can easily link these directories to the databases in our system. It is worth noticing that PostgreSQL uses the object ID of the database here. This has many advantages over using the name, because the object ID never changes and offers a good way to abstract all sorts of problems, such as issues with different character sets on the server:

```
test=# SELECT oid, datname FROM pg_database;
oid    |datname
-------+-----------
     1 | template1
```

```
 12180 | template0
 12185 | postgres
 16384 | test
(4 rows)
```

Now we can see how data is stored inside those database-specific directories. In PostgreSQL, each table is related to (at least) one data file. Let's create a table and see what happens:

```
test=# CREATE TABLE t_test (id int4);
CREATE TABLE
```

We can check the system table now to retrieve the so-called `relfilenode` variable, which represents the name of the storage file on the disk:

```
test=# SELECT relfilenode, relname
     FROM  pg_class
WHERE  relname = 't_test';
relfilenode | relname
------------+---------
     16385 | t_test
(1 row)
```

Note that `relfilenode` can change if TRUNCATE or similar commands occur on a certain table.

As soon as the table is created, PostgreSQL will create an empty file on the disk:

```
[hs@paula base]$ ls -l 16384/16385*
-rw------- 1 hs staff 0 Feb 12 12:06 16384/16385
```

Growing data files

Tables can sometimes be quite large, and therefore it is not wise to put all of the data related to a table into a single data file. To solve this problem, PostgreSQL will add more files every time 1 GB of data has been added.

So, if the file called `16385` grows beyond 1 GB, there will be a file called `16385.1`; once this has been filled, you will see a file named `16385.2`; and so on. In this way, a table in PostgreSQL can be scaled up reliably and safely without having to worry too much about the underlying filesystem limitations of some rare operating systems or embedded devices (Most modern filesystems can handle a large number of files efficiently. However, not all filesystems have been created as equals.)

Performing I/O in chunks

To improve I/O performance, PostgreSQL will usually perform I/O in 8 K chunks. Thus, you will see that your data files will always grow in steps of 8 K each. When considering physical replication, you have to make sure that both sides (master and slave) are compiled with the same block size.

 Unless you have explicitly compiled PostgreSQL on your own using different block sizes, you can always rely on the fact that block sizes will be identical and exactly 8 K.

Relation forks

Other than the data files discussed in the previous paragraph, PostgreSQL will create additional files using the same `relfilenode` number. Till now, those files have been used to store information about free space inside a table (`Free Space Map`), the so-called `Visibility Map` file, and so on. In future, more types of relation forks might be added.

global – the global data

The `global` directory will contain the global system tables. This directory is small, so you should not expect excessive storage consumption.

Dealing with standalone data files

There is one thing that is often forgotten by users: a single PostgreSQL data file is basically more or less worthless. It is hardly possible to restore data reliably if you just have a data file; trying to extract data from single data files can easily end up as hopeless guesswork. Without the transaction log infrastructure, data files are usually meaningless. So, in order to read data, you need an instance that is more or less complete.

pg_clog – the commit log

The `commit` log is an essential component of a working database instance. It stores the status of the transactions on this system. A transaction can be in four states: `TRANSACTION_STATUS_IN_PROGRESS`, `TRANSACTION_STATUS_COMMITTED`, `TRANSACTION_STATUS_ABORTED`, and `TRANSACTION_STATUS_SUB_COMMITTED`. If the commit log status for a transaction is not available, PostgreSQL will have no idea whether a row should be seen or not. The same applies to the end user, of course.

If the commit log of a database instance is broken for some reason (maybe because of filesystem corruption), you can expect some funny hours ahead.

If the commit log is broken, we recommend that you snapshot the database instance (filesystem) and fake the commit log. This can sometimes help retrieve a reasonable amount of data from the database instance in question. Faking the commit log won't fix your data — it might just bring you closer to the truth. This faking can be done by generating a file as required by the clog infrastructure (see the documentation).

pg_dynshmem – shared memory

This "shared memory" is somewhat of a misnomer, because what it is really doing is creating a bunch of files and mapping them to the PostgreSQL address space. So it is not system-wide shared memory in a classical sense. The operating system may feel obliged to synchronize the contents to the disk, even if nothing is being paged out, which will not serve us well. The user can relocate the pg_dynshmem directory to a RAM disk, if available, to avoid this problem.

pg_hba.conf – host-based network configuration

The pg_hba.conf file configures the PostgreSQL's internal firewall and represents one of the two most important configuration files in a PostgreSQL cluster. It allows users to define various types of authentication based on the source of a request. To a database administrator, understanding the pg_hba.conf file is of vital importance because this file decides whether a slave is allowed to connect to the master or not. If you happen to miss something here, you might see error messages in the slave's logs (for instance, no pg_hba.conf entry for ...).

pg_ident.conf – ident authentication

The pg_ident.conf file can be used in conjunction with the pg_hba.conf file to configure ident authentication.

pg_logical – logical decoding

The pg_logical directory, information for logical decoding is stored (snapshots and the like).

pg_multixact – multitransaction status data

The multiple-transaction-log manager handles shared row locks efficiently. There are no replication-related practical implications of this directory.

pg_notify – LISTEN/NOTIFY data

In the `pg_notify` directory, the system stores information about LISTEN/NOTIFY (the async backend interface). There are no practical implications related to replication.

pg_replslot – replication slots

Information about replication slots is stored in the `pg_replslot` directory.

pg_serial – information about committed serializable transactions

Information about serializable transactions is stored in `pg_serial` directory. We need to store information about commits of serializable transactions on the disk to ensure that long-running transactions will not bloat the memory. A simple **Segmented Least Recently Used (SLRU)** structure is used internally to keep track of these transactions.

pg_snapshot – exported snapshots

The `pg_snapshot` file consists of information needed by the PostgreSQL snapshot manager. In some cases, snapshots have to be exported to the disk to avoid going to the memory. After a crash, these exported snapshots will be cleaned out automatically.

pg_stat – permanent statistics

The `pg_stat` file contains permanent statistics for the statistics subsystem.

pg_stat_tmp – temporary statistics data

Temporary statistical data is stored in the `pg_stst_tmp` file. This information is needed for most `pg_stat_*` system views (and therefore, it is also needed for the underlying function providing the raw data).

pg_subtrans – subtransaction data

In this directory, we store information about subtransactions. The `pg_subtrans` (and `pg_clog`) directories are a permanent (on-disk) storage of transaction-related information. There are a limited number of pages of directories kept in the memory, so in many cases, there is no need to actually read from the disk. However, if there's a long-running transaction or a backend sitting idle with an open transaction, it may be necessary to be able to read and write this information to the disk. These directories also allow the information to be permanent across server restarts.

pg_tblspc – symbolic links to tablespaces

The pg_tblspc directory is a highly important directory. In PostgreSQL, a tablespace is simply an alternative storage location that is represented by a directory holding the data.

The important thing here is that if a database instance is fully replicated, we simply cannot rely on the fact that all the servers in the cluster use the same disk layout and the same storage hardware. There can easily be scenarios in which a master needs a lot more I/O power than a slave, which might just be around to function as backup or standby. To allow users to handle different disk layouts, PostgreSQL will place symlinks in the pg_tblspc directory. The database will blindly follow those symlinks to find the tablespaces, regardless of where they are.

This gives end users enormous power and flexibility. Controlling storage is essential to both replication as well as performance in general. Keep in mind that those symlinks can only be changed post transaction(users can do that if a slave server in a replicated setup does not use the same filesystem layout). This should be carefully thought over.

> We recommend using the trickery outlined in this section only when it is really needed. For most setups, it is absolutely recommended to use the same filesystem layout on the master as well as on the slave. This can greatly reduce the complexity of backups and replay. Having just one tablespace reduces the workload on the administrator.

pg_twophase – information about prepared statements

PostgreSQL has to store information about two-phase commit. While two-phase commit can be an important feature, the directory itself will be of little importance to the average system administrator.

pg_xlog – the PostgreSQL transaction log (WAL)

The PostgreSQL transaction log is the essential directory we have to discuss in this chapter. The pg_xlog log contains all the files related to the so-called XLOG. If you have used PostgreSQL in the past, you might be familiar with the term **Write-Ahead Log (WAL)**. XLOG and WAL are two names for the same thing. The same applies to the term **transaction log**. All of these three terms are widely in use, and it is important to know that they actually mean the same thing.

The `pg_xlog` directory will typically look like this:

```
[hs@paulapg_xlog]$ ls -l
total 81924
-rw------- 1 hs staff 16777216 Feb 12 16:29 000000010000000000000001
-rw------- 1 hs staff 16777216 Feb 12 16:29 000000010000000000000002
-rw------- 1 hs staff 16777216 Feb 12 16:29 000000010000000000000003
-rw------- 1 hs staff 16777216 Feb 12 16:29 000000010000000000000004
-rw------- 1 hs staff 16777216 Feb 12 16:29 000000010000000000000005
drwx------ 2 hs staff     4096 Feb 11 18:14 archive_status
```

What you see is a bunch of files that are always exactly 16 MB in size (the default setting). The filename of an XLOG file is generally 24 bytes long. The numbering is always hexadecimal. So, the system will count "… 9, A, B, C, D, E, F, 10" and so on.

One important thing to mention is that the size of the `pg_xlog` directory will not vary wildly over time, and it is totally independent of the type of transactions you are running on your system. The size of the XLOG is determined by the `postgresql.conf` parameters, which will be discussed later in this chapter. In short, no matter whether you are running small or large transactions, the size of the XLOG will be the same. You can easily run a transaction as big as 1 TB with just a handful of XLOG files. This might not be too efficient performance wise, but it is technically perfectly feasible.

postgresql.conf – the central PostgreSQL configuration file

Finally, there is the main PostgreSQL configuration file. All configuration parameters can be changed in `postgresql.conf`, and we will use this file extensively to set up replication and tune our database instances to make sure that our replicated setups provide us with superior performance.

 If you happen to use prebuilt binaries, you might not find `postgresql.conf` directly inside your data directory. It is more likely to be located in some subdirectory of `/etc/` (on Linux/Unix) or in your place of choice in Windows. The precise location is highly dependent on the type of operating system you are using. The typical location of data directories is `/var/lib/pgsql/data`, but `postgresql.conf` is often located under `/etc/postgresql/9.X/main/postgresql.conf` (as in Ubuntu and similar systems), or under `/etc` directly.

Writing one row of data

Now that we have gone through the disk layout, we will dive further into PostgreSQL and see what happens when PostgreSQL is supposed to write one line of data. Once you have mastered this chapter, you will have fully understood the concept behind the XLOG.

Note that in this section, which is about writing a row of data, we have simplified the process a little to make sure that we can stress the main point and the ideas behind the PostgreSQL XLOG.

A simple INSERT statement

Let's assume that we are using a simple INSERT statement, like the following:

```
INSERT INTO foo VALUES ('abcd'):
```

As one might imagine, the goal of an INSERT operation is to somehow add a row to an existing table. We have seen in the previous section — the section about the disk layout of PostgreSQL — that each table will be associated with a file on the disk.

Let's perform a mental experiment and assume that the table we are dealing with here is 10 TB large. PostgreSQL will see the INSERT operation and look for some spare place inside this table (either using an existing block or adding a new one). For the purpose of this example, we have simply put the data into the second block of the table.

Everything will be fine as long as the server actually survives the transaction. What happens if somebody pulls the plug after just writing abc instead of the entire data? When the server comes back up after the reboot, we will find ourselves in a situation where we have a block with an incomplete record, and to make it even funnier, we might not even have the slightest idea where this block containing the broken record might be.

In general, tables containing incomplete rows in unknown places can be considered to be corrupted tables. Of course, systematic table corruption is nothing the PostgreSQL community would ever tolerate, especially not if problems like that are caused by clear design failures.

 We have to ensure that PostgreSQL will survive interruptions at any given point in time without losing or corrupting data. Protecting your data is not something nice to have but an absolute must-have. This is what is commonly referred to as the "D" in **Atomicity, Consistency, Isolation, and Durability (ACID)**.

To fix the problem that we have just discussed, PostgreSQL uses the so-called WAL or simply XLOG. Using WAL means that a log is written ahead of data. So, before we actually write data to the table, we make log entries in a sequential order, indicating what we are planning to do to our underlying table. The following diagram shows how things work in WAL:

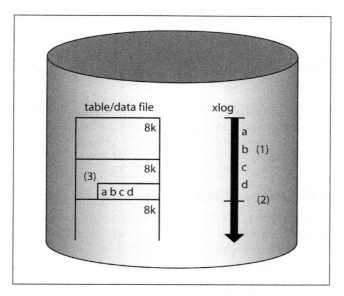

As we can see from this diagram, once we have written data to the log in **(1)**, we can go ahead and mark the transaction as done in **(2)**. After that, data can be written to the table, as marked with **(3)**.

 We have left out the memory part of the equation; this will be discussed later in this section.

Let's demonstrate the advantages of this approach with two examples:

- Crashing during WAL writing
- Crashing after WAL writing

Crashing during WAL writing

To make sure that the concept described in this chapter is rock-solid and working, we have to make sure that we can crash at any point in time without risking our data. Let's assume that we crash while writing the XLOG. What will happen in this case? Well, in this case, the end user will know that the transaction was not successful, so they will not rely on the success of the transaction anyway.

As soon as PostgreSQL starts up, it can go through the XLOG and replay everything necessary to make sure that PostgreSQL is in a consistent state. So, if we don't make it through WAL-writing, it means that something nasty has happened and we cannot expect a write to be successful.

A WAL entry will always know whether it is complete or not. Every WAL entry has a checksum inside, and therefore PostgreSQL can instantly detect problems if somebody tries to replay a broken WAL. This is especially important during a crash, when we might not be able to rely on the very latest data written to the disk. The WAL will automatically sort those problems during crash recovery.

> If PostgreSQL is configured properly (fsync = on, and so on), crashing is perfectly safe at any point in time (unless hardware is damaged of course; a malfunctioning RAM and so on are, of course, always a risk).

Crashing after WAL writing

Let's now assume we have made it through WAL writing and a crash happens shortly after that, maybe while writing to the underlying table. What if we only manage to write ab instead of the entire data (which is abcd in this example)?

Well, in this case, we will know during replay what is missing. Again, we go to the WAL and replay what is needed to make sure that all of the data is safely in our data table.

While it might be hard to find data in a table after a crash, we can always rely on the fact that we can find data in the WAL. The WAL is sequential, and if we simply keep a track of how much data has been written, we can always continue from there. The XLOG will lead us directly to the data in the table, and it always knows where a change has been made or should have been made. PostgreSQL does not have to search for data in the WAL; it just replays it from the proper point onward. Keep in mind that replaying XLOG is very efficient and can be a lot faster than the original write to the master.

> Once a transaction has made it to the WAL, it cannot be lost easily any more.

Read consistency

Now that we have seen how a simple write is performed, we will see what impact writes have on reads. The next diagram shows the basic architecture of the PostgreSQL database system:

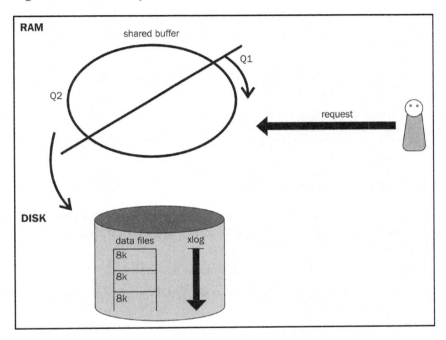

For the sake of simplicity, we can see a database instance as an entity consisting of three major components:

- PostgreSQL data files
- The transaction log
- Shared buffer

In the previous sections, we have already discussed data files. You have also read some basic information about the transaction log itself. Now we have to extend our model and bring another component into the scenery — the memory component of the game, which is the shared buffer.

The purpose of the shared buffer

The shared buffer is the I/O cache of PostgreSQL. It helps cache 8K blocks, which are read from the operating system, and also helps hold back writes to the disk to optimize efficiency (how this works will be discussed later in this chapter).

 The shared buffer is important as it affects performance.

However, performance is not the only issue we should be focused on when it comes to the shared buffer. Let's assume that we want to issue a query. For the sake of simplicity, we also assume that we need just one block to process this read request.

What happens if we perform a simple read? Maybe we are looking for something simple, such as a phone number or a username, given a certain key. The following list shows in a highly simplified way what PostgreSQL will do under the assumption that the instance has been freshly restarted:

1. PostgreSQL will look up the desired block in the cache (as stated before, this is the shared buffer). It will not find the block in the cache of a freshly started instance.

2. PostgreSQL will ask the operating system for the block.

3. Once the block has been loaded from the OS, PostgreSQL will put it into the first queue of the cache.

4. The query will be served successfully.

Let's assume that the same block will be used again, this time by a second query. In this case, things will work as follows:

1. PostgreSQL will look up the desired block and come across a cache hit.

2. Then PostgreSQL will figure out that a cached block has been reused, and move it from a lower level of cache (Q1) to a higher level of cache (Q2). Blocks that are in the second queue will stay in the cache longer, because they have proven to be more important than those that are only at the Q1 level.

How large should the shared buffer be? Under Linux, a value of up to 8 GB is usually recommended. On Windows, values below 1 GB have been proven to be useful (as of PostgreSQL9.2). From PostgreSQL 9.3 onwards, higher values might be useful and feasible under Windows. Insanely large shared buffers on Linux can actually be a deoptimization. Of course, this is only a rule of thumb; special setups might need different settings. Also keep in mind that some work goes on in PostgreSQL constantly and the best practices might vary over time.

Mixed reads and writes

Remember that in this section, it is all about understanding writes to make sure that our ultimate goal—full and deep understanding of replication—can be achieved. Therefore, we have to see how reads and writes go together:

1. A write will come in.

2. PostgreSQL will write to the transaction log to make sure that consistency can be reached.

3. Then PostgreSQL will grab a block inside the PostgreSQL shared buffer and make the change in the memory.

4. A read will come in.

5. PostgreSQL will consult the cache and look for the desired data.

6. A cache hit will be landed and the query will be served.

What is the point of this example? Well! As you might have noticed, we have never talked about actually writing to the underlying table. We talked about writing to the cache, to the XLOG, and so on, but never about the real data file.

 In this example, whether the row we have written is in the table or not is totally irrelevant. The reason is simple; if we need a block that has just been modified, we will never make it to the underlying table anyway.

It is important to understand that data is usually not sent to a data file directly after or during a write operation. It makes perfect sense to write data a lot later to increase efficiency. The reason this is important is that it has subtle implications on replication. A data file itself is worthless because it is neither necessarily complete nor correct. To run a PostgreSQL instance, you will *always* need data files along with the transaction log. Otherwise, there is no way to survive a crash.

From a consistency point of view, the shared buffer is here to complete the view a user has of the data. If something is not in the table, logically, it has to be in memory.

In the event of a crash, the memory will be lost, and so the XLOG will be consulted and replayed to turn data files into a consistent data store again. Under all circumstances, data files are only half of the story.

 In PostgreSQL 9.2 and before, the shared buffer was exclusively in the SysV/POSIX shared memory or simulated SysV on Windows. PostgreSQL 9.3 (already released at the time of writing this book) started using memory-mapped files. This is a lot faster under Windows and makes no difference in performance under Linux, but is slower under BSDs. BSD developers have already started fixing this. Moving to mmap was done to make configuration easier, because mmap is not limited by the operating system. It is unlimited as long as enough RAM is around. SysV's memory is limited and a high amount of it can usually be allocated only if the operating system is tweaked accordingly. The default configuration of shared memory varies from distribution to distribution in the case of Linux. SUSE tends to be a bit more relaxed, while Red Hat, Ubuntu, and some others tend to be more conservative.

The format of the XLOG

Many users have asked me during consulting or training sessions how the XLOG is really organized internally. As this information is rarely described in books, I decided to include a small section about this internal information here, hoping that you will find this little excursion into PostgreSQL's internals interesting and useful.

Basically, an XLOG entry identifies the object it is supposed to change using three variables:

- The OID (object id) of the database
- The OID of the tablespace
- The OID of the underlying data file

This triplet is a unique identifier for any data-carrying object in the database system. Depending on the type of operation, various types of records are used (commit records, B-tree changes, heap changes, and so on).

In general, the XLOG is a stream of records lined up one after the other. Each record is identified by the location in the stream. As already mentioned in this chapter, a typical XLOG file is 16 MB in size (unless changed at compile time). Inside those 16 MB segments, data is organized in 8 K blocks. XLOG pages contain a simple header consisting of:

- The 16-bit "magic" value
- Flag bits
- The timeline ID
- The XLOG position of this page
- The length of data remaining from the last record on the previous page

In addition to this, each segment (16 MB file) has a header consisting of various fields as well:

- System identifier
- Segment size and block size

The segment and block size are mostly available to check the correctness of the file.

Finally, each record has a special header with following contents:

- The XLOG record structure
- The total length of the record
- The transaction ID that produced the record
- The length of record-specific data, excluding header and backup blocks
- Flags
- The record type (for example, XLOG checkpoint, transaction commit, and B-tree insert)
- The start position of previous record
- The checksum of this record
- Record-specific data
- Full-page images

XLOG addresses are highly critical and must not be changed, otherwise the entire system breaks down.

The data structure outlined in this chapter is as of PostgreSQL 9.4. It is quite likely that changes will happen in PostgreSQL 9.5 and beyond.

The XLOG and replication

In this chapter, you have already learned that the transaction log of PostgreSQL has all the changes made to the database. The transaction log itself is packed into nice and easy-to-use 16 MB segments.

The idea of using this set of changes to replicate data is not farfetched. In fact, it is a logical step in the development of every relational (or maybe even a nonrelational) database system. For the rest of this book, you will see in many ways how the PostgreSQL transaction log can be used, fetched, stored, replicated, and analyzed.

In most replicated systems, the PostgreSQL transaction log is the backbone of the entire architecture (for synchronous as well as for asynchronous replication).

Understanding consistency and data loss

Digging into the PostgreSQL transaction log without thinking about consistency is impossible. In the first part of this chapter, we tried hard to explain the basic idea of the transaction log in general. You learned that it is hard, or even impossible, to keep data files in good shape without the ability to log changes beforehand.

So far, we have mostly talked about corruption. It is definitely not good to lose data files because of corrupted entries in them, but corruption is not the only issue you have to be concerned about. Two other important topics are:

- Performance
- Data loss

While these might be an obvious choice for important topics, we have the feeling that they are not well understood and honored. Therefore, they have been taken into consideration.

In our daily business as PostgreSQL consultants and trainers, we usually tend to see people who are only focused on performance.

> *Performance is everything. We want to be fast; tell us how to be fast...*

The awareness of potential data loss, or even a concept to handle it, seems to be new to many people. Let's try to put it this way: what good is higher speed if data is lost even faster? The point of this is not that performance is not important; performance is highly important. However, we simply want to point out that performance is not the only component in the bigger picture.

All the way to the disk

To understand issues related to data loss and consistency, we have to see how a chunk of data is sent to the disk. The following diagram illustrates how this happens:

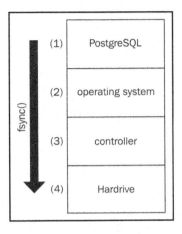

When PostgreSQL wants to read or write a block, it usually has to go through a couple of layers. When a block is written, it will be sent to the operating system. The operating system will cache the data and perform some operation on it. At some point, the operating system will decide to pass the data to some lower level. This might be the disk controller. The disk controller will cache, reorder, message the write again, and finally pass it to the disk. Inside the disk, there might be one more caching level before the data ends up on the real physical storage device.

In our example, we have used four layers. In many enterprise systems, there can be even more layers. Just imagine a virtual machine with storage mounted over the network, such as SAN, NAS, NFS, ATA-over_Ethernet, iSCSI, and so on. Many abstraction layers will pass data around, and each of them will try to do its share of optimization.

From memory to memory

What happens when PostgreSQL passes an 8 K block to the operating system? The only correct answer to this question might be, "something." When a normal write to a file is performed, there is absolutely no guarantee that the data is actually sent to the disk. In reality, writing to a file is nothing more than a copy operation from the PostgreSQL memory to some system memory. Both memory areas are in RAM, so in the event of a crash, data can be lost. Practically speaking, it makes no difference as to who loses the data if the entire RAM is gone due to a failure.

The following code snippet illustrates the basic problem we are facing:

```
test=# \d t_test
      Table "public.t_test"
 Column |  Type   | Modifiers
--------+---------+-----------
 id     | integer |


test=# BEGIN;
BEGIN
test=# INSERT INTO t_test VALUES (1);
INSERT 0 1
test=# COMMIT;
COMMIT
```

Just as in the previous chapter, we are using a table with only one column. The goal is to run a transaction inserting a single row.

If a crash happens shortly after COMMIT, no data will be in danger because nothing has happened. Even if a crash happens shortly after the INSERT statement but before COMMIT, nothing can happen. The user has not issued a COMMIT command yet, so the transaction is known to be running and thus unfinished. If a crash occurs, the application will notice that things were unsuccessful and (hopefully) react accordingly. Also keep in mind that every transaction that is not committed will eventually end up as ROLLBACK.

However, the situation is quite different if the user has issued a COMMIT statement and it has returned successfully. Whatever happens, the user will expect the committed data to be available.

> Users expect that successful writes will be available after an unexpected reboot. This persistence is also required by the ACID criteria. In computer science, ACID is a set of properties that guarantee that database transactions are processed reliably.

From the memory to the disk

To make sure that the kernel will pass data from the memory to the disk, PostgreSQL has to take some precautions. Upon a COMMIT command, a system call will be issued. It forces data to the transaction log.

PostgreSQL does not have to force data to the data files at this point because we can always repair broken data files from the XLOG. If data is stored in the XLOG safely, the transaction can be considered safe.

The system call necessary to force data to the disk is called `fsync()`. The following listing has been copied from the BSD manual page. In our opinion, it is one of the best manual pages ever written dealing with the topic:

```
FSYNC(2)              BSD System Calls Manual              FSYNC(2)


NAME
fsync -- synchronize a file's in-core state with
that on disk


SYNOPSIS
     #include <unistd.h>


int
fsync(intfildes);


DESCRIPTION
Fsync() causes all modified data and attributes of
fildes to be moved to a permanent storage device.
     This normally results in all in-core modified
copies of buffers for the associated file to be
written to a disk.


     Note that while fsync() will flush all data from
the host to the drive (i.e. the "permanent storage
device"), the drive itself may not physically
write the data to the platters for quite some time
and it may be written in an out-of-order sequence.


     Specifically, if the drive loses power or the OS
crashes, the application may find that only some
or none of their data was written.  The disk drive
may also re-order the data so that later writes
```

```
may be present, while earlier writes are not.


     This is not a theoretical edge case.  This sce-
nario is easily reproduced with real world work-
loads and drive power failures.
```

It essentially says that the kernel tries to make its image of the file in the memory consistent with the image of the file on the disk. It does so by forcing all changes to the storage device. It is also clearly stated that we are not talking about a theoretical scenario here; flushing to disk is a highly important issue.

Without a disk flush on COMMIT, you just cannot be sure that your data is safe, and this means that you can actually lose data in the event of some serious trouble.

Also, what is essentially important is speed and consistency; they can actually work against each other. Flushing changes to the disk is especially expensive because real hardware is involved. The overhead we have is not some five percent but a lot more. With the introduction of SSDs, the overhead has gone down dramatically but it is still substantial.

A word about batteries

Most production servers make use of a RAID controller to manage disks. The important point here is that disk flushes and performance are usually strongly related to RAID controllers. If the RAID controller has no battery, which is usually the case, then it takes insanely long to flush. The RAID controller has to wait for the slowest disk to return. However, if a battery is available, the RAID controller can assume that a power loss will not prevent an acknowledged disk write from completing once power is restored. So, the controller can cache a write and simply pretend to flush. Therefore, a simple battery can easily increase flush performance tenfold.

> Keep in mind that what we have outlined in this section is general knowledge, and every piece of hardware is different. We highly recommend that you check out and understand your hardware and RAID configuration to see how flushes are handled.

Beyond the fsync function

The fsync function is not the only system call that flushes data to the disk. Depending on the operating system you are using, different flush calls are available. In PostgreSQL, you can decide on your preferred flush call by changing wal_sync_method. Again, this change can be made by tweaking postgresql.conf.

The methods available are `open_datasync`, `fdatasync`, `fsync`, `fsync_writethrough`, and `open_sync`.

 If you want to change these values, we highly recommend checking out the manual pages of the operating system you are using to make sure that you have made the right choice.

PostgreSQL consistency levels

Ensuring consistency and preventing data loss is costly. Every disk flush is expensive and we should think twice before flushing to the disk. To give the user choices, PostgreSQL offers various levels of data protection. These various choices are represented by two essential parameters, which can be found in `postgresql.conf`:

- `fsync`
- `synchronous_commit`

The `fsync` parameter will control data loss, if it is used at all. In the default configuration, PostgreSQL will always flush a commit out to the disk. If `fsync` is `off`, however, there is no guarantee at all that a `COMMIT` statement will survive a crash. Data can be lost and there might even be data corruption. To protect all of your data, it is necessary to keep `fsync` at `on`. If you can afford to lose some or all of your data, you can relax flushing standards a little.

The `synchronous_commit` parameter is related to XLOG writes. Normally, PostgreSQL will wait until data has been written to the XLOG completely. Especially short transactions can suffer considerably, and therefore, different options are offered:

- `on`: PostgreSQL will wait until XLOG has been fully and successfully written. If you are storing credit card data, you would want to make sure that a financial transaction is not lost. In this case, flushing to the disk is essential.
- `off`: There will be a time difference between reporting success to the client and safely writing to the disk. In a setting like this, there can be corruption. Let's assume a database that stores information about who is currently online on a website. Suppose your system crashes and comes back up 20 minutes later. Do you really care about your data? After 20 minutes, everybody has to log in again anyway, and it is not worth sacrificing performance to protect data that will be outdated in a couple of minutes anyway.

- `local`: In the case of a replicated database instance, we will wait only for the local instance to flush to the disk. The advantage here is that you have a high level of protection because you flush to one disk. However, we can safely assume that not both servers crash at the same time, so we can relax the standards on the slave a little.

- `remote_write`: PostgreSQL will wait until a synchronous standby server reports success for a given transaction.

In contrast to setting `fsync` to `off`, changing `synchronous_commit` to `off` will not result in corruption. However, in the event of a crash we might lose a handful of transactions that have already been committed successfully. The amount of potential data loss is governed by an additional `postgresql.conf` setting called `wal_writer_delay`. In the case of setting `synchronous_commit` to `off`, we can never lose more data than defined in the `wal_writer_delay` configuration variable.

> Changing `synchronous_commit` might look like a small performance tweak; in reality, however, changing the sync behavior is one of the dominant factors when running small writing transactions. The gain might not just be a handful of percentage points. If you are lucky, it could be tenfold or even more (depending on the hardware, work load, I/O subsystem, and so on).

Keep in mind that configuring a database is not just about speed. Consistency is at least as important as speed, and therefore, you should think carefully whether you want to trade speed for potential data loss.

It is important to fully understand the consistency-related topics outlined in this chapter. When it comes to deciding on your cluster architecture, data security will be an essential part, and it is highly desirable to be able to judge whether a certain architecture makes sense for your data. After all, work on databases is all about protecting data. Full awareness of your durability requirements is definitely a big plus.

Tuning checkpoints and the XLOG

So far, this chapter has hopefully provided some insights into how PostgreSQL writes data and what the XLOG is used for in general. Given this knowledge, we can now move on and see what we can do to make our databases work even more efficiently, both in the case of replication and in the case of running just a single server.

Understanding the checkpoints

In this chapter, we have seen that data has to be written to the XLOG before it can go anywhere. The thing is that if the XLOG was never deleted, clearly, we would not write to it forever without filling up the disk at some point in time.

To solve this problem, the XLOG has to be deleted at some point. This process is called **checkpointing**.

The main question arising from this issue is, "When can the XLOG be truncated up to a certain point?" The answer is, "When PostgreSQL has put everything that is already in the XLOG into the storage files." If all the changes made to the XLOG are also made to the data files, the XLOG can be truncated.

 Keep in mind that simply writing the data is worthless. We also have to flush the data to the data tables.

In a way, the XLOG can be seen as the repairman of the data files if something undesirable happens. If everything is fully repaired, the repair instructions can be removed safely; this is exactly what happens during a checkpoint.

Configuring the checkpoints

Checkpoints are highly important for consistency, but they are also highly relevant to performance. If checkpoints are configured poorly, you might face serious performance degradations.

When it comes to configuring checkpoints, the following parameters are relevant. Note that all of these parameters can be changed in `postgresql.conf`:

```
checkpoint_segments = 3
checkpoint_timeout = 5min
checkpoint_completion_target = 0.5
checkpoint_warning = 30s
```

In the following sections, we will take a look at each of these variables.

Segments and timeouts

The `checkpoint_segments` and `checkpoint_timeout` parameters define the distance between two checkpoints. A checkpoint happens either when we run out of segments or when the timeout happens.

Remember that a segment is usually 16 MB, so three segments means that we will perform a checkpoint every 48 MB. On modern hardware, 16 MB is far from enough. In a typical production system, a checkpoint interval of 256 MB (measured in segments) or even higher is perfectly feasible.

However, when setting `checkpoint_segments`, one thing has to be present at the back of your mind: in the event of a crash, PostgreSQL has to replay all the changes since the last checkpoint. If the distance between two checkpoints is unusually large, you might notice that your failed database instance takes too long to start up again. This should be avoided for the sake of availability.

> There will always be a trade-off between performance and recovery times after a crash. You have to balance your configuration accordingly.

The `checkpoint_timeout` parameter is also highly relevant. It is the upper limit of the time allowed between two checkpoints. There is no point in increasing `checkpoint_segments` infinitely while leaving the time as it is. On large systems, increasing `checkpoint_timeout` has proven to make sense for many people.

> In PostgreSQL, you will figure out that there are a constant number of transaction log files around. Unlike other database systems, the number of XLOG files has nothing to do with the maximum size of a transaction; a transaction can easily be much larger than the distance between two checkpoints.

To write or not to write?

You learned in this chapter that at the COMMIT time, we cannot be sure whether the data is already in the data files or not.

So if the data files don't have to be consistent anyway, why not vary the point in time at which the data is written? This is exactly what we can do with the `checkpoint_completion` target. The idea is to have a setting that specifies the target of checkpoint completion as a fraction of the total time between two checkpoints.

Let's now discuss three scenarios to illustrate the purpose of the `checkpoint_completion_target` parameter.

Scenario 1 – storing stock market data

In scenario 1, we want to store the most recent stock quotes of all stocks in the **Dow Jones Industrial Average (DJIA)**. We don't want to store the history of all stock prices but only the most recent, current price.

Given the type of data we are dealing with, we can assume that we will have a workload that is dictated by UPDATE statements.

What will happen now? PostgreSQL has to update the same data over and over again. Given the fact that the DJIA consists of only 30 different stocks, the amount of data is very limited and our table will be really small. In addition to this, the price might be updated every second or even more often.

Internally, the situation is like this: when the first UPDATE command comes along, PostgreSQL will grab a block, put it into the memory, and modify it. Every subsequent UPDATE command will most likely change the same block. Logically, all writes have to go to the transaction log, but what happens with the cached blocks in the shared buffer?

The general rule is as follows: if there are many UPDATE commands (and as a result, changes made to the same block), it is wise to keep the blocks in memory as long as possible. This will greatly increase the odds of avoiding I/O by writing multiple changes in one go.

 If you want to increase the odds of having many changes in one disk I/O, consider decreasing checkpoint_completion_target. The blocks will stay in the memory longer, and therefore many changes might go into the same block before a write occurs.

In the scenario just outlined, a checkpoint_completion_target variable having value of 0.05 (or 5 percent) might be reasonable.

Scenario 2 – bulk loading

In our second scenario, we will load 1 TB of data into an empty table. If you are loading so much data at once, what are the odds of hitting a block you have hit 10 minutes ago again? The odds are basically zero. There is no point in buffering writes in this case, because we would simply miss the disk capacity lost by idling and waiting for I/O to take place.

During a bulk load, we would want to use all of the I/O capacity we have all the time. To make sure that PostgreSQL writes data instantly, we have to increase checkpoint_completion_target to a value close to 1.

Scenario 3 – I/O spikes and throughput considerations

Sharp spikes can kill you; at least, they can do serious harm, which should be avoided. What is true in the real world around you is always true in the database world as well.

In this scenario, we want to assume an application storing the so-called **Call Detail Records (CDRs)** for a phone company. You can imagine that a lot of writing will happen and people will be placing phone calls all day long. Of course, there will be people placing a phone call that is instantly followed by the next call, but we will also witness a great number of people placing just one call a week or so.

Technically, this means that there is a good chance that a block in the shared memory that has recently been changed will face a second or a third change soon, but we will also have a great deal of changes made to blocks that will never be visited again.

How will we handle this? Well, it is a good idea to write data late so that as many changes as possible will go to pages that have been modified before. But what will happen during a checkpoint? If changes (in this case, dirty pages) have been held back for too long, the checkpoint itself will be intense, and many blocks will have to be written within a fairly short period of time. This can lead to an I/O spike. During an I/O spike, you will see that your I/O system is busy. It might show poor response times, and those poor response times can be felt by your end user.

This adds a new dimension to the problem—predictable response times.

Let's put it in this way: assume you have used internet banking successfully for quite a while. You are happy. Now some guy at your bank has found a tweak that makes the database behind the internet banking 50 percent faster, but this gain comes with a downside: for two hours a day, the system will not be reachable. Clearly, from a performance point of view, the throughput will be better, as shown in this inequation:

*24 hours * 1 X < 22 hours * 1.5 X*

But are you, the customer, going to be happy? Clearly, you would not be. This is a typical use case where optimizing for maximum throughput does no good. If you can meet your performance requirements, it might be wiser to have evenly distributed response times at the cost of a small performance penalty. In our banking example, this would mean that your system is up 24x7 instead of just 22 hours a day.

 Would you pay your mortgage more frequently if your internet banking was 10 times faster? Clearly, you would not. Sometimes, it is not about optimizing for many transactions per second but to optimize in a way that you can handle a predefined amount of load in the most reasonable way.

The same concept applies to the phone application we have outlined. We are not able to write all changes during the checkpoint anymore, because this might cause latency issues during a checkpoint. It is also no good to make a change to the data files more or less instantly (which means a high `checkpoint_completion_target` value), because we would be writing too much, too often.

This is a classic example where you have got to compromise. A `checkpoint_completion_target` value of `0.5` might be the best idea in this case.

Conclusion

The conclusion that should be drawn from these three examples is that no configuration fits all purposes. You really have to think about the type of data you are dealing with in order to come up with a good and feasible configuration. For many applications, a value of `0.5` has been proven to be just fine.

Tweaking WAL buffers

In this chapter, we have already adjusted some major parameters, such as `shared_buffers`, `fsync`, and so on. There is one more parameter, however, that can have a dramatic impact on performance. The `wal_buffers` parameter has been designed to tell PostgreSQL how much memory to keep around to remember the XLOG that has not been written to the disk so far. So, if somebody pumps in a large transaction, PostgreSQL will not write any "mini" change to the table to the XLOG before COMMIT. Remember that if a non-committed transaction is lost during a crash, we won't care about it anyway because COMMIT is the only thing that really counts in everyday life. It makes perfect sense to write XLOG in larger chunks before COMMIT happens. This is exactly what `wal_buffers` does. Unless changed manually in `postgresql.conf`, it is an auto-tuned parameter (represented by `-1`) that makes PostgreSQL take three percent of `shared_buffers`, but no more than 16 MB to keep the XLOG around before writing it to the disk.

> In older versions of PostgreSQL, the `wal_buffers` parameter was at 64 kB. That was unreasonably low for modern machines. If you are running an old version, consider increasing `wal_buffers` to 16 MB. This is usually a good value for reasonably sized database instances.

Experiencing the XLOG in action

We will use the transaction log throughout this book, and to give you a deeper insight into how things work on a technical level, we have added this section dealing exclusively with the internal workings of the XLOG machinery. We will avoid going down to the C level as this would be way beyond the scope of this book, but we will provide you with insights that are hopefully deep enough.

Understanding the XLOG records

Changes made to the XLOG are record-based. What does that mean? Let's assume you are adding a row to a table:

```
test=# INSERT INTO t_test VALUES (1, 'hans');
INSERT 0 1
```

In this example, we are inserting values into a table containing two columns. For the sake of this example, we want to assume that both columns are indexed.

Remember what you learned before: the purpose of the XLOG is to keep those data files safe. So this operation will trigger a series of XLOG entries. First, the data file (or files) related to the table will be written. Then the entries related to the indexes will be created. Finally, a COMMIT record will be sent to the log.

Not all the XLOG records are equal. Various types of XLOG records exist, for example heap, B-tree, clog, storage, **Generalized Inverted Index** (**GIN**), and standby records, to name a few.

XLOG records are chained backwards so, each entry points to the previous entry in the file. In this way, we can be perfectly sure that we have found the end of a record as soon as we have found the pointer to the previous entry.

Making the XLOG deterministic

As you can see, a single change can trigger a larger number of XLOG entries. This is true for all kinds of statements; a large DELETE statement, for instance, can easily cause a million changes. The reason is that PostgreSQL cannot simply put the SQL itself into the log; it really has to log physical changes made to the table.

Why is that so? Just consider the following example:

```
test=# DELETE FROM t_test WHERE id > random();
DELETE 5335
```

The random() function has to produce a different output every time it is called, and therefore we cannot just put the SQL into the log because it is not guaranteed to provide us with the same outcome if it is executed during replay.

Making the XLOG reliable

The XLOG itself is one of the most critical and sensitive parts in the entire database instance. Therefore, we have to take special care to make sure that everything possible is done to protect it. In the event of a crash, a database instance is usually doomed if there is no XLOG around.

Internally, PostgreSQL takes some special precautions to handle the XLOG:

- Using CRC32 checksums
- Disabling signals
- Space allocation

First of all, each XLOG record contains a CRC32 checksum. This allows us to check the integrity of the log at startup. It is perfectly possible that the last write operations before a crash were not totally sound any more, and therefore a checksum can definitely help sort problems straightaway. The checksum is automatically computed by PostgreSQL and users don't have to take care of this feature explicitly.

In addition to checksums, PostgreSQL will disable signals temporarily while writing to the XLOG. This gives some extra level of security and reduces the odds of a stupid corner-case problem somewhere.

Finally, PostgreSQL uses a fixed-size XLOG. The size of the XLOG is determined by checkpoint segments as well as by `checkpoint_completion_target`.

The size of the PostgreSQL transaction log is calculated as follows:

(2 + checkpoint_completion_target) * checkpoint_segments + 1

An alternative way to calculate the size is this:

checkpoint_segments + wal_keep_segments + 1 files

An important thing to note is that if something is of fixed size, it can rarely run out of space.

 In the case of transaction-log-based replication, we *can* run out of space on the XLOG directory if the transaction log cannot be archived.

You will learn more about this topic in the next chapter.

LSNs and shared buffer interaction

If you want to repair a table, you have to make sure that you do so in the correct order; it would be a disaster if a row was deleted before it actually came into existence. Therefore, the XLOG provides you with the order of all the changes. Internally, this order is reflected through the **Logical Sequence Number (LSN)**. The LSN is essential to the XLOG. Each XLOG entry will be assigned an LSN straight away.

In one of the previous sections, we discussed consistency level. With `synchronous_commit` set to `off`, a client will get an approval even if the XLOG record has not been flushed to disk yet. Still, since a change must be reflected in cache and since the XLOG must be written before the data table, the system has to make sure that not all the blocks in the shared buffer can be written to instantly. The LSN will guarantee that we can write blocks from the shared buffer to the data file only if the corresponding change has already made it to the XLOG. Writing to the XLOG is fundamental, and a violation of this rule will certainly lead to problems after a crash.

Debugging the XLOG and putting it all together

Now that we have seen how an XLOG basically works, we can put it all together and actually look into the XLOG. As of PostgreSQL 9.2, it works as follows: we have to compile PostgreSQL from source. Before we do that, we should modify the file located at `src/include/pg_config_manual.h`. At approximately line 250, we can uncomment `WAL_DEBUG` and compile as usual. This will then allow us to set a client variable called `wal_debug`:

```
test=# SET client_min_messages TO log;
SET
test=# SET wal_debug TO on;
SET
```

In addition to this, we have to set `client_min_messages` to make sure that the LOG messages will reach our client.

We are using the following table structure for our test:

```
test=# \d t_test
    Table "public.t_test"
 Column |  Type   | Modifiers
--------+---------+-----------
 id     | integer |
 name   | text    |
Indexes:
"idx_id"btree (id)
"idx_name"btree (name)
```

Only if PostgreSQL has been compiled properly will we see some information about the XLOG on the screen:

```
test=# INSERT INTO t_test VALUES (1, 'hans');
LOG:   INSERT @ 0/17C4680: prev 0/17C4620; xid 1009; len 36: Heap -
insert(init): rel 1663/16384/16394; tid 0/1

LOG:   INSERT @ 0/17C46C8: prev 0/17C4680; xid 1009; len 20: Btree -
newroot: rel 1663/16384/16397; root 1 lev 0

LOG:   INSERT @ 0/17C4700: prev 0/17C46C8; xid 1009; len 34: Btree -
insert: rel 1663/16384/16397; tid 1/1

LOG:   INSERT @ 0/17C4748: prev 0/17C4700; xid 1009; len 20: Btree -
newroot: rel 1663/16384/16398; root 1 lev 0

LOG:   INSERT @ 0/17C4780: prev 0/17C4748; xid 1009; len 34: Btree -
insert: rel 1663/16384/16398; tid 1/1

LOG:   INSERT @ 0/17C47C8: prev 0/17C4780; xid 1009; len 12: Transaction -
commit: 2013-02-25 18:20:46.633599+01

LOG:   XLOG flush request 0/17C47F8; write 0/0; flush 0/0
```

Just as stated in this chapter, PostgreSQL will first add a row to the table itself (heap). Then the XLOG will contain all entries that are index-related. Finally, a commit record will be added.

In all, 156 bytes have made it to the XLOG. This is far more than the data we have actually added. Consistency, performance (indexes), and reliability come with a price.

Making use of replication slots

In PostgreSQL 9.4, a major new feature called "replication slots" has been introduced. The idea is to give users and tools alike a chance to connect to the transaction log stream in a standard way and consume data.

Basically, two types of replication slots exist:

- Physical replication slots
- Logical replication slots

The following two sections describe those two types of replication slots in detail.

Physical replication slots

Physical replication slots are an important new feature of PostgreSQL 9.4. The idea is that a client can create a replication slot to make sure that the server only discards what has really made it to the client. Remember that in PostgreSQL, the transaction log is normally recycled as soon as a certain amount of new XLOG has been created. To the streaming replication slaves or some other clients, this can turn out to be disastrous, because if the slave/client cannot consume the transaction log fast enough or if there is simply not enough bandwidth, it can happen that the master throws away stuff that is actually still needed in the future. By giving clients an actual name, the master knows when to recycle the XLOG and make sure that the client won't lose sight of it.

Of course, a replication slot can also be dangerous. What if a slave disconnects and does not come back within a reasonable amount of time to consume all of the XLOG kept in stock? In this case, the consequences for the master are not good, because by the time the master fills up, it might be too late.

To use replication slots in your setup, you have to tell PostgreSQL via `postgresql.conf` to allow this feature, otherwise the system will error out immediately:

```
test=# SELECT * FROM pg_create_physical_replication_slot('my_slot');
ERROR:  replication slots can only be used if max_replication_slots > 0
```

In the next example, `max_replication_slots` is set to `10` in `postgresql.conf`. Keep in mind that a restart is required:

```
max_replication_slots = 10        # max number of replication slots
                                  # (change requires restart)
```

Before the database is restarted, make sure that `wal_level` is set to at least archive to make this work. Once the database has been restarted, the replication slot can be created:

```
test=# SELECT * FROM pg_create_physical_replication_slot('my_slot');
 slot_name | xlog_position
-----------+---------------
 my_slot   |
(1 row)
```

In this scenario, a replication slot called `my_slot` has been created. So far, no XLOG position has been assigned to it yet.

In the next step, it is possible to check which replication slots already exist. In this example, there is only one, of course. To retrieve the entire list, just select from `pg_replication_slots`:

```
test=# \d pg_replication_slots
View "pg_catalog.pg_replication_slots"
     Column      |  Type   | Modifiers
-----------------+---------+-----------
 slot_name       | name    |
 plugin          | name    |
 slot_type       | text    |
 datoid          | oid     |
 database        | name    |
 active          | boolean |
 xmin            | xid     |
 catalog_xmin    | xid     |
 restart_lsn     | pg_lsn  |
```

The important thing here is that a physical replication slot has been created. It can be used to stream XLOG directly, so it is really about physical copies of the data.

If a replication slot is not needed any more, it can be deleted. To do so, the following instruction can be helpful:

```
test=# SELECT pg_drop_replication_slot('my_slot');
 pg_drop_replication_slot
--------------------------

(1 row)
```

It is important to clean out replication slots as soon as they are not needed any more. Otherwise, it might happen that the server producing the XLOG fills up and faces troubles because of filled-up filesystems. It is highly important to keep an eye on those replication slots and make sure that cleanup of spare slots really happens.

Logical replication slots

In contrast to physical replication slots, logical replication slots return decoded messages through a mechanism called **logical decoding**. The main idea is to have a means of extracting changes going on in the database directly by connecting to the XLOG. The beauty of this concept is that a plugin can be used to present data in any format desired by the administrator. The output plugin reads data through a standard API and transforms things into the desired output format. No changes to the core of PostgreSQL are required because modules can be loaded on demand.

The following example shows how a simple plugin, called `test_decoding`, can be utilized to dissect the XLOG:

```
test=# SELECT * FROM pg_create_logical_replication_slot('slot_name',
'test_decoding');
 slot_name | xlog_position
-----------+---------------
 slot_name | D/438DCEB0
(1 row)
```

As soon as the replication slot is created, the transaction log position is returned. This is important to know because from this position onward, the decoded XLOG will be sent to the client.

The replication slot is, of course, visible in the system view:

```
test=# \x
Expanded display is on.
test=# SELECT * FROM pg_replication_slots;
-[ RECORD 1 ]+--------------
slot_name    | slot_name
plugin       | test_decoding
slot_type    | logical
datoid       | 21589
database     | test
active       | f
xmin         |
catalog_xmin | 937
restart_lsn  | D/438DCE78
```

The replication slot can now be used. Logically, at this point, it won't return anything because nothing has happened in the database system so far:

```
test=# SELECT * FROM pg_logical_slot_get_changes('slot_name', NULL,
NULL);
(No rows)
```

It is now possible to generate a table and insert some data to make use of the replication slot:

```
test=# CREATE TABLE t_test (id serial, name text, PRIMARY KEY (id));
CREATE TABLE
```

For the sake of simplicity, a table consisting of only two columns is enough. In the next step, two rows are added:

```
test=# INSERT INTO t_test (name) VALUES ('hans'), ('paul') RETURNING *;
 id | name
----+------
  1 | hans
  2 | paul
(2 rows)
```

Now it is possible to fetch data from the replication slot:

```
test=# SELECT * FROM pg_logical_slot_get_changes('slot_name', NULL,
NULL);
  location  | xid |                            data
------------+-----+-----------------------------------------------------
--------
 D/438DD1C8 | 937 | BEGIN 937
 D/438FCE98 | 937 | COMMIT 937
 D/438FD030 | 938 | BEGIN 938
 D/438FD030 | 938 | table public.t_test: INSERT: id[integer]:1
name[text]:'hans'
 D/438FD138 | 938 | table public.t_test: INSERT: id[integer]:2
name[text]:'paul'
 D/438FD208 | 938 | COMMIT 938
(6 rows)
```

A couple of things need to be taken care of here. One of them is that DDLs (in our case, CREATE TABLE) are not decoded and cannot be replicated through replication slots. Therefore the 937 transaction is just an empty thing. The more important details can be seen in the 938 transaction. As data has been added in one transaction, data is also logically decoded in a single transaction.

The important thing is that data is only decoded *once*. If the function is called again, it won't return anything in this case:

```
test=# SELECT * FROM pg_logical_slot_get_changes('slot_name', NULL,
NULL);
 location | xid | data
----------+-----+------
(0 rows)
```

Let's add some more data:

```
test=# INSERT INTO t_test (name) VALUES ('john') RETURNING *;
 id | name
----+------
  3 | john
(1 row)
```

There is a function called pg_logical_slot_peek_changes. It can be used to look ahead and see what is next in the queue. It does not actually dequeue the data, so it is available for later consumption:

```
test=# SELECT * FROM pg_logical_slot_peek_changes('slot_name', NULL,
NULL);
  location  | xid |                          data
------------+-----+--------------------------------------------------------
--------
 D/438FD240 | 939 | BEGIN 939
 D/438FD240 | 939 | table public.t_test: INSERT: id[integer]:3
name[text]:'john'
 D/438FD310 | 939 | COMMIT 939
(3 rows)
```

It is possible to dequeue data multiple times. PostgreSQL also offers the opportunity to pass on a parameter to the decoding module. In this example, a timestamp is desired:

```
test=# SELECT * FROM pg_logical_slot_peek_changes('slot_name', NULL,
        NULL, 'include-timestamp', 'on');
  location  | xid |                         data
------------+-----+-----------------------------------------------------
--------
 D/438FD240 | 939 | BEGIN 939
 D/438FD240 | 939 | table public.t_test: INSERT: id[integer]:3
name[text]:'john'
 D/438FD310 | 939 | COMMIT 939 (at 2015-02-11 15:38:08.00209+01)
(3 rows)
```

The system will add a timestamp to the end of the commit record of the row.

Configuring replication identities

Starting with PostgreSQL 9.4, there is also some new functionality related to replication slots in ALTER TABLE. The idea is to give users control over the amount of transaction log created during the UPDATE command. In general, the goal of the transaction log is to allow the server to repair itself. If replication slots are used, it is necessary to know a bit more about the change.

Here is a simple UPDATE command:

```
test=# UPDATE t_test SET id = id * 10 WHERE id = 3;
UPDATE 1
```

Normally, UPDATE is presented by the replication slot as follows:

```
test=# SELECT * FROM pg_logical_slot_get_changes('slot_name', NULL,
NULL);
  location  | xid |                         data
------------+-----+-----------------------------------------------------
------------------------------------------
 D/439095E8 | 940 | BEGIN 940
 D/439095E8 | 940 | table public.t_test: UPDATE: old-key: id[integer]:3
new-tuple: id[integer]:30 name[text]:'john'
 D/43909838 | 940 | COMMIT 940
(3 rows)
```

The new and the old keys are represented. However, somebody might want to see more. To extract more information, ALTER TABLE can be called. The REPLICA IDENTITY parameter can be set to FULL:

```
test=# ALTER TABLE t_test REPLICA IDENTITY FULL;
ALTER TABLE
```

```
test=# UPDATE t_test SET id = id * 10 WHERE id = 1;
UPDATE 1
```

The UPDATE command will now create a more verbose representation of the changed row. The content is way more beefy and makes the functioning of many client applications a bit easier:

```
test=# SELECT * FROM pg_logical_slot_get_changes('slot_name', NULL,
NULL);
  location  | xid |
data

------------+-----+----------------------------------------------------
--------------------------------------------
 D/4390B818 | 944 | BEGIN 944
 D/4390B818 | 944 | table public.t_test: UPDATE: old-key: id[integer]:1
name[text]:'hans'
       new-tuple: id[integer]:10 name[text]:'hans'
 D/4390B908 | 944 | COMMIT 944
(3 rows)
```

The most important difference is that in the case of the name column, both versions (before and after) are included in the textual representation.

At this point, PostgreSQL provides four different levels of REPLICA IDENTITY:

- DEFAULT: This records the old values of the columns of the primary key, if any.
- USING INDEX: This index records the old values of the columns covered by the named index, which must be unique, not partial, and not deferrable, and must include only columns marked as NOT NULL.

- FULL: This records the old values of all the columns in the row.
- NOTHING: This records no information about the old row.

The default setting is usually fine. However, in some situations (especially auditing), a bit more information is definitely worth creating.

Summary

In this chapter, you learned about the purpose of the PostgreSQL transaction log. We talked extensively about the on-disk data format and some highly important topics, such as consistency and performance. All of them will be needed when we replicate our first database in the next chapter.

The next chapter will build on top of what you have just learned, and focus on **Point-in-time-Recovery (PITR)**. Therefore, the goal will be to make PostgreSQL return to a certain point in time and provide data as if some later transactions never happened.

Understanding Point-in-time Recovery

So far, you have endured a fair amount of theory. However, since life does not only consist of theory (as important as it may be), it is definitely time to dig into practical stuff.

The goal of this chapter is to make you understand how you can recover your database to a given point in time. When your system crashes, or when somebody just happens to drop a table accidentally, it is highly important not to replay the entire transaction log but just a fraction of it. Point-in-time Recovery will be the tool to do this kind of partial replay of the transaction log.

In this chapter, you will learn all you need to know about **Point-in-time Recovery (PITR)**, and you will be guided through practical examples. Therefore, we will apply all the concepts you have learned in *Chapter 2*, *Understanding the PostgreSQL Transaction Log*, to create some sort of incremental backup or set up a simple, rudimentary standby system.

Here is an overview of the topics we will deal with in this chapter:

- Understanding the concepts behind PITR
- Configuring PostgreSQL for PITR
- Running `pg_basebackup`
- Recovering PostgreSQL to a certain point in time

At the end of this chapter, you should be able to set up Point-in-time Recovery easily.

Understanding the purpose of PITR

PostgreSQL offers a tool called `pg_dump` to back up a database. Basically, `pg_dump` will connect to the database, read all of the data in "repeatable read" transaction isolation level and return the data as text. As we are using "repeatable read," the dump is always consistent. So, if your `pg_dump` routine starts at midnight and finishes at 6 A.M., you will have created a backup that contains all of the data as of midnight, but no further data. This kind of snapshot creation is highly convenient and perfectly feasible for small to medium amounts of data.

> A dump is always consistent. This means that all the foreign keys are intact. New data added after starting the dump will be missing. It is the most common way to perform standard backups.

But what if your data is so valuable and, maybe, so large in size that you want to back it up incrementally? Taking a snapshot from time to time might be enough for some applications, but for highly critical data, it is clearly not. In addition to that, replaying 20 TB of data in textual form is not efficient either. Point-in-time Recovery has been designed to address this problem. How does it work? Based on a snapshot of the database, the XLOG will be replayed later on. This can happen indefinitely or up to a point chosen by you. In this way, you can reach any point in time.

This method opens the door to many different approaches and features:

*   Restoring a database instance up to a given point in time
*   Creating a standby database that holds a copy of the original data
*   Creating a history of all changes

In this chapter, we will specifically focus on the incremental backup functionality and describe how you can make your data more secure by incrementally archiving changes to a medium of choice.

Moving to the bigger picture

The following diagram provides an overview of the general architecture in use for Point-in-time Recovery:

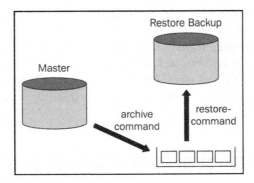

We have seen in the previous chapter that PostgreSQL produces 16 MB segments of transaction log. Every time one of those segments is filled up and ready, PostgreSQL will call the so-called `archive_command`. The aim of `archive_command` is to transport the XLOG file from the database instance to an archive. In our diagram, the archive is represented as the pot in the bottom-right corner.

The beauty of the design is that you can basically use an arbitrary shell script to archive the transaction log. Here are some ideas:

- Use some simple copy to transport data to an NFS share
- Run `rsync` to move a file
- Use a custom-made script to checksum the XLOG file and move it to an FTP server
- Copy the XLOG file to a tape
- Upload data to a cloud-based storage provider

The possible options for managing XLOG are only limited by the imagination.

The `restore_command` is the exact counterpart of `archive_command`. Its purpose is to fetch data from the archive and provide it to the instance, which is supposed to replay it (in the preceding diagram, this is labeled as **Restore Backup**). As you have seen, replay might be used for replication or simply to restore a database to a given point in time, as outlined in this chapter. Again, `restore_command` is simply a shell script doing whatever you wish file by file.

It is important to mention that you, the almighty administrator, are in charge of the archive. You have to decide how much XLOG to keep and when to delete it. The importance of this task cannot be underestimated.

Keep in mind that when `archive_command` fails for some reason, PostgreSQL will keep the XLOG file and retry after a couple of seconds. If archiving fails constantly from a certain point onwards, it might happen that the master fills up. The sequence of XLOG files must not be interrupted; if a single file is missing, you cannot continue to replay XLOG. All XLOG files must be present because PostgreSQL needs an uninterrupted sequence of XLOG files. Even if a single file is missing, the recovery process will stop there.

Archiving the transaction log

After taking a look at the big picture, we can see how things can be put to work.

The first thing you have to do when it comes to Point-in-time Recovery is archive the XLOG. PostgreSQL offers all the configuration options related to archiving through `postgresql.conf`.

Let us see step by step what has to be done in `postgresql.conf` to start archiving:

1. First of all, you should turn `archive_mode` on.
2. In the second step, you should configure your `archive_command`. The `archive_command` is a simple shell, and it needs just two parameters to operate properly:

    ° `%p`: This is a placeholder representing the XLOG file that should be archived, including its full path (source).

    ° `%f`: This variable holds the name of XLOG without the path pointing to it.

Let's set up archiving now. To do so, we should create a place to put the XLOG. Ideally, the XLOG is not stored on the same hardware as the database instance you want to archive. For the sake of this example, we assume that we want to copy an archive to `/archive`. The following changes have to be made to `postgresql.conf`:

```
wal_level = archive
        # minimal, archive, hot_standby, or logical
        # (change requires restart)
archive_mode = on
        # allows archiving to be done
        # (change requires restart)
archive_command = 'cp %p /archive/%f'
        # command to use to archive a logfile segment
        # placeholders: %p = path of file to archive
        #               %f = file name only
```

Once these changes have been made to postgresql.conf, archiving is ready for action. To activate these change, restarting the database server is necessary.

Before we restart the database instance, we want to focus your attention on `wal_level`. Currently four different `wal_level` settings are available:

- `minimal`
- `archive`
- `hot_standby`
- `logical`

The amount of transaction log produced in the case of `wal_level = minimal` is by far not enough to synchronize an entire second instance. In `wal_level=minimal`, there are some optimizations in PostgreSQL that allow XLOG writing to be skipped. The following instructions can benefit from `wal_level` being set to `minimal`: `CREATE TABLE AS`, `CREATE INDEX`, `CLUSTER`, and `COPY` (if the table was created or truncated within the same transaction).

To replay the transaction log, at least `archive` is needed. The difference between `archive` and `hot_standby` is that `archive` does not have to know about the currently running transactions. However, for streaming replication, as will be covered in the next chapters, this information is vital.

If you are planning to use logical decoding, `wal_level` must be set to `logical` to make sure that the XLOG contains even more information, which is needed to support logical decoding. Logical decoding requires the most verbose XLOG currently available in PostgreSQL.

> Restarting can either be done through `pg_ctl -D /data_directory -m fast restart` directly or through a standard `init` script.

The easiest way to check whether our archiving works is to create some useless data inside the database. The following snippet shows that a million rows can be made easily:

```
test=# CREATE TABLE t_test AS SELECT * FROM generate_series(1, 1000000);
SELECT 1000000
```

```
test=# SELECT * FROM t_test LIMIT 3;
generate_series
----------------
              1
              2
              3
(3 rows)
```

We have simply created a list of numbers. The important thing is that one million rows will trigger a fair amount of XLOG traffic. You will see that a handful of files have made it to the archive:

iMac:archivehs$ ls -l /archive/

```
total 131072
-rw------- 1 hs  wheel  16777216 Mar  5 22:31 000000010000000000000001
-rw------- 1 hs  wheel  16777216 Mar  5 22:31 000000010000000000000002
-rw------- 1 hs  wheel  16777216 Mar  5 22:31 000000010000000000000003
-rw------- 1 hs  wheel  16777216 Mar  5 22:31 000000010000000000000004
```

Those files can be easily used for future replay operations.

> If you want to save storage, you can also compress those XLOG files. Just add gzip to your archive_command. This complicates things a little, but this little complexity certainly benefits users.

Taking base backups

In the previous section, you saw that enabling archiving takes just a handful of lines and offers a great deal of flexibility. In this section, we will see how to create a so-called base backup, which can be used to apply XLOG later on. A base backup is an initial copy of data.

> Keep in mind that the XLOG itself is more or less worthless. It is only useful in combination with the initial base backup.

In PostgreSQL, there are two main options to create an initial base backup:

- Using pg_basebackup
- Traditional methods based on copy /rsync

Note that `pg_dump` cannot be used for a base backup because a binary copy of the data is required. The `pg_dump` provides a textual representation of the data and not a binary one, so it is not feasible here.

The following two sections will explain in detail how a base backup can be created.

Using pg_basebackup

The first and most common method of creating a backup of an existing server is by running a command called `pg_basebackup`, which was first introduced in PostgreSQL 9.1.0. Previously, other techniques that are described later in this book were available. Basically, `pg_basebackup` is able to fetch a database base backup directly over a database connection. When executed on the slave, `pg_basebackup` will connect to the database server of your choice, and copy all the data files in the data directory to your machine. There is no need to log in to the box anymore, and all it takes is one line of code to run it; `pg_basebackup` will do all the rest for you.

In this example, we will assume that we want to take a base backup of a host called `sample.postgresql-support.de`. The following steps must be performed:

1. Modify `pg_hba.conf` to allow replication
2. Signal the master to take the `pg_hba.conf` changes into account
3. Call `pg_basebackup`

Modifying pg_hba.conf

To allow remote boxes to log in to a PostgreSQL server and stream XLOG, you have to explicitly allow replication.

In PostgreSQL, there is a file called `pg_hba.conf` that tells the server which boxes are allowed to connect using which type of credentials. Entire IP ranges can be allowed or simply discarded through `pg_hba.conf`.

To enable replication, we have to add one line for each IP range we want to allow. The following listing contains an example of a valid configuration:

```
# TYPE  DATABASE     USER     ADDRESS              METHOD
host  replication   all     192.168.0.34/32       md5
```

In this case, we allow replication connections starting from `192.168.0.34`. The IP range is identified by `32` (which simply represents a single server in our case). We have decided to use MD5 as our authentication method. This means that `pg_basebackup` has to supply a password to the server. If you are doing this in a non-security-critical environment, using `trust` as authentication method might also be an option.

What happens if you actually have a database called `replication` in your system? Basically, setting the database to `replication` will just configure your streaming behavior. If you want to put in rules dealing with the database called `replication`, you have to quote the database name as follows: `"replication"`. However, we strongly advise you not to do this kind of trickery to avoid confusion.

Signaling the master server

Once `pg_hba.conf` has been changed, we can tell PostgreSQL to reload the configuration. There is no need to restart the database completely. We have three options to make PostgreSQL reload `pg_hba.conf`:

- By running a SQL command: `SELECT pg_reload_conf();`
- By sending a signal to the master: `kill -HUP 4711` (with `4711` being the process ID of the master)
- By calling `pg_ctl`: `pg_ctl -D $PGDATA reload` (with `$PGDATA` being the home directory of your database instance)

Once we have told the server acting as data source to accept streaming connections, we can move forward and run `pg_basebackup`.

pg_basebackup – basic features

The `pg_basebackup` tool is a very simple to use command-line tool for PostgreSQL. It has to be called on the target system, and will provide you with a ready to use base backup, which is ready to consume the transaction log for Point-in-time Recovery.

The syntax of `pg_basebackup` is as follows:

```
hs@chantal:~$ pg_basebackup --help
pg_basebackup takes a base backup of a running PostgreSQL server.

Usage:
  pg_basebackup [OPTION]...

Options controlling the output:
  -D, --pgdata=DIRECTORY receive base backup into directory
  -F, --format=p|t       output format (plain (default), tar)
  -r, --max-rate=RATE    maximum transfer rate to transfer data directory
                         (in kB/s, or use suffix "k" or "M")
```

```
-R, --write-recovery-conf
                        write recovery.conf after backup
-T, --tablespace-mapping=OLDDIR=NEWDIR
                        relocate tablespace in OLDDIR to NEWDIR
-x, --xlog              include required WAL files in backup (fetch
mode)
-X, --xlog-method=fetch|stream
                        include required WAL files with specified method
    --xlogdir=XLOGDIR   location for the transaction log directory
-z, --gzip              compress tar output
-Z, --compress=0-9      compress tar output with given compression level


General options:
-c, --checkpoint=fast|spread
                        set fast or spread checkpointing
-l, --label=LABEL       set backup label
-P, --progress          show progress information
-v, --verbose           output verbose messages
-V, --version           output version information, then exit
-?, --help              show this help, then exit


Connection options:
-d, --dbname=CONNSTR    connection string
-h, --host=HOSTNAME     database server host or socket directory
-p, --port=PORT         database server port number
-s, --status-interval=INTERVAL
                        time between status packets sent to server (in
seconds)
-U, --username=NAME     connect as specified database user
-w, --no-password       never prompt for password
-W, --password          force password prompt (should happen
automatically)
```

A basic call to pg_basebackup would look like this:

```
chantal:dbhs$ pg_basebackup -D /target_directory \
-h sample.postgresql-support.de
```

In this example, we will fetch the base backup from `sample.postgresql-support.de`, and put it into our local directory called `/target_directory`. It just takes this simple line to copy an entire database instance to the target system.

When we create a base backup as shown in this section, `pg_basebackup` will connect to the server and wait for a checkpoint to happen before the actual copy process is started. In this mode, this is necessary because the replay process will start exactly at this point in the XLOG. The problem is that it might take a while until a checkpoint kicks in; `pg_basebackup` does not enforce a checkpoint on the source server straightaway so as to make sure that normal operations are not disturbed.

 If you don't want to wait on a checkpoint, consider using `--checkpoint=fast`. This will enforce a checkpoint and `pg_basebackup` will start copying instantly.

By default, a plain base backup will be created. It will consist of all the files in directories found on the source server. If the base backup has to be stored on a tape, we recommend that you give `--format=t` a try. It will automatically create a `tar` archive (maybe on a tape). If you want to move data to a tape, you can easily save an intermediate step in this way. When using `tar`, it is usually quite beneficial to use it in combination with `--gzip` to reduce the size of the base backup on the disk.

 There is also a way to see a progress bar while performing the base backup, but we don't recommend using this option (`--progress`) because it requires `pg_basebackup` to determine the size of the source instance first, which can be costly.

Backup throttling

If your master has only a weak I/O subsystem, it can happen that a *full blown* base backup creates so much load on the master's I/O system that normal transactions begin to suffer. Performance goes down and latency goes up. This is clearly an undesirable thing. Therefore, `pg_basebackup` allows backup speeds to be reduced. By reducing the throughput of the backup tool, the master will have more capacity left to serve normal requests.

To reduce the speed of the backup, you can use the `-r` (`--max-rate`) command-line switch. The expected unit is in KB. However, megabytes are also possible. Just pass the desired throughput as a parameter and stretch the backup to make sure that your master server does not suffer from the backup. The optimal value for these settings highly depends on your hardware infrastructure and performance requirements, so administrators have to determine the right speed as needed.

pg_basebackup – self-sufficient backups

Usually, a base backup without XLOG is pretty worthless. This is because the base backup is taken while the master is fully operational. While the backup is taken, the storage files in the database instance might have been modified heavily. The purpose of the XLOG is to fix those potential issues in the data files reliably.

But what if we want to create a base backup that can live without (explicitly archived) XLOG? In such a case, we can use the --xlog-method=stream option. If this option has been chosen, pg_basebackup will not only copy the data as it is, but also stream the XLOG being created during the base backup to our destination server. This will provide us with just enough XLOG to allow us to start a base backup made directly. It is self-sufficient and does not need additional XLOG files. This is not Point-in-time Recovery, but it can come in handy if there is trouble. Having a base backup, which can be started right away, is usually a good thing and it comes at fairly low cost.

> Note that --xlog-method=stream will require two database connections to the source server, not just one. You have to keep that in mind when adjusting max_wal_senders on the source server.

If you are planning to use Point-in-time Recovery and if there is absolutely no need to start the backup as it is, you can safely skip the XLOG and save some space this way (default mode).

Making use of traditional methods to create base backups

These days, pg_basebackup is the most common way of getting an initial copy of a database server. This has not always been the case. Traditionally, a different method was used, which worked as follows:

1. Call SELECT pg_start_backup('some label');.
2. Copy all data files to the remote box through rsync or any other means.
3. Run SELECT pg_stop_backup();.

The main advantage of this old method is that there is no need to open a database connection, and no need to configure the XLOG streaming infrastructure on the source server.

Another main advantage is that you can make use of features such as ZFS snapshots or similar means that can help reduce dramatically the amount of I/O needed to create an initial backup.

Once you have started `pg_start_backup`, there is no need to hurry. It is not necessary, and not even desirable, to leave the backup mode soon. Nothing will happen if you are in backup mode for days. PostgreSQL will archive the transaction log as usual, and the user won't face any kind of downside. Of course, it is a bad habit not to close backups soon and properly. However, the way PostgreSQL works internally does not change when a base backup is running. There is nothing filling up, no disk I/O delayed, or anything of this sort. The `pg_basebackup` tool just copies files to the slave, and therefore it is not invasive at all.

Tablespace issues

If you happen to use more than one tablespace, `pg_basebackup` will handle this just fine, provided the filesystem layout on the target box is identical to the filesystem layout on the master. However, if your target system does not use the same filesystem layout, there will be a bit more work to do. Using the traditional way of doing the base backup might be beneficial in this case.

If you are using `--format=t` (for `tar`), you will be provided with one `tar` file per tablespace.

Keeping an eye on the network bandwidth

In the previous section, it has already been not that a weak server can easily fall victim to fast backups consuming all of the I/O capacity. The solution to the problem is the `--max-rate` setting. Throttling the backup is also highly recommended when using rsync as the desired backup method.

If you want to limit `rsync` to, say, 20 MB/sec, you can simply use `rsync --bwlimit=20000`. This will definitely cause creation of the base backup to take longer, but it will make sure that your client apps don't face problems. In general, we recommend a dedicated network which connects the master and slave to make sure that a base backup does not affect normal operations.

Of course, you can use any other tools to copy data and achieve similar results.

 If you are using `gzip` compression with `--gzip`, it can work as an implicit speed brake. However, this is mainly a workaround.

Replaying the transaction log

Once we have created ourselves a shiny initial base backup, we can collect the XLOG files created by the database. When the time comes, we can take all of those XLOG files and perform our desired recovery process. This works as described in this section.

Performing a basic recovery

In PostgreSQL, the entire recovery process is governed by a file named `recovery. conf`, which has to reside in the main directory of the base backup. It is read during startup and tells the database server where to find the XLOG archive, when to end the replay, and so forth.

To get you started, we have decided to include a simple `recovery.conf` sample file for performing a basic recovery process:

```
restore_command = 'cp /archive/%f %p'
recovery_target_time = '2015-10-10 13:43:12'
```

The `restore_command` is essentially the exact counterpart of the `archive_command` you have seen before. While `archive_command` is supposed to put data into the archive, `restore_command` is supposed to provide the recovering instance with the data file by file. The `restore_command` is called for every file requested by the starting slave/replica. Again, it is a simple shell command or a simple shell script providing one chunk of XLOG after the other. The options you have here are only limited by the imagination. All that PostgreSQL does is it checks for the return code of the code you have written and replays the data provided by your script.

Just as in `postgresql.conf`, we have used `%p` and `%f` as placeholders. The meaning of those two placeholders is exactly the same.

To tell the system when to stop recovery, we can set `recovery_target_time`. This variable is actually optional. If it has not been specified, PostgreSQL will recover until it runs out of XLOG. In many cases, simply consuming the entire XLOG is a highly desirable process. If something crashes, you would want to restore as much data as possible, but this is not always so. If you want to make PostgreSQL stop recovery at a specific point in time, you simply have to put in the proper date. The crucial part here is actually to know how far you want to replay XLOG. In a real work scenario, this has proven to be the trickiest question to answer.

> If you happen to specify `recovery_target_time`, which is in the future, don't worry. PostgreSQL will start at the very last transaction available in your XLOG and simply stop recovery. The database instance will still be consistent and ready for action. You cannot break PostgreSQL, but you might break your applications if data is lost because of missing XLOG.

Before starting PostgreSQL, you have to run `chmod 700` on the directory containing the base backup, otherwise PostgreSQL will error out:

```
iMac:target_directoryhs$ pg_ctl -D /target_directory \
  start
server starting
FATAL:  data directory "/target_directory" has group or world access
DETAIL:  Permissions should be u=rwx (0700).
```

This additional security check is supposed to make sure that your data directory cannot be read by some user accidentally. Therefore, an explicit permission change is definitely an advantage from a security point of view (better safe than sorry).

Now that we have all the pieces in place, we can start the replay process by starting PostgreSQL:

```
iMac:target_directoryhs$ pg_ctl -D /target_directory \
start
server starting
LOG:  database system was interrupted; last known up at 2015-03-10
18:04:29 CET
LOG:  creating missing WAL directory "pg_xlog/archive_status"
```

```
LOG:    starting point-in-time recovery to 2015-10-10 13:43:12+02
LOG:    restored log file "000000010000000000000006" from archive
LOG:    redo starts at 0/6000020
LOG:    consistent recovery state reached at 0/60000B8
LOG:    restored log file "000000010000000000000007" from archive
LOG:    restored log file "000000010000000000000008" from archive
LOG:    restored log file "000000010000000000000009" from archive
LOG:    restored log file "00000001000000000000000A" from archive
cp: /tmp/archive/00000001000000000000000B: No such file or directory
LOG:    could not open file "pg_xlog/00000001000000000000000B" (log file 0,
segment 11): No such file or directory
LOG:    redo done at 0/AD5CE40
LOG:    last completed transaction was at log time 2015-03-10
18:05:33.852992+01
LOG:    restored log file "00000001000000000000000A" from archive
cp: /tmp/archive/00000002.history: No such file or directory
LOG:    selected new timeline ID: 2
cp: /tmp/archive/00000001.history: No such file or directory
LOG:    archive recovery complete
LOG:    database system is ready to accept connections
LOG:    autovacuum launcher started
```

The amount of log produced by the database tells us everything we need to know about the restoration process, and it is definitely worth investigating this information in detail.

The first line indicates that PostgreSQL has realized that it has been interrupted and has to start recovery. From the database instance point of view, a base backup looks more or less like a crash needing some instant care by replaying XLOG. This is precisely what we want.

The next couple of lines (`restored log file ...`) indicate that we are replaying one XLOG file after the other. These files have been created since the base backup. It is worth mentioning that the replay process starts at the sixth file. The base backup knows where to start, so PostgreSQL will automatically look for the right XLOG file.

The message displayed after PostgreSQL reaches the sixth file (`consistent recovery state reached at 0/60000B8`) is important. PostgreSQL states that it has reached a consistent state. The reason is that the data files inside a base backup are actually broken by definition (refer to *Chapter 2, Understanding the PostgreSQL Transaction Log* in the *The XLOG and replication* section), but the data files are not broken beyond repair. As long as we have enough XLOG to recover, we are very well off. If you cannot reach a consistent state, your database instance will not be usable and your recovery cannot work without providing additional XLOG.

> Practically speaking, not being able to reach a consistent state usually indicates a problem somewhere in your archiving process and your system setup. If everything so far has been working properly, there is no reason for not reaching a consistent state. Keep in mind that having an untested backup is the same as having no backup at all. It is really essential to make sure that the XLOGs are complete.

Once we have reached a consistent state, one file after another will be replayed successfully until the system finally looks for the `00000001000000000000000B` file. The problem is that this file has not been created by the source database instance. Logically, an error pops up.

> Not finding the last file is absolutely normal. This type of error is expected if `recovery_target_time` does not ask PostgreSQL to stop recovery before it reaches the end of the XLOG stream. Don't worry! Your system is actually fine. The error just indicates that you have run out of XLOG. You have successfully replayed everything to the file that shows up exactly before the error message.

As soon as all of the XLOG has been consumed and the error message discussed earlier has been issued, PostgreSQL reports the last transaction that it was able to or supposed to replay and starts up. You now have a fully recovered database instance and can connect to the database instantly. As soon as the recovery has ended, `recovery.conf` will be renamed by PostgreSQL to `recovery.done` to make sure that it does not do any harm when the new instance is restarted later on at some point.

More sophisticated positioning in the XLOG

So far, we have recovered a database up to the very latest moment available in our 16 MB chunks of transaction log. We have also seen that you can define the desired recovery timestamp. But the question now is: how do you know which point in time to perform the recovery to? Just imagine that somebody has deleted a table during the day. What if you cannot easily determine the recovery timestamp right away? What if you want to recover to a certain transaction?

The `recovery.conf` file has all you need. If you want to replay up to a certain transaction, you can refer to `recovery_target_xid`. Just specify the transaction you need and configure `recovery_target_inclusive` to include that very transaction mentioned in `recovery_target_xid` or not to include it. Using this setting is technically easy, but as mentioned before, it can be really difficult to find a specific transaction ID.

In a typical setup, the best way to find a reasonable point to stop recovery is to use `pause_at_recovery_target`. If this is set to true, PostgreSQL will not automatically turn into a productive instance if the recovery point has been reached. Instead, it will wait for further instructions from the database administrator. This is especially useful if you don't know exactly how far to replay. You can replay, log in, see how far the database is, change to the next target time, and continue replaying in small steps.

 You have to set `hot_standby = on` in `postgresql.conf` to allow reading during recovery.

Resuming recovery after PostgreSQL has paused can be done by calling a simple SQL statement— `SELECT pg_xlog_replay_resume()`. This will make the instance move to the next position you have set in `recovery.conf`. Once you have found the right place, you can set `pause_at_recovery_target` back to false and call `pg_xlog_replay_resume`. Alternatively, you can simply utilize `pg_ctl -D ... promote` to stop the recovery and make the instance operational.

Was this explanation too complicated? Let us boil it down to a simple list:

1. Add `restore_command` to the `recovery.conf` file.
2. Add `recovery_target_time` to the `recovery.conf` file.
3. Set `pause_at_recovery_target` to `true` in the `recovery.conf` file.
4. Then set `hot_standby` to on in the `postgresql.conf` file.
5. Start the instance to be recovered.
6. Connect to the instance once it has reached a consistent state and as soon as it stops recovering
7. Check whether you have already recovered
8. If you are not:
   1. Change `recovery_target_time`
   2. Run `SELECT pg_xlog_replay_resume()`
   3. Check again and repeat this section if necessary

> Keep in mind that once the recovery has completed and once PostgreSQL has started up as a normal database instance, there is (as of 9.4) no way to replay XLOG later on. Instead of going through this process, you can—of course—always use filesystem snapshots. A filesystem snapshot will always work with PostgreSQL because when you restart a "snapshotted" database instance, it will simply believe that it had crashed before and recover normally.

Cleaning up the XLOG on the way

Once you have configured archiving, you have to store the XLOG being created by the source server. Logically, this cannot happen forever. At some point, you really have to get rid of this XLOG. It is essential to have a sane and sustainable cleanup policy for your files.

Keep in mind, however, that you must keep enough XLOG so that you can always perform recovery from the latest base backup. But if you are certain that a specific base backup is not needed anymore, you can safely clean out all of the XLOG that is older than the base backup you want to keep.

How can an administrator figure out what to delete? The best method is to simply take a look at their archive directory:

```
000000010000000000000005
000000010000000000000006
000000010000000000000006.00000020.backup
000000010000000000000007
000000010000000000000008
```

Check out the filename in the middle of the listing. The .backup file has been created by the base backup. It contains some information about the way the base backup has been made, and tells the system where to continue replaying the XLOG. If the backup file belongs to the oldest base backup you need to keep around, you can safely erase all contents of the XLOG files lower than file number 6. In this case, file number 5 can be safely deleted.

In our case, 000000010000000000000006.00000020.backup contains the following information:

```
START WAL LOCATION: 0/6000020 (file 000000010000000000000006)
STOP WAL LOCATION: 0/60000E0 (file 000000010000000000000006)
CHECKPOINT LOCATION: 0/6000058
BACKUP METHOD: streamed
```

```
BACKUP FROM: master
START TIME: 2015-03-10 18:04:29 CET
LABEL: pg_basebackup base backup
STOP TIME: 2015-03-10 18:04:30 CET
```

The `.backup` file will also provide you with relevant information, such as the time the base backup has been made. It is plainly shown there, and so it should be easy for ordinary users to read this information.

Also, you can add the `recovery_end_command` command to your `recovery.conf` file. The goal of `recovery_end_command` is to allow you to automatically trigger some action as soon as the recovery ends. Again, PostgreSQL will call a script that does precisely what you want. You can easily misuse this setting to clean up the old XLOG when the database declares itself active.

Switching the XLOG files

If you are going for an XLOG-file-based recovery, you many have seen that one XLOG will be archived every 16 MB. What would happen if you never manage to create 16 MB of changes? What if you have a small supermarket that makes just 50 sales a day? Your system will never manage to take up 16 MB in time.

However, if your system crashes, the potential data loss can be seen as the amount of data in your last unfinished XLOG file. Maybe, this is not good enough for you.

A `postgresql.conf` setting on the source database might help. The `archive_timeout` variable tells PostgreSQL to create a new XLOG file at least every *x* seconds. So, if you have this little supermarket, you can ask the database to create a new XLOG file every day shortly before you are heading for home. In this case, you can be sure that the day's data will be present safely on your backup device.

It is also possible to make PostgreSQL switch to the next XLOG file manually. A procedure named `pg_switch_xlog()` is provided by the server to do this job:

```
test=# SELECT pg_switch_xlog();

pg_switch_xlog
----------------
 0/17C0EF8

(1 row)
```

You might want to call this procedure when some important patch job has finished, or if you want to make sure that a certain chunk of data is safely in your XLOG archive.

Summary

In this chapter, you learned about Point-in-time Recovery, which is a safe and easy way to restore your PostgreSQL database to any desired point in time. PITR will help you implement better backup policies and make your setups more robust.

In the next chapter, we will extend this topic and turn to asynchronous replication. You will learn how to replicate an entire database instance using the PostgreSQL transaction log.

4
Setting Up Asynchronous Replication

After performing our first PITR, we are ready to work on a real replication setup. In this chapter, you will learn how to set up asynchronous replication and streaming. The goal is to make sure that you can achieve higher availability and higher data security.

In this chapter, we will cover the following topics:

- Configuring asynchronous replication
- Understanding streaming
- Combining streaming and archives
- Managing timelines

At the end of this chapter, you will be able to easily set up streaming replication in a couple of minutes.

Setting up streaming replication

In the previous chapter, we recovered data from simple 16 MB XLOG files. Logically, the replay process can only replay 16 MB at a time. This can lead to latency in your replication setup, because you have to wait until the 16 MB have been created by the master database instance. In many cases, this kind of delay might not be acceptable.

 Missing the last XLOG file, which has not been finalized (and thus not sent to the archive and lost because of the crash), is often the core reason that people report data loss in the case of PITR.

In this scenario, streaming replication will be the solution to your problem. With streaming replication, the replication delay will be minimal and you can enjoy an extra level of protection for your data.

Let's talk about the general architecture of the PostgreSQL streaming infrastructure. The following diagram illustrates the basic system design:

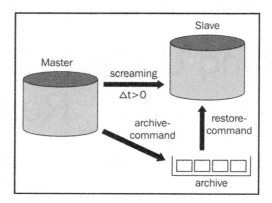

You have already seen this type of architecture. What we have added here is the streaming connection. It is basically a normal database connection, just as you would use in any other application. The only difference is that in the case of a streaming connection, the connection will be in a special mode so as to be able to carry the XLOG.

Tweaking the config files on the master

The question now is: how can you make a streaming connection come into existence? Most of the infrastructure has already been made in the previous chapter. On the master, the following must be set:

- The `wal_level` parameter must be set to `hot_standby`
- The `max_wal_senders` parameter must be at a reasonably high value to support enough slaves

How about `archive_mode` and `archive_command`? Many people use streaming replication to make their systems replicate more data to a slave as soon as possible. In addition to that, file-based replication is often utilized to make sure that there is an extra layer of security. Basically, both mechanisms use the same techniques; just the source of XLOG differs in the cases of streaming-based and archive-based recovery.

Now that the master knows that it is supposed to produce enough XLOG, handle XLOG senders, and so on, we can move on to the next step.

For security reasons, you must configure the master to enable streaming replication connections. This requires changing `pg_hba.conf` as shown in the previous chapter. Again, this is needed to run `pg_basebackup` and the subsequent streaming connection. Even if you are using a traditional method to take the base backup, you still have to allow replication connections to stream the XLOG, so this step is mandatory.

Once your master has been successfully configured, you can restart the database (to make `wal_level` and `max_wal_senders` work) and continue working on the slave.

Handling pg_basebackup and recovery.conf

So far, you have seen that the replication process is absolutely identical to performing a normal PITR. The only different thing so far is `wal_level`, which has to be configured differently for a normal PITR. Other than that, it is the same technique; there's no difference.

To fetch the base backup, we can use `pg_basebackup`, just as was shown in the previous chapter. Here is an example:

```
iMac:dbhs$ pg_basebackup -D /target_directory \
-h sample.postgresql-support.de\
--xlog-method=stream
```

Now that we have taken a base backup, we can move ahead and configure streaming. To do so, we have to write a file called `recovery.conf` (just like before). Here is a simple example:

```
standby_mode = on
primary_conninfo= ' host=sample.postgresql-support.de port=5432 '
```

Note that from PostgreSQL 9.3 onwards, there is a `-R` flag for `pg_basebackup`, which is capable of automatically generating `recovery.conf`. In other words, a new slave can be generated using just one command.

We have two new settings:

* `standby_mode`: This setting will make sure that PostgreSQL does not stop once it runs out of XLOG. Instead, it will wait for new XLOG to arrive. This setting is essential in order to make the second server a standby, which replays XLOG constantly.

- `primary_conninfo`: This setting will tell our slave where to find the master. You have to put a standard PostgreSQL connect string (just like in `libpq`) here. The `primary_conninfo` variable is central and tells PostgreSQL to stream XLOG.

For a basic setup, these two settings are totally sufficient. All we have to do now is to fire up the slave, just like starting a normal database instance:

```
iMac:slavehs$ pg_ctl -D / start
server starting
LOG:   database system was interrupted; last known up
at 2015-03-17 21:08:39 CET
LOG:   creating missing WAL directory
       "pg_XLOG/archive_status"
LOG:   entering standby mode
LOG:   streaming replication successfully connected
to primary
LOG:   redo starts at 0/2000020
LOG:   consistent recovery state reached at 0/3000000
```

The database instance has successfully started. It detects that normal operations have been interrupted. Then it enters standby mode and starts to stream XLOG from the primary system. PostgreSQL then reaches a consistent state and the system is ready for action.

Making the slave readable

So far, we have only set up streaming. The slave is already consuming the transaction log from the master, but it is not readable yet. If you try to connect to the instance, you will face the following scenario:

```
iMac:slavehs$ psql -l
FATAL:  the database system is starting up
psql: FATAL:  the database system is starting up
```

This is the default configuration. The slave instance is constantly in backup mode and keeps replaying XLOG.

If you want to make the slave readable, you have to adapt `postgresql.conf` on the slave system; `hot_standby` must be set to `on`. You can set this straightaway, but you can also make this change later on and simply restart the slave instance when you want this feature to be enabled:

```
iMac:slavehs$ pg_ctl -D ./target_directory restart
waiting for server to shut down....
LOG:  received smart shutdown request
FATAL:  terminating walreceiver process due to administrator command
LOG:  shutting down
LOG:  database system is shut down
done
server stopped
server starting
LOG:  database system was shut down in recovery at 2015-03-17 21:56:12
CET
LOG:  entering standby mode
LOG:  consistent recovery state reached at 0/3000578
LOG:  redo starts at 0/30004E0
LOG:  record with zero length at 0/3000578
LOG:  database system is ready to accept read only connections
LOG:  streaming replication successfully connected to primary
```

The restart will shut down the server and fire it back up again. This is not too much of a surprise; however, it is worth taking a look at the log. You can see that a process called walreceiver is terminated.

Once we are back up and running, we can connect to the server. Logically, we are only allowed to perform read-only operations:

```
test=# CREATE TABLE x (id int4);
ERROR:  cannot execute CREATE TABLE in a read-only transaction
```

The server will not accept writes, as expected. Remember, slaves are read-only.

The underlying protocol

When using streaming replication, you should keep an eye on two processes:

- wal_sender
- wal_receiver

The wal_sender instances are processes on the master instance that serve XLOG to their counterpart on the slave, called wal_receiver. Each slave has exactly one wal_receiver parameter, and this process is connected to exactly one wal_sender parameter on the data source.

How does this entire thing work internally? As we have stated before, the connection from the slave to the master is basically a normal database connection. The transaction log uses more or less the same method as a COPY command would do. Inside the COPY mode, PostgreSQL uses a little micro language to ship information back and forth. The main advantage is that this little language has its own parser, and so it is possible to add functionality fast and in a fairly easy, non-intrusive way. As of PostgreSQL 9.4, the following commands are supported:

- IDENTIFY_SYSTEM: This requires the server to identify itself. The server replies with four fields (systemid, timeline, xlogpos, dbname).

- TIMELINE_HISTORY tli: This requests the server to send the timeline history file for a given timeline. The response consists of the filename and content.

- CREATE_REPLICATION_SLOT slot_name {PHYSICAL | LOGICAL output_plugin}: This creates a replication slot (physical or logical). In the case of a logical replication slot, an output plugin for formatting the data returned by the replication slot is mandatory.

- START_REPLICATION [SLOT slot_name] [PHYSICAL] xxx/xxx [TIMELINE tli]: This tells the server to start WAL streaming for a given replication slot at a certain position for a certain timeline.

- START_REPLICATION SLOT slot_name LOGICAL XXX/XXX [(option_name [option_value] [, ...])]: This starts logical streaming from a certain position onwards.

- DROP_REPLICATION_SLOT slot_name: This drops a replication slot.

- BASE_BACKUP [LABEL 'label'] [PROGRESS] [FAST] [WAL] [NOWAIT] [MAX_RATE rate]: This performs a base backup, given certain optional parameters.

What you see is that the protocol level is pretty close to what pg_basebackup offers as command-line flags.

Configuring a cascaded replication

As you have already seen in this chapter, setting up streaming replication is really easy. All it takes is setting a handful of parameters, taking a base backup, and enjoying your replication setup.

In many cases, however, the situation is a bit more delicate. Let's assume for this example that we want to use a master to spread data to dozens of servers. The overhead of replication is actually very small (common wisdom says that the overhead of a slave is around 3 percent of overall performance—however, this is just a rough estimate), but if you do something small often enough, it can still be an issue.

It is definitely not very beneficial for the master to have, say, 100 slaves.

An additional use case is as follows: having a master in one location and a couple of slaves in some other location. It does not make sense to send a lot of data over a long distance over and over again. It is a lot better to send it once and dispatch it to the other side.

To make sure that not all servers have to consume the transaction log from a single master, you can make use of cascaded replication. Cascading means that a master can stream its transaction log to a slave, which will then serve as the dispatcher and stream the transaction log to further slaves.

 To use cascaded replication, you need at least PostgreSQL 9.2.

The following diagram illustrates the basic architecture of cascaded replication:

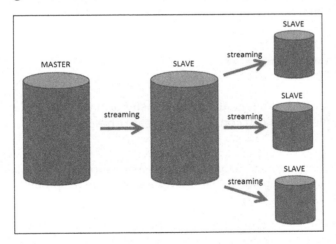

The slaves to the far right of the diagram could serve as dispatchers again. With this very simple method, you can basically create a system of infinite size.

The procedure to set things up is basically the same as that for setting up a single slave. You can easily take base backups from an operational slave (`postgresql.conf` and `pg_hba.conf` have to be configured just as in the case of a single master).

 Be aware of timeline switches; these can easily cause issues in the event of a failover. Check out the *Dealing with the timelines* section to find out more.

Turning slaves into masters

A slave can be a wonderful thing if you want to scale up reads or get a backup of your data. But a slave might not always have to remain a slave. At some point, you might need to turn a slave into a master. In classic cases, this happens when the original master crashes or the hardware has to be changed.

 Be careful when promoting a slave. It cannot easily be demoted anymore. Once a slave has turned into a master, it can be a slave again only after performing a complete resync or after running pg_rewind, which will be available by default in PostgreSQL 9.5.

PostgreSQL offers some simple ways to do this. The first way, and most likely the most convenient way, to turn a slave into a master is by using pg_ctl:

```
iMac:slavehs$ pg_ctl -D /target_directory promote
server promoting
iMac:slavehs$ psql test
psql (9.2.4)
Type "help" for help.
test=# CREATE TABLE sample (id int4);
CREATE TABLE
```

The promote command will signal the postmaster and turn your slave into a master. Once this is complete, you can connect and create objects.

 If you've got more than one slave, make sure that those slaves are manually repointed to the new master before the promotion.

In addition to the promote command, there is a second option to turn a slave into a master. Especially when you are trying to integrate PostgreSQL with high-availability software of your choice, it can be easier to create a simple file than to call an init script.

To use the file-based method, you can add the trigger_file command to your recovery.conf file:

```
trigger_file = '/some_path/start_me_up.txt'
```

In our case, PostgreSQL will wait for a file called /some_path/start_me_up.txt to come into existence. The content of this file is totally irrelevant; PostgreSQL simply checks whether the file is present, and if it is, PostgreSQL stops recovery and turns itself into a master.

Creating an empty file is a rather simple task:

```
iMac:slavehs$ touch /some_path/start_me_up.txt
```

The database system will react to the new file, `start_me_up.txt`:

```
FATAL:   terminating walreceiver proced fire up:
LOG:   trigger file found: /some_path/start_ss due to
administrator command
LOG:   redo done at 0/50000E0
LOG:   selected new timeline ID: 2
LOG:   archive recovery complete
LOG:   database system is ready to accept connections
LOG:   autovacuum launcher started
```

PostgreSQL will check for the file you have defined in `recovery.conf` every 5 seconds. For most cases, this is perfectly fine, and fast enough by far..

Mixing streaming-based and file-based recovery

Life is not always just black or white. Sometimes, there are also some shades of gray. For some cases, streaming replication might be just perfect. In some other cases, file-based replication and PITR are all you need. But there are also many cases in which you need a bit of both. One example would be like this: when you interrupt replication for a long period of time, you might want to resync the slave using the archive again instead of performing a full base backup. It might also be useful to keep an archive around for some later investigation or replay operation.

The good news is that PostgreSQL allows you to actually mix file-based and streaming-based replication. You don't have to decide whether streaming-based or file-based is better. You can have the best of both worlds at the very same time.

How can you do that? In fact, you have already seen all the ingredients; we just have to put them together in the right way.

To make this easier for you, we have compiled a complete example.

The master configuration

On the master, we can use the following configuration in `postgresql.conf`:

```
wal_level = hot_standby
archive_mode = on
        # allows archiving to be done
        # (change requires restart)
archive_command = 'cp %p /archive/%f'
        # command to use to archive a logfile segment
        # placeholders: %p = path of file to archive
        #               %f = file name only
max_wal_senders = 5
        # we used five here to have some spare capacity
```

In addition to this, we have to add some configuration lines to `pg_hba.conf` to allow streaming. Here is an example:

```
# Allow replication connections from localhost, by a user with the
# replication privilege.
local   replication     hs   trust
host    replication     hs   127.0.0.1/32      trust
host    replication     hs   ::1/128           trust


host    replication     all  192.168.0.0/16    md5
```

In our case, we have simply opened an entire network to allow replication (to keep the example simple).

Once we have made these changes, we can restart the master and take a base backup as shown earlier in this chapter.

The slave configuration

Once we have configured our master and taken a base backup, we can start configuring our slave system. Let's assume for the sake of simplicity that we are using only a single slave; we will not cascade replication to other systems.

We only have to change a single line in `postgresql.conf` on the slave:

```
hot_standby = on       # to make the slave readable
```

In the next step, we can write a simple `recovery.conf` file and put it into the main data directory:

```
restore_command = 'cp /archive/%f %p'
standby_mode = on
primary_conninfo = ' host=sample.postgresql-support.de port=5432 '
trigger_file = '/some_path/start_me_up.txt'
```

When we fire up the slave, the following will happen:

1. PostgreSQL will call `restore_command` to fetch the transaction log from the archive.
2. It will do so until no more files can be found in the archive.
3. PostgreSQL will try to establish a streaming connection.
4. It will stream if data exists.

You can keep streaming as long as necessary. If you want to turn the slave into a master, you can again use `pg_ctl promote` or the `trigger_file` file defined in `recovery.conf`.

Error scenarios

The most important advantage of a dual strategy is that you can create a cluster that offers a higher level of security than just plain streaming-based or plain file-based replay. If streaming does not work for some reason, you can always fall back on the files.

In this section, we will discuss some typical error scenarios in a dual strategy cluster.

Network connection between the master and slave is dead

If the network is dead, the master might not be able to perform the `archive_command` operation successfully anymore. The history of the XLOG files must remain continuous, so the master has to queue up those XLOG files for later archiving. This can be a dangerous (yet necessary) scenario, because you might run out of space for XLOG on the master if the stream of files is interrupted permanently.

If the streaming connection fails, PostgreSQL will try to keep syncing itself through the file-based channel. Should the file-based channel also fail, the slave will sit there and wait for the network connection to come back. It will then try to fetch XLOG and simply continue once this is possible again.

Keep in mind that the slave needs an uninterrupted stream of XLOG. It can continue to replay XLOG only if no single XLOG file is missing, or if the streaming connection can still provide the slave with the XLOG that it needs to operate.

Rebooting the slave

Rebooting the slave will not do any harm as long as the archive has XLOG required to bring the slave back up. The slave will simply start up again and try to get the XLOG from any source available. There won't be corruption or any other problem of this sort.

Rebooting the master

If the master reboots, the situation is pretty non-critical as well. The slave will notice through the streaming connection that the master is gone. It will try to fetch the XLOG through both channels, but it won't be successful until the master is back. Again, nothing bad, such as corruption, can happen. Operations can simply resume after the box reboots.

Corrupted XLOG in the archive

If the XLOG in the archive is corrupted, we have to distinguish between two scenarios:

1. In the first scenario, the slave is streaming. If the stream is okay and intact, the slave will not notice that some XLOG file somehow became corrupted in the archive. The slaves never need to read from the XLOG files as long as the streaming connection is operational.

2. If we are not streaming but replaying from a file, PostgreSQL will inspect every XLOG record and see whether its checksum is correct. If anything goes wrong, the slave will not continue to replay the corrupted XLOG. This will ensure that no problems can propagate and no broken XLOG can be replayed. Your database might not be complete, but it will be the same and consistent up to the point of the erroneous XLOG file.

Surely, there is a lot more that can go wrong, but given those likely cases, you can see clearly that the design has been made as reliable as possible.

Making streaming-only replication more robust

The first thing a slave has to do when connecting to a master is to play catch up. But can this always work? We have already seen that we can use a mixed setup consisting of a streaming-based and a file-based component. This gives us some extra security if streaming does not work.

In many real-world scenarios, two ways of transporting the XLOG might be too complicated. In many cases, it is enough to have just streaming. The point is that in a normal setup, as described already, the master can throw the XLOG away as soon as it is not needed to repair the master anymore. Depending on your checkpoint configuration, the XLOG might be around for quite a while or only a short time. The trouble is that if your slave connects to the master, it might happen that the desired XLOG is not around anymore. The slave cannot resync itself in this scenario. You might find this a little annoying, because it implicitly limits the maximum downtime of your slave to your master's checkpoint behavior.

Two choices are available to solve the problem:

- `wal_keep_segments`: Keep some XLOG files on the master
- Physical replication slots: Teach the master to recycle the XLOG only when it has been consumed

Using wal_keep_segments

To make your setup much more robust, we recommend making heavy use of `wal_keep_segments`. The idea of this `postgresql.conf` setting (on the master) is to teach the master to keep more XLOG files around than theoretically necessary. If you set this variable to `1000`, it essentially means that the master will keep 16 GB of more XLOG than needed. In other words, your slave can be gone for 16 GB (in terms of changes to the master) longer than usual. This greatly increases the odds that a slave can join the cluster without having to completely resync itself from scratch. For a 500 MB database, this is not worth mentioning, but if your setup has to hold hundreds of gigabytes or terabytes, it becomes an enormous advantage. Producing a base backup of a 20 TB instance is a lengthy process. You might not want to do this too often, and you definitely won't want to do this over and over again.

 If you want to update a large base backup, it might be beneficial to incrementally update it using `rsync` and the traditional method of taking base backups.

What are the reasonable values for `wal_keep_segments`? As always, this largely depends on your workloads. From experience, we can tell that a multi-GB implicit archive on the master is definitely an investment worth considering. Very low values for `wal_keep_segments` might be risky and not worth the effort. Nowadays, pace is usually cheap. Small systems might not need this setting, and large ones should have sufficient spare capacity to absorb the extra requirements. Personally, I am always in favor of using at least some extra XLOG segments.

Utilizing replication slots

With the introduction of PostgreSQL 9.4, a more sophisticated solution to the problem of deleted XLOG has been introduced — physical replication slots. As already outlined earlier in this book, replication slots make sure that the master deletes XLOG only when it has been safely consumed by the replica. In the case of the cleanup problem outlined in this section, this is exactly what is needed here.

The question now is: how can a replication slot be used? Basically, it is very simple. All that has to be done is create the replication slot on the master and tell the slave which slots to use through `recovery.conf`.

Here is how it works on the master:

```
postgres=# SELECT * FROM pg_create_physical_replication_slot('repl_slot);
  slot_name  | xlog_position
-------------+---------------
 repl_slot |


postgres=# SELECT * FROM pg_replication_slots;
  slot_name  | slot_type | datoid | database | active | xmin | restart_
lsn
-------------+-----------+--------+----------+--------+------+----------
---
 repl_slot | physical  |        |          | f      |      |
(1 row)
```

Once the base backup has happened, the slave can be configured easily:

```
standby_mode = 'on'
primary_conninfo = 'host=master.postgresql-support.de port=5432 user=hans
password=hanspass'
primary_slot_name = 'repl_slot'
```

The configuration is just as if there were no replication slots. The only change is that the `primary_slot_name` variable has been added. The slave will pass the name of the replication slot to the master, and the master knows when to recycle the transaction log. As mentioned already, if a slave is not in use anymore, make sure that the replication slot is properly deleted to avoid trouble on the master (running out of disk space and other troubles). The problem is that this is incredibly insidious. Slaves, being optional, are not always monitored as they should be. As such, it might be a good idea to recommend that you regularly compare `pg_stat_replication` with `pg_replication_slots` for mismatches worthy of further investigation.

Efficient cleanup and the end of recovery

In recent years, `recovery.conf` has become more and more powerful. Back in the early days (that is, before PostgreSQL 9.0), there was barely anything more than `restore_command` and some setting related to `recovery_target_time`. More modern versions of PostgreSQL already offer a lot more and give you the chance to control your replay process in a nice and professional way.

In this section, you will learn what kind of settings there are and how you can make use of those features easily.

Gaining control over the restart points

So far, we have archived the XLOG indefinitely. Just like in real life, infinity is a concept that causes trouble. As John Maynard Keynes stated in his famous book, *The General Theory of Employment, Interest, and Money*:

> *"In the long run, we are all dead."*

What applies to Keynesian stimulus is equally true in the case of XLOG archiving; you simply cannot keep doing it forever. At some point, the XLOG has to be thrown away.

To make cleanup easy, you can put `archive_cleanup_command` into `recovery.conf`. Just like most other commands (for example, `restore_command`), this is a generic shell script. The script you will put in here will be executed at every restart point. What is a restart point? Every time PostgreSQL switches from file-based replay to streaming-based replay, you face a restart point. In fact, starting streaming again is considered to be a restart point.

You can make PostgreSQL execute some cleanup routine (or anything else) as soon as the restart point is reached. It is easily possible to clean the older XLOG or trigger some notifications.

The following script shows how you can clean any XLOG that is older than a day:

```
#!/bin/sh
find /archive "-type f -mtime +1 -exec rm -f {} \;
```

Keep in mind that your script can be of any kind of complexity. You have to decide on a proper policy to handle the XLOG. Every business case is different, and you have all the flexibility to control your archives and replication behavior.

Tweaking the end of your recovery

The `recovery_end_command` parameter serves purposes similar to `archive_cleanup_command`. It triggers some script execution when your recovery (or XLOG streaming) has completed.

Again, you can use this to clean the old XLOG, send out notifications, or perform any other kind of desired action.

Conflict management

In PostgreSQL, the streaming replication data flows in one direction only. The XLOG is provided by the master to a handful of slaves, which consume the transaction log and provide you with a nice copy of the data. You might wonder how this could ever lead to conflicts. Well, there can be conflicts.

Consider the following scenario: as you know, data is replicated with a very small delay. So, the XLOG ends up at the slave *after* it has been made on the master. This tiny delay can cause the scenario shown in the following diagram:

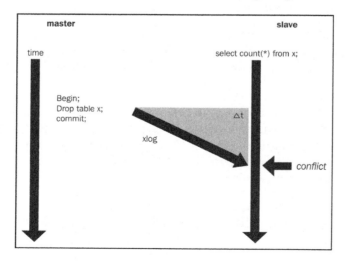

Let's assume that a slave starts to read a table. It is a long read operation. In the meantime, the master receives a request to actually drop the table. This is a bit of a problem, because the slave will still need this data to perform its SELECT statement. On the other hand, all the requests coming from the master have to be obeyed under any circumstances. This is a classic conflict.

 In the event of a conflict, PostgreSQL will issue the **Terminating connection due to conflict with recovery** error message.

There are two ways to solve the problem:

- Don't replay the conflicting transaction log before the slave has terminated the operation in question
- Kill the query on the slave to resolve the problem

The first option might lead to ugly delays during the replay process, especially if the slave performs fairly long operations. The second option might frequently kill queries on the slave. The database instance cannot know by itself what is best for your application, so you have to find a proper balance between delaying the replay and killing queries.

To find this delicate balance, PostgreSQL offers two parameters in postgresql. conf:

```
max_standby_archive_delay = 30s
    # max delay before canceling queries
    # when reading WAL from archive;
    # -1 allows indefinite delay
max_standby_streaming_delay = 30s
    # max delay before canceling queries
    # when reading streaming WAL;
    # -1 allows indefinite delay
```

The max_standby_archive_delay parameter will tell the system how long to suspend the XLOG replay when there is a conflicting operation. In the default setting, the slave will delay the XLOG replay for up to 30 seconds if a conflict is found. This setting is valid if the slave is replaying the transaction log from the files.

The `max_standby_streaming_delay` parameter tells the slave how long it should suspend the XLOG replay if the XLOG is coming in through streaming. If the time has expired and the conflict is still there, PostgreSQL will cancel the statement due to a problem with recovery, causing a problem in the slave system and resuming the XLOG recovery to catch up. These settings cover a cumulative delay. That is, if there are ten queries pending, they don't get 30 seconds each to delay replication. So, a query might run for 10 milliseconds and get canceled because it was unlucky to be at the end of an existing delay, causing the user to wonder what happened.

In the previous example, we have shown that a conflict may show up if a table is dropped. This is an obvious scenario; however, it is by no means the most common one. It is much more likely that a row is removed by VACUUM or HOT-UPDATE somewhere, causing conflicts on the slave.

Conflicts popping up once in a while can be really annoying and trigger bad behavior of your applications. In other words, if possible, conflicts should be avoided. We have already seen how replaying the XLOG can be delayed. These are not the only mechanisms provided by PostgreSQL. There are two more settings we can use.

The first, and older one of the two, is the setting called `vacuum_defer_cleanup_age`. It is measured in transactions, and tells PostgreSQL when to remove a line of data. Normally, a line of data can be removed by VACUUM if no more transactions can see the data anymore. The `vacuum_defer_cleanup_age` parameter tells VACUUM to not clean up a row immediately but wait for some more transactions before it can go away. Deferring cleanups will keep a row around a little longer than needed. This helps the slave to complete queries that are relying on old rows. Especially if your slave is the one handling some analytical work, this will help a lot in making sure that no queries have to die in vain.

One more method of controlling conflicts is by making use of `hot_standby_feedback`. The idea is that a slave reports transaction IDs to the master, which in turn can use this information to defer VACUUM. This is one of the easiest methods of avoiding cleanup conflicts on the slave.

 Keep in mind, however, that deferring cleanups can lead to increased space consumption and some other side effects, which have to be kept in mind under any circumstances. The effect is basically the same as running a long transaction on the master.

Dealing with timelines

Timelines are an important concept you have to be aware of, especially when you are planning a large-scale setup.

So what is a timeline? In fact, it is a certain branch of the XLOG. Normally, a database instance that has been freshly set up utilizes timeline number 1. Let's assume that we are starting to replicate our master database to a slave system. The slave will also operate in timeline 1. At some point, your master might die and your slave will be promoted to a new master. This is the time when a timeline switch happens. The new master will create a transaction log of its own now. Logically, we want to make sure that its XLOG is not mixed with some other XLOG made in the good old times.

How can we figure out that the timeline has advanced? Let's take a look at the XLOG directory of a system that was just turned into a master:

```
00000002.history
000000020000000000000006
000000020000000000000007
000000020000000000000008
```

The first part of the XLOG files is an interesting thing. You can observe that so far, there was always a 1 near the beginning of our filename. This is not so anymore. By checking the first part of the XLOG filename, you can see that the number has changed over time (after turning the slave into a master, we have reached timeline number 2).

It is important to mention that (as of PostgreSQL 9.4) you cannot simply pump the XLOG of timeline 5 into a database instance that is already at timeline 9. It is simply not possible.

In PostgreSQL 9.3, we are able to handle these timelines a little more flexibly. This means that timeline changes will be put to the transaction log, and a slave can follow a timeline shift easily.

 Timelines are especially something to be aware of when cascading replication and working with many slaves. After all, you have to connect your slaves to some server if your master fails.

Delayed replicas

So far, two main scenarios have been discussed in this book:

- **Point-in-time Recovery (PITR)**: Replaying the transaction log as soon as something nasty has happened
- **Asynchronous replication**: Replaying the transaction log as soon as possible

Both scenarios are highly useful and can serve people's needs nicely. However, what happens if databases, and especially change volumes, start being really large? What if a 20 TB database has produced 10 TB of changes and something drastic happens? Somebody might have accidentally dropped a table or deleted a couple of million rows, or maybe somebody set data to a wrong value. Taking a base backup and performing a recovery might be way too time consuming, because the amount of data is just too large to be handled nicely.

The same applies to performing frequent base backups. Creating a 20 TB base backup is just too large, and storing all those backups might be pretty space consuming. Of course, there is always the possibility of getting around certain problems on the filesystem level. However, it might be fairly complex to avoid all of those pitfalls in a critical setup.

Since PostgreSQL 9.4, the database platform provides an additional, easy-to-use feature. It is possible to tell PostgreSQL that the slave is supposed to stay a couple of minutes/hours/days behind the master. If a transaction commits on the master, it is not instantly replayed on the slave but applied some time later (for example, 6 hours). The gap between the master and the slave can be controlled easily, and if the master crashes, the administrator has a convenient 6-hour window (in my example) to roll forward to a desired point in time. The main advantage is that there is already a base backup in place (the lagging standby in this case), and in addition to that, the time frame, which has to be recovered, is fairly small. This leads to less downtime and faster recovery. Replaying only a small time frame is way more desirable than having to fiddle around with large base backups and maybe even a larger amount of XLOG. Having a slave that lags behind is of course no substitute for a proper backup; however, it can definitely help.

To configure a slave that lags behind, `recovery_min_apply_delay` can be added to `recovery.conf`. Just use replication slots and set the desired value of `recovery_min_apply`. Then your system will work as expected.

Keep in mind that normal *Hot-Standby* is definitely a wise option. The purpose of a lagging slave is to protect yourself against unexpected DROP TABLE statements, accidental deletions of data, and so on. It allows users to jump back in time when really needed without having to touch too much data. A lagging slave can be seen as a form of backup that constantly updates itself.

Handling crashes

It is generally wise to use a transaction log archive when using a lagging slave. In addition to that, a crash of the master itself has to be handled wisely. If the master crashes, the administrator should make sure that they decide on a point in time to recover to. Once this point has been found (which is usually the hardest part of the exercise), recovery_target_time can be added to recovery.conf. Once the slave has been restarted, the system will recover to this desired point in time and go live. If the time frames have been chosen wisely, this is the fastest way to recover a system.

In a way, recovery_min_apply_delay is a mixture of classical *PITR* and *Hot-Standby-Slaves*.

Summary

In this chapter, you learned about streaming replication. We saw how a streaming connection can be created, and what you can do to configure streaming to your needs. We also briefly discussed how things work behind the scenes.

It is important to keep in mind that replication can indeed cause conflicts, which need proper treatment.

In the next chapter, it will be time to focus our attention on synchronous replication, which is logically the next step. You will learn to replicate data without potential data loss.

Setting Up Synchronous Replication

5

So far, we have dealt with file-based replication (or **log shipping**, as it is often called) and a simple streaming-based asynchronous setup. In both cases, data is submitted and received by the slave (or slaves) *after* the transaction has been committed on the master. During the time between the master's commit and the point when the slave actually has fully received the data, it can still be lost.

In this chapter, you will learn about the following topics:

- Making sure that no single transaction can be lost
- Configuring PostgreSQL for synchronous replication
- Understanding and using application_name
- The performance impact of synchronous replication
- Optimizing replication for speed

Synchronous replication can be the cornerstone of your replication setup, providing a system that ensures zero data loss.

Synchronous replication setup

As mentioned before, synchronous replication has been made to protect your data at all costs. The core idea of synchronous replication is that a transaction must be on at least two servers before the master returns success to the client. Making sure that data is on at least two nodes is a key requirement to ensure no data loss in the event of a crash.

Setting up synchronous replication works just like setting up asynchronous replication. Just a handful of parameters discussed in this chapter have to be changed to enjoy the blessings of synchronous replication. However, if you are about to create a setup based on synchronous replication, we recommend getting started with an asynchronous setup and gradually extending your configuration and turning it into synchronous replication. This will allow you to debug things more easily and avoid problems down the road.

Understanding the downside to synchronous replication

The most important thing you have to know about synchronous replication is that it is simply expensive. Do you remember our first chapter about the CAP theory, about the speed of light, and so on? Synchronous replication and its downsides are two of the core reasons for which we have decided to include all this background information in this book. It is essential to understand the physical limitations of synchronous replication, otherwise you could end up in deep trouble.

When setting up synchronous replication, try to keep the following things in mind:

- Minimize the latency
- Make sure you have redundant connections
- Synchronous replication is more expensive than asynchronous replication
- Always cross-check twice whether there is a real need for synchronous replication

In many cases, it is perfectly fine to lose a couple of rows in the event of a crash. Synchronous replication can safely be skipped in this case. However, if there is zero tolerance, synchronous replication is a tool that should be used.

Understanding the application_name parameter

In order to understand a synchronous setup, a config variable called `application_name` is essential, and it plays an important role in a synchronous setup. In a typical application, people use the `application_name` parameter for debugging purposes, as it allows users to assign a name to their database connection. It can help track bugs, identify what an application is doing, and so on:

```
test=# SHOW application_name;
```

```
application_name

-----------------

psql
(1 row)


test=# SET application_name TO 'whatever';
SET
test=# SHOW application_name;
application_name

-----------------

 whatever

(1 row)
```

As you can see, it is possible to set the application_name parameter freely.
The setting is valid for the session we are in, and will be gone as soon as we
disconnect. The question now is: What does application_name have to do
with synchronous replication?

Well, the story goes like this: if this application_name value happens to be part
of synchronous_standby_names, the slave will be a synchronous one. In addition
to that, to be a synchronous standby, it has to be:

- connected
- streaming data in real-time (that is, not fetching old WAL records)

Once a standby becomes synced, it remains in that position until disconnection.

 In the case of cascaded replication (which means that a slave is again
connected to a slave), the cascaded slave is not treated synchronously
anymore. Only the first server is considered to be synchronous.

With all of this information in mind, we can move forward and configure our first
synchronous replication.

Making synchronous replication work

To show you how synchronous replication works, this chapter will include a full,
working example outlining all the relevant configuration parameters.

A couple of changes have to be made to the master. The following settings will be needed in `postgresql.conf` on the master:

```
wal_level = hot_standby
max_wal_senders = 5      # or any number
synchronous_standby_names = 'book_sample'
hot_standby = on
# on the slave to make it readable
```

Then we have to adapt `pg_hba.conf`, just as we have already seen in previous chapters. After that, the server can be restarted and the master is ready for action.

> We recommend that you set `wal_keep_segments` as well to keep more transaction logs. We also recommend setting `wal_keep_segments` to keep more transaction logs on the master database. This makes the entire setup way more robust.
>
> It is also possible to utilize replication slots, as outlined in the previous chapter.

In the next step, we can perform a base backup just as we have done before. We have to call `pg_basebackup` on the slave. Ideally, we already include the transaction log when doing the base backup. The `--xlog-method=stream` parameter allows us to fire things up quickly and without any greater risks.

> The `--xlog-method=stream` and `wal_keep_segments` parameters are a good combo, and in our opinion, should be used in most cases to ensure that a setup works flawlessly and safely.

We have already recommended setting `hot_standby` on the master. The `config` file will be replicated anyway, so you save yourself one trip to `postgresql.conf` to change this setting. Of course, this is not fine art but an easy and pragmatic approach.

Once the base backup has been performed, we can move ahead and write a simple `recovery.conf` file suitable for synchronous replication, as follows:

```
iMac:slavehs$ cat recovery.conf
primary_conninfo = 'host=localhost
                    application_name=book_sample
                    port=5432'

standby_mode = on
```

The `config` file looks just like before. The only difference is that we have added `application_name` to the scenery. Note that the `application_name` parameter must be identical to the `synchronous_standby_names` setting on the master.

Once we have finished writing `recovery.conf`, we can fire up the slave.

In our example, the slave is on the same server as the master. In this case, you have to ensure that those two instances will use different TCP ports, otherwise the instance that starts second will not be able to fire up. The port can easily be changed in `postgresql.conf`.

After these steps, the database instance can be started. The slave will check out its connection information and connect to the master. Once it has replayed all the relevant transaction logs, it will be in synchronous state. The master and the slave will hold exactly the same data from then on.

Checking the replication

Now that we have started the database instance, we can connect to the system and see whether things are working properly.

To check for replication, we can connect to the master and take a look at `pg_stat_replication`. For this check, we can connect to any database inside our (master) instance, as follows:

```
postgres=# \x
Expanded display is on.
postgres=# SELECT * FROM pg_stat_replication;
-[ RECORD 1 ]----+-------------------------------
pid              | 62871
usesysid         | 10
usename          | hs
application_name | book_sample
client_addr      | ::1
client_hostname  |
client_port      | 59235
backend_start    | 2013-03-29 14:53:52.352741+01
state            | streaming
sent_location    | 0/30001E8
```

```
write_location   | 0/30001E8
flush_location   | 0/30001E8
replay_location  | 0/30001E8
sync_priority    | 1
sync_state       | sync
```

This system view will show exactly one line per slave attached to your master system.

> The \x command will make the output more readable for you. If you don't use \x to transpose the output, the lines will be so long that it will be pretty hard for you to comprehend the content of this table. In expanded display mode, each column will be in one line instead.

You can see that the application_name parameter has been taken from the connect string passed to the master by the slave (which is book_sample in our example). As the application_name parameter matches the master's synchronous_standby_names setting, we have convinced the system to replicate synchronously. No transaction can be lost anymore because every transaction will end up on two servers instantly. The sync_state setting will tell you precisely how data is moving from the master to the slave.

> You can also use a list of application names, or simply a * sign in synchronous_standby_names to indicate that the first slave has to be synchronous.

Understanding performance issues

At various points in this book, we have already pointed out that synchronous replication is an expensive thing to do. Remember that we have to wait for a remote server and not just the local system. The network between those two nodes is definitely not something that is going to speed things up. Writing to more than one node is always more expensive than writing to only one node. Therefore, we definitely have to keep an eye on speed, otherwise we might face some pretty nasty surprises.

> Consider what you have learned about the CAP theory earlier in this book. Synchronous replication is exactly where it should be, with the serious impact that the physical limitations will have on performance.

The main question you really have to ask yourself is: do I really want to replicate all transactions synchronously? In many cases, you don't. To prove our point, let's imagine a typical scenario: a bank wants to store accounting-related data as well as some logging data. We definitely don't want to lose a couple of million dollars just because a database node goes down. This kind of data might be worth the effort of replicating synchronously. The logging data is quite different, however. It might be far too expensive to cope with the overhead of synchronous replication. So, we want to replicate this data in an asynchronous way to ensure maximum throughput.

How can we configure a system to handle important as well as not-so-important transactions nicely? The answer lies in a variable you have already seen earlier in the book — the `synchronous_commit` variable.

Setting synchronous_commit to on

In the default PostgreSQL configuration, `synchronous_commit` has been set to `on`. In this case, commits will wait until a reply from the current synchronous standby indicates that it has received the commit record of the transaction and has flushed it to the disk. In other words, both servers must report that the data has been written safely. Unless both servers crash at the same time, your data will survive potential problems (crashing of both servers should be pretty unlikely).

Setting synchronous_commit to remote_write

Flushing to both disks can be highly expensive. In many cases, it is enough to know that the remote server has accepted the XLOG and passed it on to the operating system without flushing things to the disk on the slave. As we can be pretty certain that we don't lose two servers at the very same time, this is a reasonable compromise between performance and consistency with respect to data protection.

Setting synchronous_commit to off

We have already dealt with setting `synchronous_commit` to `off` in *Chapter 2, Understanding the PostgreSQL Transaction Log*. The idea is to delay WAL writing to reduce disk flushes. This can be used if performance is more important than durability. In the case of replication, it means that we are not replicating in a fully synchronous way.

Keep in mind that this can have a serious impact on your application. Imagine a transaction committing on the master and you wanting to query that data instantly on one of the slaves. There would still be a tiny window during which you can actually get outdated data.

Setting synchronous_commit to local

The local value will flush locally but not wait for the replica to respond. In other words, it will turn your transaction into an asynchronous one.

Setting synchronous_commit to local can also cause a small time delay window, during which the slave can actually return slightly outdated data. This phenomenon has to be kept in mind when you decide to offload reads to the slave.

In short, if you want to replicate synchronously, you have to ensure that synchronous_commit is set to either on or remote_write.

Changing durability settings on the fly

Changing the way data is replicated on the fly is easy and highly important to many applications, as it allows the user to control durability on the fly. Not all data has been created equal, and therefore, more important data should be written in a safer way than data that is not as important (such as log files). In this chapter, we have already set up a full synchronous replication infrastructure by adjusting synchronous_standby_names (master) along with the application_name (slave) parameter. The good thing about PostgreSQL is that you can change your durability requirements on the fly:

```
test=# BEGIN;
BEGIN
test=# CREATE TABLE t_test (id int4);
CREATE TABLE
test=# SET synchronous_commit TO local;
SET
test=# \x
Expanded display is on.
test=# SELECT * FROM pg_stat_replication;
-[ RECORD 1 ]----+------------------------------
pid              | 62871
usesysid         | 10
usename          | hs
application_name | book_sample
client_addr      | ::1
client_hostname  |
client_port      | 59235
```

```
backend_start      | 2013-03-29 14:53:52.352741+01
state              | streaming
sent_location      | 0/3026258
write_location     | 0/3026258
flush_location     | 0/3026258
replay_location    | 0/3026258
sync_priority      | 1
sync_state         | sync
```

```
test=# COMMIT;
COMMIT
```

In this example, we changed the durability requirements on the fly. This will make sure that this very specific transaction will not wait for the slave to flush to the disk. Note, as you can see, `sync_state` has *not* changed. Don't be fooled by what you see here; you can completely rely on the behavior outlined in this section. PostgreSQL is perfectly able to handle each transaction separately. This is a unique feature of this wonderful open source database; it puts you in control and lets you decide which kind of durability requirements you want.

Understanding the practical implications and performance

In this chapter, we have already talked about practical implications as well as performance implications. But what good is a theoretical example? Let's do a simple benchmark and see how replication behaves. We are performing this kind of testing to show you that various levels of durability are not just a minor topic; they are the key to performance.

Let's assume a simple test: in the following scenario, we have connected two equally powerful machines (3 GHz, 8 GB RAM) over a 1 Gbit network. The two machines are next to each other. To demonstrate the impact of synchronous replication, we have left `shared_buffers` and all other memory parameters as default, and only changed `fsync` to `off` to make sure that the effect of disk wait is reduced to practically zero.

The test is simple: we use a one-column table with only one integer field and 10,000 single transactions consisting of just one `INSERT` statement:

```
INSERT INTO t_test VALUES (1);
```

We can try this with full, synchronous replication (`synchronous_commit = on`):

```
real    0m6.043s
user    0m0.131s
sys     0m0.169s
```

As you can see, the test has taken around 6 seconds to complete. This test can be repeated with `synchronous_commit = local` now (which effectively means asynchronous replication):

```
real    0m0.909s
user    0m0.101s
sys     0m0.142s
```

In this simple test, you can see that the speed has gone up by us much as six times. Of course, this is a brute-force example, which does not fully reflect reality (this was not the goal anyway). What is important to understand, however, is that synchronous versus asynchronous replication is not a matter of a couple of percentage points or so. This should stress our point even more: replicate synchronously only if it is really needed, and if you really have to use synchronous replication, make sure that you limit the number of synchronous transactions to an absolute minimum.

Also, please make sure that your network is up to the job. Replicating data synchronously over network connections with high latency will kill your system performance like nothing else. Keep in mind that throwing expensive hardware at the problem will not solve the problem. Doubling the clock speed of your servers will do practically nothing for you because the real limitation will always come from network latency.

> The performance penalty with just one connection is definitely a lot larger than that with many connections. Remember that things can be done in parallel, and network latency does not make us more I/O or CPU bound, so we can reduce the impact of slow transactions by firing up more concurrent work.

When synchronous replication is used, how can you still make sure that performance does not suffer too much? Basically, there are a couple of important suggestions that have proven to be helpful:

- **Use longer transactions**: Remember that the system must ensure on commit that the data is available on two servers. We don't care what happens in the middle of a transaction, because anybody outside our transaction cannot see the data anyway. A longer transaction will dramatically reduce network communication.

- **Run stuff concurrently**: If you have more than one transaction going on at the same time, it will be beneficial to performance. The reason for this is that the remote server will return the position inside the XLOG that is considered to be processed safely (flushed or accepted). This method ensures that many transactions can be confirmed at the same time.

Redundancy and stopping replication

When talking about synchronous replication, there is one phenomenon that must not be left out. Imagine we have a two-node cluster replicating synchronously. What happens if the slave dies? The answer is that the master cannot distinguish between a slow and a dead slave easily, so it will start waiting for the slave to come back.

At first glance, this looks like nonsense, but if you think about it more deeply, you will figure out that synchronous replication is actually the only correct thing to do. If somebody decides to go for synchronous replication, the data in the system must be worth something, so it must not be at risk. It is better to refuse data and cry out to the end user than to risk data and silently ignore the requirements of high durability.

If you decide to use synchronous replication, you must consider using at least three nodes in your cluster. Otherwise, it will be very risky, and you cannot afford to lose a single node without facing significant downtime or risking data loss.

Summary

In this chapter, we outlined the basic concept of synchronous replication, and showed how data can be replicated synchronously. We also showed how durability requirements can be changed on the fly by modifying PostgreSQL runtime parameters. PostgreSQL gives users the choice of how a transaction should be replicated, and which level of durability is necessary for a certain transaction.

In the next chapter, we will dive into monitoring and see how we can figure out whether our replicated setup is working as expected.

6

Monitoring Your Setup

In previous chapters of this book, you learned about various kinds of replication and how to configure various types of scenarios. Now it's time to make your setup more reliable by adding monitoring. Monitoring is a key component of every critical system, and therefore a deep and thorough understanding of it is essential in order to keep your database system up and running.

In this chapter, you will learn what to monitor and how to implement reasonable monitoring policies. You will learn how to do the following:

- Check your XLOG archive
- Check the `pg_stat_replication` system view
- Check for replication-related processes at the OS level

At the end of this chapter, you should be able to monitor any kind of replication setup properly.

Checking your archive

If you are planning to use PITR or if you want to use an XLOG archive to assist in your streaming setup, various things can go wrong, for example:

- Pushing of the XLOG might fail
- Cleanup of the archive might fail

Of course, there are countless other things that can go wrong. However, in this chapter, our goal is to focus on the most common issues people face.

Checking archive_command

A failing `archive_command` variable might be one of the greatest showstoppers in your setup. The purpose of `archive_command` is to push XLOG to some archive and store the data there. But what happens if those XLOG files cannot be pushed for some reason?

The answer is quite simple: the master has to keep these XLOG files to ensure that no XLOG files can be lost. There must always be an uninterrupted sequence of XLOG files. Even if a single file in the sequence of files is missing, your slave won't be able to recover anymore. For example, if your network has failed, the master will accumulate those files and keep them. Logically, this cannot be done forever, and so, at some point, you will face disk space shortages on your master server.

This can be dangerous, because if you are running out of disk space, there is no way to keep writing to the database. While reads might still be possible, most writes will definitely fail and cause serious disruptions on your system. PostgreSQL won't fail and your instance will be intact after a disk has filled up, but—as stated before—your service will be interrupted.

To prevent this from happening, it is recommended to monitor your `pg_xlog` directory and check for:

- An unusually high number of XLOG files
- Free disk space on the partition hosting `pg_xlog`

The core question here is: what would be a reasonable number to check for? In a standard configuration, PostgreSQL should not use more XLOG files than *checkpoint_segments * 2 + wal_keep_segments*. If the number of XLOG files starts skyrocketing , you can expect some weird problem.

So, make sure that `archive_command` works properly.

If you perform these checks properly, nothing bad can happen on this front. But if you fail to check these parameters, you are risking doomsday!

Monitoring the transaction log archive

The master is not the only place that can run out of space. The same thing can happen to your archive. So, it is advisable to monitor the disk space there as well.

Apart from disk space, which has to be monitored anyway, there is one more thing you should keep on your radar. You have to come up with a decent policy to handle base backups. Remember that you are allowed to delete XLOG only if it is older than the oldest base backup that you want to preserve. This tiny thing can undermine your disk space monitoring. It is highly recommended to make sure that your archive has enough spare capacity. This is important if your database system has to write many transaction logs.

Checking pg_stat_replication

Checking the archive and `archive_command` is primarily for Point-In-Time-Recovery. If you want to monitor a streaming-based setup, it is advised to keep an eye on a system view called `pg_stat_replication`. This view contains the following information:

```
test=# \d pg_stat_replication
          View "pg_catalog.pg_stat_replication"
      Column       |            Type             | Modifiers
-------------------+-----------------------------+-----------
 pid               | integer                     |
 usesysid          | oid                         |
 usename           | name                        |
 application_name  | text                        |
 client_addr       | inet                        |
 client_hostname   | text                        |
 client_port       | integer                     |
 backend_start     | timestamp with time zone    |
 backend_xmin      | xid                         |
 state             | text                        |
 sent_location     | pg_lsn                      |
 write_location    | pg_lsn                      |
 flush_location    | pg_lsn                      |
 replay_location   | pg_lsn                      |
 sync_priority     | integer                     |
 sync_state        | text                        |
```

For each slave connected to our system via streaming, the view listed here will return exactly one line of data. You will see precisely what your slaves are doing.

Relevant fields in pg_stat_replication

The following fields are available for monitoring the system. Let's discuss these fields in detail:

- `pid`: This represents the process ID of the `wal_receiver` process in charge of this streaming connection. If you check the process table in your operating system, you should find a PostgreSQL process with exactly this number.

- `usesysid`: Internally, every user has a unique number. The system works pretty much like it would on UNIX. The `usesysid` is a unique identifier for the (PostgreSQL) user connecting to the system.

- `usename`: This (not username; mind the missing "r") stores the name of the user related to `usesysid`. It is what the client has put into the connection string.

- `application_name`: This is usually set when people decide to go for synchronous replication. It can be passed to the master through the connection string.

- `client_addr`: This will tell you where the streaming connection comes from. It holds the IP address of the client.

- `client_hostname`: In addition to the client's IP, you can also identify a client via its hostname, if you chose to do so. You can enable reverse DNS lookups by turning `log_hostname` on in the `postgresql.conf` file on the master.

- `client_port`: This is the TCP port number the client is using for communication with the particular WAL sender. `-1` will be shown if local UNIX sockets are used.

- `backend_start`: This tells us when the relevant streaming connection has been created by the slave.

- `backend_xmin`: The transaction ID reported by `hot_standby_feedback` (which is the oldest transaction ID on a slave). It can make sense to monitor the difference between the current transaction ID on the master and the oldest one reported by the slave as well, to check whether there are unusually high differences.

- `state`: This column informs us about the state of the database connection. If things are going as planned, it should contain `streaming`.

- `sent_location`: This represents the last transaction log position sent to the connection.

- `write_location`: This is the last transaction log position written to the disk on the standby system.

- flush_location: This is the last location that was flushed to the standby system. Mind the difference between writing and flushing here. Writing does not imply flushing (refer *A simple INSERT statement* section in *Chapter 2, Understanding the PostgreSQL Transaction Log* about durability requirements).

- replay_location: This is the last transaction log position that is replayed on the slave.

- sync_priority: This field is relevant only if you are replicating synchronously. Each sync replica will choose a priority — sync_priority — that will tell you which priority has been chosen.

- sync_state: Finally, you can see which state the slave is in. The state can be async, sync, or potential. PostgreSQL will mark a slave as potential when there is a sync slave with a higher priority.

Remember that each record in this system view represents exactly one slave. So, you can see at the first glance who is connected and what task is being done. The pg_stat_replication variable is also a good way to check whether a slave is connected in the first place.

Checking for operating system processes

Once we have checked the archives and our system views, we are ready to check for system processes. Checking for system processes might look a little crude, but it has been proven to be highly effective.

On the master, we can simply check for a process called wal_sender. On the slave, we have to check for a process called wal_receiver.

Let's check out what we are supposed to see on the master first. The following command does the job:

```
ps ax | grep "wal sender"
```

Here is the output:

```
9314   ??  Ss     0:00.00 postgres: wal sender process
hs ::1(61498) idle
```

On Linux, we can see that the process carries not only its purpose (in this case, wal_sender) but also the name of the end user and network-related information. In our case, we can see that somebody has connected from localhost through port 61498.

The situation on the slave is pretty simple as well:

```
9313    ??  Ss      0:00.00 postgres: wal receiver process
```

All we see is a process informing us that we are consuming XLOG.

If both the processes on master and slave are here, you have already got a pretty good indicator that your replication setup is working nicely.

Checking for replication slots

Starting from PostgreSQL 9.4, it is also necessary and useful to check for leftover replication slots. The core issue is that if somebody forgets to drop a replication slot, XLOG can accumulate, just as it does in the case of broken archive commands. Therefore, it is essential to keep an eye on useless replication slots (physical as well as logical).

Here is how you can retrieve a list of existing replication slots:

```
test=# \d pg_replication_slots
View "pg_catalog.pg_replication_slots"
    Column     |  Type   | Modifiers
---------------+---------+-----------
 slot_name     | name    |
 plugin        | name    |
 slot_type     | text    |
 datoid        | oid     |
 database      | name    |
 active        | boolean |
 xmin          | xid     |
 catalog_xmin  | xid     |
 restart_lsn   | pg_lsn  |
```

To read data from the view, you can simply use TABLE pg_replication_slots.

The main problem is that an administrator has to know about those replication slots that are still needed and in use. The authors are not aware of any automated, feasible methods to clean up replication slots that are not in use anymore. At this point, it really boils down to knowledge about the system.

What you should do is to periodically check the difference between the current transaction ID and the transaction ID listed for the replication slot. In addition to that the LSNs can be checked. Unusually high differences can be reported by the monitoring system.

Actually, it is not so easy to determine what the usual range is as it might vary. In most cases, the difference in range will be very close to zero. However, if a large index is built and the network is slow, the difference might peak temporarily, making it hard to determine a good value for the threshold.

To calculate the difference between two LSNs, the pg_xlog_location_diff function can be called. The following example shows how this can be done:

```
test=# SELECT pg_xlog_location_diff('0/234234', '0/123232');
 pg_xlog_location_diff
-----------------------
               1118210
(1 row)
```

The result is in bytes. Note that if the replication lag (or difference) constantly grows, it might indicate that the replication has stopped.

If the age of a certain transaction ID is needed, the age function can be used:

```
test=# SELECT age('223'::xid);
 age
-----
 722
(1 row)
```

In this example, transaction ID 223 is 722 transactions old. If a replication slot is really old, the age of the transaction is a nice indicator, which can trigger soft alerts.

If a replication slot still provides a very old transaction log, it might not be in use anymore. Again, dropping a replication slot should be done only after thorough checking.

Dealing with monitoring tools

There are a couple of monitoring tools around these days that make your life easier.

One of the most popular monitoring tools around is Nagios. It is widely used and supports a variety of software components.

If you want to use Nagios to monitor your PostgreSQL cluster, it is necessary to install a plugin capable of running tests relevant to replication. Such plugins are also available for PostgreSQL, and can be downloaded for free from http://bucardo.org/wiki/Check_postgres. The Bucardo plugins for Nagios are not just able to test replication but are also a standard software component for monitoring PostgreSQL as a whole.

Installing check_postgres

Once you have downloaded the plugin from the Bucardo website, it is easy to install it, as follows:

1. The first step is to extract the `.tar` archive:

   ```
   tar xvfz check_postgres.tar.gz
   ```

2. Now you can enter the newly created directory and run Perl `Makefile`:

   ```
   perl Makefile.PL
   ```

3. Finally, you can compile and install the code:

   ```
   make
   make install
   ```

> The last step must be performed as the `root` user. Otherwise, you will most likely not have enough permissions to deploy the code on your system.

4. In our case, the binaries have been installed at `/usr/local/bin`. We can easily check whether the installation has been successful by running the following command:

   ```
   /usr/local/bin/check_postgres.pl --help
   ```

Starting `check_postgres.pl` directly is also a way to call those plugins from the command-line prompt and checking whether the results make sense.

We want to focus your attention on the `custom_query` functionality. If there are checks missing — checks that are needed but are not available — `custom_query` will always be there to help you. Users might want to determine the average transaction rate, check the data turnover or run application-specific checks, shedding some light on what is really going on in the database. A good custom query can provide users with valuable insights.

Deciding on a monitoring strategy

People often ask which of the countless Nagios checks that are available they should use to configure their database systems. For us, the answer to this question can only be, "It depends." If you happen to run a large analysis database that will be used only by a handful of people, checking for the number of open database connections might be of no use. If you happen to run a high-performance OLTP system serving thousands of users, checking for open connections might be a very good idea.

It really depends on the type of application you are running, so you have to think yourself and come up with a reasonable set of checks and thresholds. Logically, the same applies to any other monitoring software you can potentially think of. The rules are always the same: think about what your application does, and consider things that can go wrong. Based on this information, you can then select proper checks. A list of all available checks can be found at `http://bucardo.org/check_postgres/check_postgres.pl.html`.

It is important to mention that certain checks that are not related to PostgreSQL are always useful. The following list contains a — nowhere complete — list of suggestions:

- CPU usage
- Disk space consumption and free space
- Memory consumption
- Disk wait
- Operating system swap usage
- General availability of the desired services

Summary

In this chapter, you learned a lot about monitoring. We saw what to check for in the archive and how to interpret the PostgreSQL internal system views. Finally, we saw which processes to check for at the operating system level.

In general, it is recommended to use professional monitoring software, such as Zabbix, Nagios, and others, that is capable of running automated tests and issuing notifications.

All of these checks will, together, provide you with a pretty nice safety net for your database setup.

The next chapter is dedicated exclusively to High Availability. You will be taught the important concepts related to High Availability, and we will guide you through the fundamentals.

7
Understanding Linux High Availability

High Availability (HA) is not just an industry term. The fact that something needs to be available usually also means that it is super important, and that the service must be available to clients, no matter the cost.

High Availability is important in the PostgreSQL world. A database is the central component of most setups, and therefore, availability of the service is the key.

In this chapter, the following topics will be covered:

- Understanding the purpose of High Availability
- Measuring availability
- Linux-HA (Heartbeat), STONITH, and Pacemaker
- Terminology and concepts
- PostgreSQL and High Availability

Understanding the purpose of High Availability

To quote Murphy's law:

> *"Anything that can go wrong will go wrong."*

"Anything" really includes everything in life. This is well understood by all service providers who intend to retain their customers. Customers usually aren't satisfied if the service they want is not continuous, or not available. Availability is also called **uptime**, and its opposite is called **downtime**.

Depending on the service, downtime can be more or less tolerated. For example, if a house is heated using wood or coal, the homeowner can stack up a lot of it before winter to avoid depending on the availability of shipping during the winter. However, if the house is heated using natural gas, availability is a lot more important. Uninterrupted service (there should be enough pressure in the gas pipe coming into the house) and a certain heating quality of the gas are expected from the provider.

The provider must minimize downtime as much as possible. If possible, downtime should be completely eliminated. The complete lack of downtime is called **High Availability**.

Also, we will talk about the perception of High Availability when the downtime is hidden.

Measuring availability

The idea behind availability is that the service provider tries to guarantee a certain level of it, and clients can then expect that or more. In some cases (depending on service contracts), a penalty fee or a decreased subscription fee is the consequence of an unexpected downtime.

The quality of availability is measured in fraction of percentages, for example, 99.99 percent or 99.999 percent, which are referred to as "four nines" and "five nines" respectively. These values are considered pretty good availability values, but there is a small trick in computing this value. If the provider has a planned downtime that is announced in advance; for example, the annual or bi-annual maintenance for water pipes in a town doesn't make the availability number worse, then availability is only measured outside the planned maintenance window.

However, let's consider the 0.001 percent downtime for the "five nines" case. Users experience denied or delayed service only 5 minutes and 15 seconds in total (that is, 864 milliseconds every day) during the entire year, which may not be noticed at all. Because of this, the service is perceived to be uninterrupted.

The second and third examples show that no matter what the provider does, there is a minimum downtime, and the uptime converges to the maximum that can be provided.

Let's see what planned downtime means and what can be done to hide it. Let's take a theoretical factory and its workers. The workers operate on certain machinery and they expect it to work during their work hours. The factory can have different shifts, so the machinery may not be turned off at all, except for one week of maintenance. The workers are told to take their vacation during this time period. If there is really no other downtime, everyone is happy. On the other hand, if there is downtime, it means lost income for the factory and wasted time and lower wages for the workers.

Let's look at the "one hour every day" downtime. It amounts to more than two weeks in total, which is kind of surprising. It's actually quite a lot if added together. But in some cases, the service is really not needed for that single hour during the whole day. For example, a back office database can have automatic maintenance scheduled for the night, when there are no users in the office. In this way, there is no perceived downtime; the system is always up when the users need it.

Another example of this "one hour downtime every day" is a non-stop hypermarket. Cash registers usually have to be switched to daily report mode before the first payment on the next day; otherwise, they refuse to accept further payments. These reports must be printed for accounting and the tax office. Being a non-stop hypermarket, it doesn't actually close its doors, but the customers cannot pay and leave until the cash registers are switched back to service mode.

Durability and availability

When designing data storage systems, it is important to distinguish between the properties of availability and durability. Availability is a measure of the probability that the system is able to accept reads and writes at any given point in time. Durability is a measure of the probability that once a write has been accepted (in PostgreSQL, this means a successful transaction commit), that information will not be lost. All real systems must pick a compromise between availability, durability, performance, and cost.

For a simple example, we can consider a cluster consisting of two database servers. One is running as the primary server, accepting writes from our application. The other one is running as a standby, replicating to the primary changes if something bad, such as a crash, happens. The question we have to answer now is how many changes we can afford to lose and how often. In some systems, such as those collecting sensor statistics, it's not a huge tragedy, or even noticeable, if a couple of minutes' worth of work goes missing occasionally. In other cases, such as financial systems, we will be in deep trouble if even a single transaction goes missing.

If losing some data is okay, then the primary system can report a success as soon as it has successfully processed the data. This is called asynchronous replication. If the primary fails in this system, there is a pretty good chance that a few transactions will not be replicated and will therefore be lost.

On the other hand, if we need to ensure that no data is lost under any circumstances, we would want to wait for a confirmation that the standby has successfully written the data to the disk. What happens if the standby fails? If losing data in any single failure is not acceptable, then our system must stop accepting write transactions once either of the nodes fails. The system will remain unavailable until a new standby is set up, which can take a considerable amount of time. If both High Availability and high durability are required, then at least three database nodes are a must.

There are many compromises to be made. PostgreSQL's replication system even allows you to set up a replication cluster where the guarantee of durability is provided by streaming transaction logs to a dedicated storage system, and availability is provided by a hot standby.

Detecting failures

For a system to be highly available, failures need to be detected and corrective action needs to be taken. For systems requiring lesser availability, it is acceptable to page the database administrator when anomalies occur and have them wake up and figure out what happened. To provide High Availability, you will need a rotation of database administrators sitting on guard in case something bad happens, in order to have even a remote chance of reacting fast enough. Obviously, automation is required here.

At first glance, it might seem that automating failovers is easy enough—just have the standby server run a script that checks whether the primary is still there, and if not, promote itself to primary. This will actually work okay in most common scenarios. However, to get High Availability, thinking about common scenarios is not enough. You have to make the system behave correctly in the most unusual situations you can think of, and even more importantly also in situations that you can't think of. This is because Murphy's law means that all those situations will happen in your case.

What happens if the primary is only temporarily blocked and starts receiving connections again? Will you have two primary servers then? What happens if, due to a network failure or misconfiguration, the two cluster nodes can't communicate with each other, but can communicate with the application? Will you be able to avoid repeated failovers? Is your system correctly handling timeouts? This is where using a tool that implements some of these concerns becomes handy. Pacemaker and the Linux-HA stack are two such tools.

The split-brain syndrome

Segal's law states that "A man with a watch knows what time it is. A man with two watches is never sure." Similar considerations apply to databases. It is extremely important to avoid situations where more than one database instance could be accepting writes from your application. Your data will end up in two places, and you will not be able to merge the two databases back together without a large data recovery effort. In effect, this causes you to lose data, so you fail on your durability guarantees. This situation is called a split-brain, and all cluster management systems must have ways to avoid it. The tools used to avoid split-brain are called quorum and fencing.

To understand quorum, consider what happens if the network breaks in a way that applications can see all the cluster members but the cluster members are split into two groups that can't communicate with each other. The nodes on each side must understand what has happened to correctly handle the situation. There is no way for the cluster members to distinguish between the other half of the cluster suddenly crashing due to a power failure, and it simply becoming unavailable due to a network error. So, there needs to be some mechanism that gives exactly one group the right to decide to take up the duties of the primary. In HA parlance, this is called providing a **quorum**.

The simplest and most common way to provide quorum is to say that whenever a group of nodes consists of a majority (more than 50 percent), this group has quorum. This system isn't very useful in a two-node cluster, as the smallest number that can have majority is 2, which means that quorum is lost once either of the nodes goes down. This is great for guaranteeing durability, but not so good for availability. There are some ways to securely run a two node cluster, but the simplest solution is to add a third node that has the sole duty of being a tiebreaker in a network split. Just remember that if the tiebreaker node shares a single point of failure with either of the two database nodes, that point becomes a point of failure for the entire cluster. So, don't put it into a small VM that shares a physical server with one of the database nodes.

Quorum means that the winning side knows that it has the right to run the primary, but this is only half of the story. The cluster also needs a way to make sure that the servers that become unresponsive are truly down, not just temporarily incapacitated. This is called fencing the node, or sometimes, a more gruesome acronym: **shoot the other node in the head** (**STONITH**). There are many fencing mechanisms, but one of the most effective mechanisms is the use of an integrated management computer in the target server, or a remotely controllable power delivery unit to just turn the power off and on again. This ensures that the cluster can quickly determine with certainty that the old primary is no longer there, and promote a new one.

Understanding Linux-HA

The Linux-HA stack is built from a set of modular components that provide services. The major parts of this stack are the messaging layer (**Corosync**), the cluster manager (**Pacemaker**), application adaptor scripts (**resource agents**), fencing adaptors for STONITH (**fence agents**), and command-line tools for configuring all of this (**pcs**). The details on how this stack is put together have varied over time and across distributions, so if you are using an older distribution, you might have some differences compared to what is being described here. For newer distributions, the digital world seems to be stabilizing and you shouldn't have major differences.

Corosync

The Corosync messaging layer is responsible for knowing which nodes are up and part of the clusters, handling reliable communications between nodes, and storing the cluster state in a reliable and consistent in-memory database.

Corosync uses a shared key for communications, which you need to generate when setting up your cluster using the **corosync-keygen** tool. The cluster members can be configured to communicate in different ways. The most common way requires that you pick a multicast address and port for multicast communications, and make sure that the multicast UDP traffic actually works on your network. By using this method, you don't need to configure a list of nodes in your configuration. Alternatively, you can set up the system to use a unicast communication method called udpu. When you use this method, you need to list all the cluster nodes in your corosync.conf file.

When using RHEL6 and derivative distributions, you will need to set up CMAN using cluster.conf, and CMAN will take care of starting Corosync for you.

Pacemaker

Pacemaker is the brain of the system. It is the portion that makes decisions on what to fail over and where. Pacemaker uses Corosync to vote one system to be the designated controller node. This node is then responsible for instructing all the other nodes on what to do.

The most important part to understand about Pacemaker is that you don't have to tell Pacemaker what to do. Instead, you have to describe what you would like the cluster to look like, and Pacemaker does its best to deliver within the given constraints. You do this by describing the resources you want to be running, and assigning scores that tell Pacemaker how the resources need to be placed and in what order they need to start and stop. Pacemaker uses this information to figure out what the desired state is and what actions need to be taken to get there. If something changes (for example, a node fails), the plan is recalculated and the corresponding corrective action is taken.

Resource agents / fence agents

Pacemaker has several methods of managing resources. For simple resources
that don't need any cluster awareness, it's possible to use plain LSB `init` scripts.

For things where you want the cluster to pass configuration parameters, or things
that need more complex cluster awareness, **Open Cluster Framework (OCF)** resource
agents are used. Resource agents can, in principle, be written in any language, but
are mostly written as shell scripts. There exists an official `resource-agents` package
that contains most of the common scripts you would want to use, including a `pgsql`
resource agent for managing PostgreSQL database clusters.

If a suitable resource agent is not available, don't be afraid to write your own.
The Linux-HA website has a comprehensive development guide for resource
agents, and you can pick any of the existing ones as an example to get you started.

Fence agents are similar to resource agents, but are only used for adapting different
fencing mechanisms. They too are freestanding executables that follow a specific
calling convention. The methods used include turning off the power through a
networked power switch, issuing a hard reset through a server management interface,
resetting a VM through the hypervisor, and calling a cloud API requesting a reset or
waiting for an operator to manually toggle a switch and tell the cluster that fencing has
been done. The scripts can also be stacked, so the less disruptive methods can be tried
first, and the bigger guns should come out only when trying to be nice fails.

PCS

Internally, Pacemaker's configuration database is stored as an XML document.
While it is possible to change the configuration by directly modifying the XML,
most people prefer to retain their sanity and use a tool that presents a friendlier
interface. The latest and greatest such tool is called **PCS**. On older systems, you
might have encountered a tool called **Crmsh**. The core concepts are the same, so
don't worry too much if you are not able to use PCS.

The PostgreSQL resource agent

The **PostgreSQL resource agent (PG RA)** contains the management of High
Availability for PostgreSQL. It is an OCF-compatible resource agent that implements
a multistate cloneable resource. It also supports an arbitrary number of clones of a
DB instance, async replication, and sync replication.

Because of the way Pacemaker handles multistate resources, when a resource is automatically started (for example, upon the first creation or after being manually stopped for some reason), both the nodes are started as slave instances. Then one of them is picked and promoted to master. This approach has the benefit of creating a new WAL timeline ID every time a new master is chosen, eliminating certain possible data loss cases that can arise from mishandling the cluster.

When picking the node to promote to master, the resource agent checks the WAL positions of all the nodes and picks the one furthest ahead. This avoids losing transactions when both the nodes go down and are come up again at the same time. This algorithm also eliminates the necessity to reimage a node lacking transactions that are not on the main timeline. However, at the same time, it does mean that sometimes, an undesirable node can be chosen to become the master. In this case, the preferred procedure is to force a failover manually (see the later section on enforcing a failover).

When promoting a node to master, PG RA creates a lock file called `PGSQL.lock` to mark the node as containing a data directory that has recently been running as the master. If the lock file is there, PG RA refuses to start up the database on this node in order to avoid possible data loss. Suppose the server with the master instance crashes, is shut down, or becomes inaccessible before all the transactions are replicated. The data directory can contain some unique transactions, and therefore, the affected node should not be brought back as a slave automatically. In other words, such a *fork in the timeline* addresses a data loss issue (transactions may contain some important information) and also prevents the server from coming up with a data directory containing some different data from a new timeline. The situation cannot be automatically corrected, so the lock file is used to highlight the fact that the system administrator's intervention is required. However, this lock file is retained even when the resource is stopped gracefully in a controlled failover scenario (even though a graceful stop has no chance of failing to replicate any transaction).

> This is *important*, take care to remove this lock file after your maintenance operations are completed in order to allow a slave server to start up.

In addition, if the data-status of a slave is set to `DISCONNECTED`, it means that a machine will not be promoted. This is done in order to save you from situations where replication breaks, the slave falls a large amount of time behind, and the master fails. Then the options are either to promote the slave and deal with a huge amount of data that only remains on the failed master timeline, or to fail on availability. PG RA chooses to keep data safe and fail on availability.

If both the slaves have the DISCONNECTED status, it means that something is seriously broken, and it is recommended to manually check the control file's XLOG position and the timeline history files on both hosts to find out exactly what is going on. Then, update the cluster state manually (using the crm_attr ibute utility), like this for example:

```
crm_attribute -N <node name> -n "pgsql-data-status" -v "LATEST"
```

Setting up a simple HA cluster

We will now go through setting up a simple database cluster. For this setup, we will need two database nodes, one extra node for providing quorum, and a cluster IP that will be assigned to the node that is running as the primary. Each database node will store the database on a local filesystem.

Preparing the servers

Install the operating system as you would normally. You should prefer fresher Linux distributions because Linux-HA support has really matured in distributions such as Red Hat Enterprise Linux 7 and its derivatives.

For the network setup, it is really important that the hostnames are set properly before you start setting up High Availability. Pacemaker uses hostnames to identify systems, and that makes changing a node's hostname a rather painful procedure. Make sure that the hostname lookup works properly on all nodes, either by using a DNS server or by adding entries to /etc/hosts on all the nodes. Set reasonably short hostnames and avoid including too much metadata in the name, as that makes life easier when operating the cluster. The prod-db123 instance is nice and easy to type and doesn't need to be changed when stuff gets shuffled around, database1-vhost418-rack7. datacenter-europe.production.mycompany.org is not so easy. Don't name one database node primary and the other standby, as after a failover, that will no longer be true and will create unnecessary confusion in an already tricky situation.

For our example, we will call the nodes db1, db2, and quorum1. The corresponding IPs of the hosts are 10.1.1.11, 10.1.1.12, and 10.1.1.13.

You will also need to pick a cluster IP address. You don't need to do anything special with the address; just ensure that nothing else is using it and that the address you pick is in the same network as the database nodes. This cluster IP will be managed by Pacemaker and added as a secondary IP to the host with the primary. For our example, we will pick 10.1.1.100 as the IP address.

You can see the list of IP addresses assigned to an interface using the
`ip addr` command:

```
[root@db1 ~]# ip addr show eth02: eth0: <BROADCAST,MULTICAST,UP,LOWER_
UP> mtu 1500 qdisc pfifo_fast state UP group default qlen 1000link/
ether 50:e5:49:38:da:c8 brd ff:ff:ff:ff:ff:ffinet 10.1.1.11/24 brd
10.1.1.255 scope global eth0  valid_lft forever preferred_lft foreverinet
10.1.1.100/24 brd 10.1.1.255 scope global eth0  valid_lft forever
preferred_lft forever
```

Installing the necessary software

What specifically needs to be installed for Linux-HA and where to get the packages
from depends heavily on your Linux distribution. However, in most cases, it will be
enough to instruct your package manager to install the `pacemaker` and `pcs` packages.
The rest of the stack will get installed automatically via dependencies, except
possibly fence agents. For them, look up your package repository for packages
starting with `fence-agents-...`, and pick up the packages you plan to use. For
the example here, version 2.0 or later of Corosync is assumed. Earlier versions have
some differences in the initial setup.

You will, of course, also need to install PostgreSQL. Make sure that PostgreSQL
is not automatically started by the operating system. This interferes with normal
cluster operations and can cause split-brain scenarios.

Once you have the packages installed, you need to start the pcsd service, enable
it to be started at boot-up time, and set a password for the hacluster user added
by the `pcs` package. Remember to do this on all nodes.

It's possible to run the cluster without running the pcsd service. Then you will
have to set up Corosync keys and configurations by yourself.

Configuring the clustering software

First, we need to authenticate ourselves to the cluster members so that we are
allowed to configure the cluster. To do this, we use the `pcs cluster auth`
command:

```
[root@db1 ~]# pcs cluster auth db1 db2 quorum1
Username: hacluster
Password:
db1: Authorized
db2: Authorized
quorum1: Authorized
```

Then we set up the cluster using the default settings. You can also adjust the cluster communication method here, or configure multiple redundant network interfaces for communication. Refer to the documentation for more details:

```
[root@db1 ~]# pcs cluster setup --name pgcluster db1 db2 quorum1
Shutting down pacemaker/corosync services...
Redirecting to /bin/systemctl stop  pacemaker.service
Redirecting to /bin/systemctl stop  corosync.service
Killing any remaining services...
Removing all cluster configuration files...
db1: Succeeded
db2: Succeeded
quorum1: Succeeded
```

Finally, we can start the clustering software and verify that it has started up:

```
[root@db1 ~]# pcs cluster start --all
db1: Starting Cluster...
db2: Starting Cluster...
quorum1: Starting Cluster...
[root@db1 ~]# pcs status corosync
Membership information
--------------------------
    Nodeid      Votes Name
         1.         1 db1 (local)
         2.         1 db2
         3.         1 quorum1
```

Preparing for the PostgreSQL installation

Setting up PostgreSQL is mostly similar to how you would do it normally. Pick a place where you want the database to reside, create separate filesystems and mounts if desired, run initdb, configure postgresql.conf and pg_hba.conf, and so on.

In our example, the database will be set up in the /pgsql/data directory, and will run under the operating system user postgres, so we change the filesystem privileges correspondingly:

```
[root@db1 ~]# mkdir /pgsql
[root@db1 ~]# mkdir /pgsql/data
[root@db1 ~]# chown postgres /pgsql/data
```

For the `pgsql` resource agent, you also need to create a directory for some runtime files:

```
[root@db1 ~]# mkdir /pgsql/run
[root@db1 ~]# chown postgres /pgsql/run
```

Create these directories on the other host too.

There are a couple of things to keep in mind when configuring your database. In addition to the changes that every new installation needs, in `postgresql.conf`, you would want to set the following replication-specific settings:

```
wal_level = hot_standby
```

The transaction logging needs to be adjusted to a setting that supports streaming replication. On PostgreSQL 9.4 and later, logical is also an acceptable setting:

```
max_wal_senders = 8
```

We need at least 1 WAL sender to support the replication, but as they don't really cost much, we might as well add a few spare ones for future expansion:

```
wal_keep_segments = 1000
```

Setting this parameter correctly is tricky. If the standby goes offline for a while, during maintenance for example, we need the primary to keep enough transaction logs around so that when the standby comes back, it can continue where it left off. If the necessary transaction logs are no longer available, the slave needs to be reimaged from the master.

This parameter specifies how much data the primary will keep around, the unit being a 16 MB chunk of log. The proper value depends on how long maintenance intervals the system should tolerate, how much transaction log is generated, and how much disk space is available.

Alternatively, with PostgreSQL 9.4 and later, and with a new enough version of the pgsql resource agent, it is possible to use replication slots to make the primary keep enough transaction logs around:

```
max_replication_slots = 8
```

We only need one slot, but similarly to `max_wal_senders`, increasing this value doesn't really cost anything significant, so we might as well add some headroom:

```
hot_standby = on
```

Setting the `hot_standby` parameter to `on` is required so that at the very least, the cluster-monitoring command can verify that the standby is functioning correctly.

For replication, the standby needs to be able to connect to the primary, so you need to have a database user for replication and add an entry to `pg_hba.conf` that allows that user to connect for replication. The automatically created postgres superuser account will work for this, but is undesirable from a security standpoint.

For our example, we will create a user called `standby_repl` and set a password. The following `pg_hba.conf` entry will allow that user to connect from our sample network:

```
# TYPE  DATABASE       USER          ADDRESS      METHOD
  host  replication    standby_repl  samenet      md5
```

We also need the pgsql resource-agent to be able to connect locally to the database. By default, it uses the `postgres` user to connect locally. This is fine for us, so we just enable it to connect without a password:

```
# TYPE   DATABASE      USER          ADDRESS      METHOD
  local  postgres      postgres      trust
```

Syncing the standby

Before we can start handing over database management to Pacemaker, we need both the hosts to be in a ready-to-run state. The simplest way to do this is by shutting down the database we configured in the previous step and simply copying it over using `scp` or `rsync`.

An alternative option is to use `pg_basebackup` to take a snapshot of the primary. The advantage of `pg_basebackup` is that you will know immediately whether the replication connection between the hosts is set up correctly:

```
[root@db2 ~]# pg_basebackup --pgdata=/pgsql/data --xlog \    --host=db1
--username=standby_repl \    --checkpoint=fast --progress
```

Configuring the cluster

Cluster configuration commands can be run on any node in the cluster.

As a first step, we will turn off fencing until we get that setup correctly.

```
pcs property set stonith-enabled=false
```

By default, Pacemaker allows resources that you create to run anywhere in the cluster, unless you explicitly forbid it. For clusters that have databases with local storage, this default doesn't really make sense. Every time we add a node, we would need to tell Pacemaker that the database can't run there. Instead, we want to explicitly allow the resources to run on specific nodes. This is achieved by turning off the `symmetric-cluster` property:

```
pcs property set symmetric-cluster=false
```

Configuring cluster resources

We are now ready to create cluster resources. We will start with PostgreSQL, as it's the most interesting one. The way to do this is as follows:

```
pcs resource create pgsql ocf:heartbeat:pgsql \
    pgctl="/usr/pgsql-9.4/bin/pg_ctl" \
    psql="/usr/pgsql-9.4/bin/psql" \
    pgdata="/pgsql/data" \
    logfile="/pgsql/startup.log" \
    config="/pgsql/data/postgresql.conf" \
    tmpdir="/pgsql/run/" \
    rep_mode="sync" \
    node_list="db1 db2" \
    master_ip="10.1.1.100" \
    repuser="standby_repl" \
    primary_conninfo_opt="password=example" \
    stop_escalate="110" \
    \
    op start timeout=120s on-fail=restart \
    op stop timeout=120s on-fail=fence \
    op monitor interval=3s timeout=10s on-fail=restart \
    op monitor interval=2s role=Master timeout=10s on-fail=fence \
    op promote timeout=120s on-fail=block \
    op demote timeout=120s on-fail=fence \
    meta migration-threshold=2 \
    --master clone-max=2 clone-node-max=1
```

This can be a bit too much to take in, so let's split it up and go through it in smaller pieces:

```
pcs resource create pgsql ocf:heartbeat:pgsql \
```

This line means that we are creating a new resource. The name of that resource will be `pgsql`, and it will use the pgsql resource-agent from the OCF resource agents, under the heartbeat directory. The following lines show the configuration parameters for the resource agent:

```
pgctl="/usr/pgsql-9.4/bin/pg_ctl" \
psql="/usr/pgsql-9.4/bin/psql" \
```

Here, we tell pgsql to use PostgreSQL which is installed at `/usr/pgsql-9.4`.

```
pgdata="/pgsql/data" \
logfile="/pgsql/startup.log" \
config="/pgsql/data/postgresql.conf" \
tmpdir="/pgsql/run/" \
```

In the preceding lines, we tell where various PostgreSQL-related directories and files will reside in the filesystem:

```
rep_mode="sync" \
node_list="db1 db2" \
```

Using these options, we tell pgsql that we want to use synchronous replication. We also need to tell pgsql separately which nodes are expected to be running PostgreSQL:

```
master_ip="10.1.1.100" \
repuser="standby_repl" \
primary_conninfo_opt="password=example" \
```

This block of options specified how to connect to the primary. The IP address we use here needs to be the clustered IP address:

```
stop_escalate="110" \
```

When PostgreSQL doesn't want to stop quickly enough, the resource agent will try to just crash it. That sounds bad, but given that otherwise we would have to reboot the whole operating system, it is a lesser evil. To be effective, this timeout needs to be smaller than the "stop operation" timeout.

This completes the parameters of the resource agent. You can specify many other parameters. To see what parameters are available, run `pcs resource describe ocf:heartbeat:pgsql`.

The next section specifies the parameters of different operations that the resource agent can perform:

```
op start timeout=120s on-fail=restart \
```

The `start` operation is performed when PostgreSQL is not running but should be. The timeout parameter specifies how long we will wait for PostgreSQL to come up, and on-fail specifies that when starting PostgreSQL fails, Pacemaker should try to stop it and then try starting again:

```
op stop timeout=120s on-fail=fence \
```

The `stop` operation is performed when Pacemaker needs to stop PostgreSQL, usually when bringing a node down for maintenance. The `on-fail=fence` parameter here means that if stopping PostgreSQL fails or times out, Pacemaker will reboot the server to expedite the process:

```
op monitor interval=3s timeout=10s on-fail=restart \
op monitor interval=2s role=Master timeout=10s on-fail=fence \
```

The `monitor` operation is performed to detect whether PostgreSQL is still running. It will try to connect to PostgreSQL and run a simple query. When Pacemaker thinks that a resource should be running, it schedules the monitor operation to run every `interval` seconds. The second line specifies special behavior for the server that runs the database primary.

As for the slave, we can afford to try to gracefully restart it, as nobody is really waiting for it. When the primary stops responding, applications are waiting and the quickest thing we can do is just pull the plug on the server and immediately promote the slave. Because we are using synchronous replication, there will be no data lost:

```
op promote timeout=120s on-fail=block \
op demote timeout=120s on-fail=fence \
```

The `promote` and `demote` functions are called when a standby needs to become a master, and vice-versa.

Pacemaker always starts multistate resources as slaves before figuring out which one to promote. When promotion is required, the pgsql resource agent is able to query the databases to figure out which one has the latest data, and request that the correct database be promoted. This has a nice side benefit that every time a node becomes master, there is a WAL timeline switch, and PostgreSQL can use the timeline history to detect when an operator error would result in data corruption. When a promotion fails, we request that Pacemaker keep its hands off so that the situation can be disentangled manually.

For demotion, PostgreSQL doesn't have any way other than shutting itself down. The same considerations apply here as in the stop operation case:

```
meta migration-threshold=2 \
```

This line specifies the `meta` attributes. These are guidelines for pacemaker on how to manage this resource. By setting `migration-threshold` to 2, we tell Pacemaker to give up on starting the node if after starting, it fails twice. Giving up avoids endless retries, which can cause nasty problems.

Once the system administrator has eliminated the cause of the failure, the resource can be re-enabled by clearing the fail count:

```
--master clone-max=2
```

Finally, we tell Pacemaker that the resource needs to be run as a master-slave cluster with two nodes. The default settings will want to run on the instance on each node.

The second resource for Pacemaker to manage is the IP alias for the clustered address:

```
pcs resource create master-ip ocf:heartbeat:IPaddr2 \
    ip="10.1.1.100" iflabel="master" \
    op monitor interval=5s
```

This resource is significantly simpler. We only need to specify the desired IP address and a label here. We also increase the monitoring frequency, to be on the safe side.

Configuring the constraints

Once the resources are set up, we can configure the constraints. We want the master IP to be located where the pgsql master is. For this, we use a `colocation` constraint:

```
pcs constraint colocation add master-ip with master pgsql-master
```

There are some things to note here. The first is that we have to refer to the PostgreSQL resource as `pgsql-master`. This is just an internal convention of how master-slave resource naming works in Pacemaker. The second is the `master` keyword, and it means that this constraint only refers to a pgsql instance running as primary.

The order in which we specify the resources is important here. Pacemaker will first decide where the target, pgsql master, should run and only then will it try to find a place `master-ip` variable. We omitted the `score` attribute in this command, which results in a score of *infinity*, making it a mandatory rule for Pacemaker. This means that if this rule can't be satisfied, `master-ip` will not be allowed to run.

Next up is the ordering constraint. We want to try to promote a node only once we have successfully started the cluster IP address there. Also, when we are doing a graceful failover (bringing primary down for maintenance), we would want to give PostgreSQL an opportunity to ship out the unsent transaction logs before we move the cluster IP to the other host. This results in the following ordering constraint:

```
pcs constraint order start master-ip then promote pgsql-master
```

Ordering constraints are symmetrical by default, which means that this constraint also makes Pacemaker to get a constraint that wants to demote pgsql-master before stopping master-ip.

Finally, we set up the location constraints to allow the pgsql resource and the master-ip resource to run on the database nodes:

```
pcs constraint location pgsql prefers db1=0 db2=0
pcs constraint location master-ip prefers db1=0 db2=0
```

We set the score to 0 here to allow the location score to be modified by Pacemaker.

Setting up fencing

The specifics of how to set up fencing depend on what kind of fencing method is available to you. For demonstration purposes, we are going to set up IPMI-based fencing, which uses a rather common management interface standard to toggle power.

The package that contains this specific agent is fence-agents-ipmilan in Red Hat / Fedora derivatives.

The first step is to create the resources:

```
pcs stonith create db1-fence fence_ipmilan \
    auth=md5 ipaddr=... passwd=... lanplus=1 login=root method=cycle \
    pcmk_host_check=static-list \
    pcmk_host_list=db1
pcs stonith create db2-fence fence_ipmilan \
    auth=md5 ipaddr=... passwd=... lanplus=1 login=root method=cycle \
    pcmk_host_check=static-list \
    pcmk_host_list=db2
```

We don't use a fence agent for the quorum host, as nothing is allowed to run on it.

We then add location constraints that allow the fence agents to run on hosts other than the node that this specific resource is tasked with fencing:

```
pcs constraint location db1-fence prefers db2=0 quorum1=0
pcs constraint location db2-fence prefers db1=0 quorum1=0
```

Then we register the fencing methods with pacemaker:

```
pcs stonith level add 1 db1 db1-fence
pcs stonith level add 1 db2 db2-fence
```

Finally, we can turn fencing on again in cluster properties:

```
pcs property set stonith-enabled=true
```

Verifying the setup

At this point, the cluster should be up and running. You can use the `crm_mon -1A` command to check what the cluster status is. The output should look something similar to the following.

First comes the header. It shows general information about the cluster. The most interesting part here is the line that tells us which node is the current **designated controller** (DC). The cluster logs on that node will contain information about what Pacemaker decided to do and why:

```
Cluster name: pgcluster
Last updated: Thu Jul 16 01:31:12 2015
Last change: Wed Jul 15 23:23:21 2015
Stack: corosync
Current DC: db1 (1) - partition with quorum
Version: 1.1.12-a9c8177
3 Nodes configured
5 Resources configured
```

Next, we have the list of nodes:

```
Online: [ db1 db2 quorum1 ]
```

Then comes the resource that we have configured:

```
Full list of resources:
master-ip   (ocf::heartbeat:IPaddr2):   Started db1
Master/Slave Set: pgsql-master [pgsql]
    Masters: [ db1 ]
    Slaves: [ db2 ]
node1fence (stonith:fence_ipmilan):   Started quorum1
node2fence (stonith:fence_ipmilan):   Started quorum1
```

In this example, we see that db1 is running as the master, db2 is running as the slave, and master-ip has been moved to the correct host.

Finally, there are the node attributes:

```
Node Attributes:
* Node db1:
    + master-pgsql                          : 1000
```

This is the master promotion score that controls which node gets picked by Pacemaker to be the master. The values are assigned by pgsql resource agents, and their semantics are as follows:

- -INF: This instance has fallen behind and should not be considered to be a candidate for the master.

- 100: This instance is eligible for promotion when the master fails.

- 1000: This is the desired master node.

- pgsql-data-status: This is the most important attribute specifying whether the node is eligible to be promoted or not.

- STREAMING|SYNC: This instance is connected to the master and streams WAL data synchronously. It is eligible for promotion.

- DISCONNECTED: This instance is disconnected from the master and is not eligible for promotion when the master fails.

- LATEST: This instance is/was running as the master and is the preferred candidate for promotion.

Then follow the pgsql RA attributes:

```
pgsql-master-baseline                       : 000000003C7027D0
    + pgsql-status                          : PRI
    + pgsql-xlog-loc                        : 000000003C7027D0
```

The pgsql-master-baseline and pgsql-xlog-loc attributes are the attributes that pgsql RA uses to decide which node to promote. The pgsql-status attribute is an informational attribute specifying what the cluster thinks the status of the particular instance is. This value can occasionally be stale. The PRI keyword means running as master, HS:sync means running as a hot standby slave connected to the master, and HS:alone means running as a hot standby slave but not connected to the master, as shown here:

```
* Node db2:
    + master-pgsql                          : 100
    + pgsql-data-status                     : STREAMING|SYNC
    + pgsql-status                          : HS:sync
    + pgsql-xlog-loc                        : 000000003C701020
```

According to the attributes for the standby server, pgsql RA thinks that it is connected to the primary, is replicating synchronously, and is eligible to be promoted to master.

Common maintenance tasks

Let's now take a look at some common maintenance tasks.

Performing maintenance on a single node

Pacemaker has a built-in notion of bringing a node down for maintenance. This is called standby mode. This mode is also used for enforced failover.

You can activate it like this:

```
pcs cluster standby db1
```

If this command is issued on the master, it causes Pacemaker to try to gracefully shut down PostgreSQL. If the shutdown takes more than 110 seconds, a forced kill of PostgreSQL is tried. If this fails, the node is rebooted. Then Pacemaker moves the master IP over to the other node and promotes the chosen PostgreSQL slave to the master role. It is recommended that you issue a CHECKPOINT command on the master prior to doing this step in order to minimize downtime.

For slave nodes, this directive only stops PostgreSQL.

Then wait for the failover to complete:

```
crm_mon
```

At this point, your maintenance tasks can be performed.

 Important! Remember to remove /pgsql/run/PGSQL.lock after completing maintenance operations.

This is how the lock file can be removed:

```
rm /pgsql/run/PGSQL.lock
```

When everything is ready, instruct Pacemaker to re-enable the node:

```
pcs cluster unstandby db1
```

This node is then put back into a cluster as a slave node.

Forcing a failover

To force a failover, you can just bring the master server down for maintenance and then immediately bring it back up again.

Recovering from failed PostgreSQL starts

When PostgreSQL fails to start on a node, it is marked as failed and Pacemaker does not try to restart it. To fix this situation, the administrator must diagnose and correct the root cause. Common problems are configuration issues and having the master lock file present. Once PostgreSQL is able to to start, order Pacemaker to forget about the PostgreSQL resource failures:

```
pcs resource cleanup pgsql
```

Performing cluster-wide maintenance

For tasks where Pacemaker cluster management must be completely subverted, it is useful to turn on the maintenance mode for the entire cluster:

```
pcs property set maintenance-mode=true
```

Once the maintenance mode is enabled, Pacemaker does not perform any actions on the cluster, and you are free to perform any reconfigurations. At the same time, you are also responsible for maintaining High Availability.

If the master role is changed during the maintenance interval or you have started/ stopped PostgreSQL, you need to tell Pacemaker to forget about any state and manually assign the preferred master to the node where the master PostgreSQL is currently running. Failing to do so can cause spurious failovers, or even extended downtime, when the cluster can't correctly detect which node to promote to master.

To reset the cluster state, use the following commands:

```
# Clean up resource information
pcs resource cleanup pgsql
pcs resource cleanup master-ip
# Assign PostgreSQL master score 1000 to the node that is currently
mastercrm_attribute -l reboot -N db1 -n master-pgsql -v 1000
# Disable promotion on the slave node
crm_attribute -l reboot -N db2 -n master-pgsql -v -INF
```

When ready to go, disable the maintenance mode with the following command:

```
pcs property set maintenance-mode=false
```

It is advisable that you monitor the system with crm_mon for some time to see whether anything unexpected happens.

Resynchronizing after master failure

As was already mentioned, when the master server crashes, its state can be ahead of the slave server. In order to address this issue, you should resynchronize the database using regular backup tools (`pg_basebackup`, or enable backup mode and use `rsync`), or using `pg_rewind` *before* removing the `PGSQL.lock` file.

The following commands can be used to reset a failed PostgreSQL master to a slave with minimal network traffic.

The `pg_rewind` tool needs the database to be in a safely shut down state. If we are doing this, it is probably in a crashed state. We remove `recovery.conf`, start it as a master in single user mode, and quit immediately after the recovery is done:

```
rm -f /pgsql/data/recovery.confsudo -u postgres /usr/pgsql-9.4/bin/
postgres --single \-D /pgsql/data/ < /dev/null
```

Fetch the out-of-sync data from the current master. The same parameters should be used here as used in replication:

```
sudo -u postgres /usr/pgsql-9.4/bin/pg_rewind \--target-pgdata=/pgsql/
data/ \--source-server="host=10.1.1.100 user=standby_repl"
```

The server is now safe to start as a slave. Remove the lock file and tell Pacemaker to retry starting it.

```
rm -f /pgsql/tmp/PGSQL.lockpcs resource cleanup pgsql
```

Summary

In this chapter, you learned how to set up a PostgreSQL HA cluster using tools that are commonly available in Linux. In addition to that, the most frequent issues, such as split-brain and fencing, were discussed in great detail.

8
Working with PgBouncer

When you are working with a large-scale installation, it is sometimes quite likely that you have to deal with many concurrent open connections. Nobody will put up 10 servers to serve just two concurrent users; in many cases, this simply makes no sense. A large installation will usually have to deal with hundreds, or even thousands, of concurrent connections. Introducing a connection pooler, such as PgBouncer, will help improve performance of your systems. PgBouncer is really the classic workhorse when it comes to connection pooling. It is rock solid and it has already been around for many years.

Usually creating thousands and thousands of connections can be quite an overhead, because every time a connection to PostgreSQL is created, a `fork()` call is required. If a connection is only used for a short period of time, this can be expensive to do. This is exactly when PgBouncer should be used. Basically, PgBouncer is not a replication-related tool. However, we have decided to include it in this book because it is often used in combination with replication to make it work more efficiently.

In this chapter, we will take a deep look at PgBouncer and see how it can be installed and used to speed up our installation. This chapter is not meant to be a comprehensive guide to PgBouncer, and it can in no way replace the official documentation (`https://pgbouncer.github.io/overview.html`).

The following topics will be covered in this chapter:

- The purpose of PgBouncer
- Fundamental concepts of connection pooling
- Installing PgBouncer
- Configuring and administering PgBouncer
- Performance tuning
- Making PgBouncer work with Java

Understanding the fundamental PgBouncer concepts

As stated before, the basic idea of PgBouncer is to save connection-related costs. When a user creates a new database connection, it usually means burning a couple of hundred kilobytes of memory. This consists of approximately 20 KB of shared memory and the amount of memory used by the process serving the connection itself. While the memory consumption itself might not be a problem, the actual creation process of the connection can be comparatively time consuming. What does "time consuming" mean? Well, if you create a connection and use it, you might not even notice the time PostgreSQL needs to fork a connection. But let's take into account what a typical website does. It opens a connection, fires a handful of simple statements, and disconnects. Even though creating a connection can be barely noticed, it is still a fair amount of work compared to all the rest. How long can looking up a handful of phone numbers or some other trivial information take, after all? So, the less the work a single connection has to do in its life cycle, the more important the time taken to actually create the connection becomes.

PgBouncer solves this problem by placing itself between the actual database server and the heavily used application. To the application, PgBouncer looks just like a PostgreSQL server. Internally, PgBouncer will simply keep an array of open connections and pool them. Whenever a connection is requested by the application, PgBouncer will take the request and assign a pooled connection. In short, it is some sort of proxy.

The main advantage here is that PgBouncer can quickly provide a connection to the application, because the real database connection already exists behind the scenes. In addition to this, a very low memory footprint can be observed. Users have reported a footprint that is as small as 2 KB per connection. This makes PgBouncer ideal for very large connection pools.

Installing PgBouncer

Before we dig into the details, we will see how PgBouncer can be installed. Just as with PostgreSQL, you can take two routes. You can either install binary packages or simply compile from source. In our case, we will show you how a source installation can be performed:

1. The first thing you have to do is download PgBouncer from the official website at `http://pgfoundry.org/projects/pgbouncer`.

2. Once you have downloaded the .tar archive, you can safely unpack it using the following command:

```
tar xvfz pgbouncer-1.5.4.tar.gz
```

3. Once you are done with extracting the package, you can enter the newly created directory and run configure. Expect this to fail due to missing packages. In many cases, you have to install libevent (the development package) first before you can successfully run configure.

 On Debian (or Debian-based distributions), the easiest way to install the libevent development package is to run apt-get install libevent-dev.

4. Once you have successfully executed configure, you can move forward and run make. This will compile the source and turn it into binaries. Once this is done, you can finally switch to root and run make install to deploy those binaries. Keep in mind that the build process needs PostgreSQL server development packages, as access to pg_config (a tool used to configure external software) is needed.

You have now successfully installed PgBouncer.

Configuring your first PgBouncer setup

Once we have compiled and installed PgBouncer, we can easily fire it up. To do so, we have set up two databases on a local instance (p0 and p1). The idea behind the setup performed in this example is to use PgBouncer as a proxy.

Writing a simple config file and starting PgBouncer up

To make PgBouncer work, we can write a simple config file, and this file can be fed to PgBouncer:

```
[databases]
p0 = host=localhost dbname=p0
p1 = host=localhost dbname=p1

[pgbouncer]
logfile = /var/log/pgbouncer.log
pidfile = /var/log/pgbouncer.pid
listen_addr = 127.0.0.1
```

```
listen_port = 6432
auth_type = trust
auth_file = /etc/pgbouncer/userlist.txt
pool_mode = session
server_reset_query = DISCARD ALL
max_client_conn = 100
default_pool_size = 20
```

Using the same database name is not required here. You can map any database name to any connect strings. We have just found it useful to use identical names.

Once we have written this config file, we can safely start PgBouncer and see what happens:

```
hs@iMac:/etc$ pgbouncer bouncer.ini

2013-04-25 17:57:15.992 22550 LOG File descriptor limit: 1024 (H:4096),
max_client_conn: 100, max fds possible: 150

2013-04-25 17:57:15.994 22550 LOG listening on 127.0.0.1:6432

2013-04-25 17:57:15.994 22550 LOG listening on unix:/tmp/.s.PGSQL.6432

2013-04-25 17:57:15.995 22550 LOG process up: pgbouncer 1.5.4, libevent
2.0.16-stable (epoll), adns: evdns2
```

In production, you would configure authentication first, but let's do it step by step.

Dispatching requests

The first thing we have to configure when dealing with PgBouncer is the database servers we want to connect to. In our example, we simply create links to p0 and p1. We put the connect strings in, and they tell PgBouncer where to connect to. As PgBouncer is essentially some sort of proxy, we can also map connections to make things more flexible. In this case, mapping means that the database holding the data does not necessarily have the same name as the virtual database exposed by PgBouncer.

The following connection parameters are allowed: dbname, host, port, user, password, client_encoding, datestyle, timezone, pool_size, and connect_query. Everything up to the password is what you would use in any PostgreSQL connect string. The rest is used to adjust PgBouncer for your needs. The most important setting here is the pool size, which defines the maximum number of connections allowed to this very specific PgBouncer virtual database.

Note that the size of the pool is not necessarily related to the number of connections to PostgreSQL. There can be more than just one pending connection to PgBouncer waiting for a connection to PostgreSQL.

The important thing here is that you can use PgBouncer to relay to various different databases on many different hosts. It is not necessary that all databases reside on the same host, so PgBouncer can also help centralize your network configuration.

Note that we connect to PgBouncer using separate passwords. As all connections are in the pool, we don't authenticate against PostgreSQL itself.

Finally, we can configure an optional `connect_query` parameter. Using this setting, we can define a query that has to be executed as soon as the connection has been passed on to the application. What is this good for? Well, you might want to set some variables in your database, clean it, or simply change some runtime parameters straightaway.

Sometimes, you simply don't want to list all database connections. Especially if there are many databases, this can come in handy. The idea is to direct all requests that have not been listed before to the fallback server:

```
* = host=fallbackserver
```

Connections to `p0` and `p1` will be handled as before. Everything else will go to the fallback connect string.

More basic settings

In our example, PgBouncer will listen on port `6432`. We have set `listen_addr` to `127.0.0.1`, so for now, only local connections are allowed. Basically, `listen_addr` works just like `listen_addresses` in `postgresql.conf`. We can define where to listen for IP addresses.

> In most cases, you might want to use * for `listen_addr`, because you might want to take all bound network addresses into consideration. The idea is to exclude networks and make sure that PgBouncer does not listen to all of them.

In our setup, PgBouncer will produce a fair amount of log entries. To channel this log into a log file, we have used the `logfile` directive in our config. It is highly recommended to write log files to make sure that you can track all the relevant data going on in your bouncer.

Handling pool sizes

So far, only two parameters for controlling the pool size have been used. However, there are more settings that can be used to control the behavior of PgBouncer. The following list of parameters is essential.

max_client_conn

The `max_client_conn` setting has already been described briefly. The theoretical maximum used is as follows:

*max_client_conn + (max_pool_size * total_databases * total_users)*

If a database user is specified in the connect string (all users connect under the same username), the theoretical maximum is this:

*max_client_conn + (max_pool_size * total_databases)*

The theoretical maximum should be never reached, unless somebody deliberately tries to come up with a special workload to reach the upper border.

default_pool_size

The `default_pool_size` setting specifies the default number of connections allowed for each user/database pair.

The default setting can be overwritten for a certain database.

min_pool_size

The `min_pool_size` setting will make sure that new connections to the databases are added as soon as the number of spare connections drops below the threshold due to inactivity. If the load spikes rapidly, `min_pool_size` is vital to keep the performance up.

reserve_pool_size

The `reserve_pool_size` setting specifies the number of additional connections that can be allowed to a pool.

pool_size

The `pool_size` parameter sets the maximum pool size for this database. If the variable is not set, the `default_pool_size` parameter is used.

Authentication

Once we have configured our databases and other basic settings, we can turn our attention to authentication. As you have already seen, this local config points to the databases in your setup. All applications will point to PgBouncer, so all authentication-related proceeding will actually be handled by the bouncer. How does it work? Well, PgBouncer accepts the same authentication methods supported by PostgreSQL, such as MD5 (the auth_file may contain passwords encrypted with MD5), crypt (plain-text passwords in auth_file), plain (clear-text passwords), trust (no authentication), and any (which is like trust, but ignores usernames).

The auth_file file itself has a very simple format:

```
"hs"    "15359fe57eb03432bf5ab838e5a7c24f"
"zb"    "15359fe57eb03432bf5ab838e5a7c24f"
```

The first column holds the username, then comes a tab, and finally there is either a plain text string or a password encrypted with MD5. If you want to encrypt as a password, PostgreSQL offers the following command:

```
test=# SELECT md5('abc');
              md5
----------------------------------
 900150983cd24fb0d6963f7d28e17f72
(1 row)
```

Connecting to PgBouncer

Once we have written this basic config and started up the system, we can safely connect to one of the databases listed:

```
hs@iMac:~$ psql -p 6432 p1 -U hs
psql (9.4.4)
Type "help" for help.


p1=#
```

In our example, we are connecting to the database called p1. We can see that the shell has been opened normally, and we can move on and issue the SQL we want just as if we were connected to a normal database.

The log file will also reflect our efforts to connect to the database and state:

```
2013-04-25 18:10:34.830 22598 LOG C-0xbca010: p1/hs@unix:6432 login
attempt: db=p1 user=hs
2013-04-25 18:10:34.830 22598 LOG S-0xbe79c0: p1/hs@127.0.0.1:5432 new
connection to server
```

For each connection, we get various log entries so that an administrator can easily check what is going on.

Java issues

If you happen to use Java as the frontend, there are some points that have to be taken into consideration. Java tends to pass some parameters to the server as part of the connection string. One of those parameters is `extra_float_digits`. This `postgresql.conf` parameter governs the floating-point behavior of PostgreSQL, and is set by Java to make things more deterministic.

The problem is that PgBouncer will only accept the tokens listed in the previous section, otherwise it will error out.

To get around this issue, you can add a directive to your bouncer config (the PgBouncer section of the file):

```
ignore_startup_parameters = extra_float_digits
```

This will ignore the JDBC setting and allow PgBouncer to handle the connection normally. If you want to use Java, we recommend putting those parameters into `postgresql.conf` directly to make sure that no nasty issues will pop up during production.

Pool modes

In the configuration, you might have also seen a config variable called `pool_mode`, which has not been described yet. The reason is that pool modes are so important that we have dedicated an entire section to them.

In general, three different pool modes are available:

- `session`
- `transaction`
- `statement`

The session mode is the default mode of PgBouncer. A connection will go back to the pool as soon as the application disconnects from the bouncer. In many cases, this is the desired mode because we simply want to save on connection overhead—and nothing more.

Nowadays, many programming languages' frameworks come with some sort of connection management of their own. So, it is actually quite rare to find a modern application that just opens a connection, executes some small transactions, and disconnects.

However, in some cases, it might be useful to return sessions to the pool faster. This is especially important if there are lags between various transactions. In the transaction mode, PgBouncer will immediately return a connection to the pool at the end of a transaction (and not when the connection ends). The advantage of this is that we can still enjoy the benefits of transactions, but connections are returned much sooner, and therefore, we can use those open connections more efficiently. For most web applications, this can be a big advantage because the lifetime of a session has to be very short. In the transaction mode, some commands, such as SET, RESET, LOAD, and so on, are not fully supported due to side effects.

The third pooling option, statement, allows us to return a connection immediately at the end of a statement. This is a highly aggressive setting, and has basically been designed to serve high-concurrency setups in which transactions are not relevant at all. To make sure that nothing can go wrong in this setup, long transactions spanning more than one statement are not allowed.

Most people will stick to the default mode here, but you have to keep in mind that other options exist.

Cleanup issues

One advantage of a clean and fresh connection after PostgreSQL calls fork() is the fact that the connection does not contain any faulty settings, open cursors, or other leftovers whatsoever. This makes a fresh connection safe to use and avoids side effects of other connections.

As you have learned in this chapter, PgBouncer will reuse connections to avoid those fork() calls. The question now is, "How can we ensure that some application does not suffer from side effects caused by some other connection?"

The answer to this problem is `server_reset_query`. Whenever a connection is returned to the pool, PgBouncer is able to run a query or a set of queries designed to clean up your database connection. This could be basically any query. In practical setups, it has been proven to be wise to call `DISCARD ALL`. The `DISCARD ALL` command is a PostgreSQL instruction that has been designed to clean out an existing connection by closing all cursors, resetting parameters, and so on. After `DISCARD ALL`, a connection is as fresh as after a `fork()` call and can be reused safely by a future request.

Keep in mind that there is no need to run an explicit `ROLLBACK` command before a connection goes back to the pool or after it is fetched from the pool. Rolling back transactions is already done by PgBouncer automatically, so you can be perfectly sure that a connection is never inside a transaction.

Improving performance

Performance is one of the key factors when considering PgBouncer in the first place. To make sure that performance stays high, some issues have to be taken seriously.

First of all, it is recommended to make sure that all nodes participating in your setup are fairly close to each other. This greatly helps reduce network round trip times, and thus boosts performance. There is no point in reducing the overhead of calling `fork()` and paying for this gain with network time. Just as in most scenarios, reducing network time and latency is definitely a huge benefit.

Basically, PgBouncer can be placed on a dedicated PgBouncer server, on the database node directly, or on the web server. In general, it is recommended to avoid putting database infrastructure onto the web server. If you have a larger setup, a dedicated server might be a good option. Mixing up things too much can lead to nasty side effects. If one component of the system starts to go crazy, it might have horrible side effects and harm others. Therefore, isolating components in containers or having things on different servers might be a good idea in many cases.

One additional issue, which is often forgotten, is related to pooling itself. As we have already stated, the idea of PgBouncer is to speed up the process of getting a database connection. But what if the pool is short of connections? If there are no spare database connections idling around, what will happen? Well, you will spend a lot of time making those connections by forking them in the backend. To fix this problem, it is recommended that you set `min_pool_size` to a reasonable value. This is especially important if many connections created at the same time (if a web server is restarted, for example). Always make sure that your pool is reasonably sized to sustain high performance (in terms of creating new connections).

The perfect value of min_pool_size will depend on the type of application you are running. However, we have good experience with values substantially higher than the default. To figure out how to set this value, check out the PgBouncer system statistics and see the maximum number of connections used, the number of connections in use at the moment, and so on. Based on this statistical information, a wise choice can be made.

A simple benchmark

In this chapter, we have already outlined that it is very beneficial to use PgBouncer if many short-lived connections have to be created by an application. To prove our point, we have compiled an extreme example. The goal is to run a test doing as little as possible. We want to measure merely how much time we spend in opening a connection. To do so, we have set up a virtual machine with just one CPU.

The test itself will be performed using pgbench (a contribution module widely used to benchmark PostgreSQL).

We can easily create ourselves a nice and shiny test database:

```
pgbench -i p1
```

Then we have to write ourselves a nice sample SQL command that should be executed repeatedly:

```
SELECT 1;
```

Now we can run an extreme test against our standard PostgreSQL installation:

```
hs@VM:test$ pgbench -t 1000 -c 20 -S p1 -C -f select.sql
starting vacuum...end.
transaction type: Custom query
scaling factor: 1
query mode: simple
number of clients: 20
number of threads: 1
number of transactions per client: 1000
number of transactions actually processed: 20000/20000
tps = 67.540663 (including connections establishing)
tps = 15423.090062 (excluding connections establishing)
```

We want to run 20 concurrent connections. They all execute 1,000 single transactions. The -c option indicates that after every single transaction, the benchmark will close the open connection and create a new one. This is a typical case on a web server without pooling — each page might be a separate connection.

Now keep in mind that this test has been designed to look ugly. We may observe that keeping the connection alive will make sure that we can execute roughly 15,000 transactions per second on our single VM CPU. If we have to fork a connection each time, we will drop to just 67 transactions per second, as we have stated before. This kind of overhead is worth thinking about.

Let's now repeat the test and connect to PostgreSQL through PgBouncer:

```
hs@VM:test$ pgbench -t 1000 -c 20 -S p1 -C -f select.sql -p 6432
starting vacuum...end.
transaction type: Custom query
scaling factor: 1
query mode: simple
number of clients: 20
number of threads: 1
number of transactions per client: 1000
number of transactions actually processed: 20000/20000
tps = 1013.264853 (including connections establishing)
tps = 2765.711593 (excluding connections establishing)
```

As you can see, our throughput has risen to 1,013 transactions per second. This is 15 times more than before — indeed a nice gain.

However, we also have to see whether our performance level has dropped since we did not close the connection to PgBouncer. Remember that the bouncer, the benchmark tool, and PostgreSQL are all running on the same single CPU. This does have an impact here (context switches are not too cheap in a virtualized environment).

Keep in mind that this is an extreme example. If you repeat the same test with longer transactions, you will see that the gap logically becomes much smaller. Our example has been designed to demonstrate our point.

Maintaining PgBouncer

In addition to what we have already described in this chapter, PgBouncer has a nice interactive administration interface capable of performing basic administration and monitoring tasks.

How does it work? PgBouncer provides you with a fake database called pgbouncer. It cannot be used for queries, as it only provides a simple syntax for handling basic administrative tasks.

 If you are using PgBouncer, please don't use a normal database called pgbouncer. It will just amount to confusion and yield zero benefits.

Configuring the admin interface

To configure this interface, we have to adapt our config file. In our example, we will simply add one line to the config (in the PgBouncer section of the file):

```
admin_users = zb
```

We want Zoltan, whose username is zb, to be in charge of the admin database, so we simply add him here. If we want many users to get access to the system, we can list them one after another (separated by commas).

After restarting PgBouncer, we can try connecting to the system:

```
psql -p 6432 -U zb pgbouncer
psql (9.4.4, server 1.5.4/bouncer)
WARNING: psql version 9.4, server version 1.5.
        Some psql features might not work.
Type "help" for help.
```

Don't worry about the warning message; it is just telling us that we have connected to something that does not look like a native PostgreSQL 9.4 database instance.

Using the management database

Once we have connected to this virtual management database, we can check which commands are available there. To do so, we can run SHOW HELP:

```
pgbouncer=# SHOW HELP;
NOTICE:  Console usage
DETAIL:
  SHOW HELP|CONFIG|DATABASES|POOLS|CLIENTS|SERVERS|VERSION
  SHOW STATS|FDS|SOCKETS|ACTIVE_SOCKETS|LISTS|MEM
  SHOW DNS_HOSTS|DNS_ZONES
  SET key = arg
```

```
    RELOAD
    PAUSE [<db>]
    RESUME [<db>]
    KILL <db>
    SUSPEND
    SHUTDOWN
SHOW
```

As we have mentioned, the system will only accept administrative commands; normal SELECT statements are not possible in this virtual database:

```
pgbouncer=# SELECT 1+1;
ERROR:  invalid command 'SELECT 1+1;', use SHOW HELP;
```

Extracting runtime information

One important thing you can do with the management interface is figure out which databases have been configured for the system. To do that, you can call the SHOW DATABASES command:

```
pgbouncer=# \x
Expanded display is on.
pgbouncer=# SHOW DATABASES;
-[ RECORD 1 ]+----------
name         | p0
host         | localhost
port         | 5432
database     | p0
force_user   |
pool_size    | 20
reserve_pool | 0
-[ RECORD 2 ]+----------
name         | p1
host         | localhost
port         | 5432
database     | p1
force_user   |
pool_size    | 20
```

```
reserve_pool | 0
-[ RECORD 3 ]+----------
name         | pgbouncer
host         |
port         | 6432
database     | pgbouncer
force_user   | pgbouncer
pool_size    | 2
reserve_pool | 0
```

As you can see, we have two productive databases and the virtual pgbouncer database. What is important here to see is that the listing contains the pool size as well as the size of the reserved pool. It is a good check to see what is going on in your bouncer setup.

Once you have checked the list of databases on your system, you can turn your attention to the active clients in your system. To extract the list of active clients, PgBouncer offers the SHOW CLIENTS instruction:

```
pgbouncer=# \x
Expanded display is on.
pgbouncer=# SHOW CLIENTS;
-[ RECORD 1 ]+--------------------
type         | C
user         | zb
database     | pgbouncer
state        | active
addr         | unix
port         | 6432
local_addr   | unix
local_port   | 6432
connect_time | 2013-04-29 11:08:54
request_time | 2013-04-29 11:10:39
ptr          | 0x19e3000
link         |
```

At the moment, we have exactly one user connection to the pgbouncer database. We can see nicely where the connection comes from and when it has been created. SHOW CLIENTS is especially important if there are hundreds, or even thousands, of servers on the system.

Sometimes, it can be useful to extract aggregated information from the system. The SHOW STATS parameter will provide you with statistics about what is going on in your system. It shows how many requests have been performed, and how many queries have been performed on an average:

```
pgbouncer=# SHOW STATS;
-[ RECORD 1 ]----+----------
database         | pgbouncer
total_requests   | 3
total_received   | 0
total_sent       | 0
total_query_time | 0
avg_req          | 0
avg_recv         | 0
avg_sent         | 0
avg_query        | 0
```

Finally, we can take a look at the memory consumption we are facing. PgBouncer will return this information if SHOW MEM is executed:

```
pgbouncer=# SHOW MEM;
name          | size | used | free | memtotal
--------------+------+------+------+----------
user_cache    | 184  | 4    | 85   | 16376
db_cache      | 160  | 3    | 99   | 16320
pool_cache    | 408  | 1    | 49   | 20400
server_cache  | 360  | 0    | 0    | 0
client_cache  | 360  | 1    | 49   | 18000
iobuf_cache   | 2064 | 1    | 49   | 103200
(6 rows)
```

As you can see, PgBouncer is really lightweight and does not consume much memory as other connection pools do.

> It is important to see that all information is returned by PgBouncer as a table. This makes it really easy to process this data and use it in some kind of application.

Suspending and resuming operations

One of the core reasons for using the interactive virtual database is to be able to suspend and resume normal operations. It is also possible to reload the config on the fly, as shown in the following example:

```
pgbouncer=# RELOAD;
RELOAD
```

The RELOAD command will reread the config, so there will be no need to restart the entire PgBouncer tool for most small changes. This is especially useful if there is just a new user.

An additional feature of PgBouncer is the ability to stop operations for a while. But why would anybody want to stop queries for some time? Well, let's assume you want to perform a small change somewhere in your infrastructure. Just interrupt operations briefly without actually throwing errors. Of course, you have to be a little careful to make sure that your frontend infrastructure can handle such an interruption nicely. From the database side, however, it can come in handy.

To temporarily stop queries, we can call SUSPEND:

```
pgbouncer=# SUSPEND;
SUSPEND
```

Once you are done with your changes, you can resume normal operations easily:

```
pgbouncer=# RESUME;
RESUME
```

Once this has been called, you can continue sending queries to the server.

Finally, you can even stop PgBouncer entirely from the interactive shell, but it is highly recommended that you be careful when doing this:

```
pgbouncer=# SHUTDOWN;
The connection to the server was lost. Attempting reset: Failed.
!>
```

The system will shut down instantly.

Summary

In this chapter, you learned how to use PgBouncer for highly scalable web applications to reduce the overhead of permanent creation of connections. We saw how to configure the system and how we can utilize a virtual management database.

In the next chapter, you will be introduced to pgpool, a tool used to perform replication and connection pooling. Just like PgBouncer, pgpool is open source and can be used along with PostgreSQL to improve your cluster setups.

9
Working with pgpool

In the previous chapter, we looked at PgBouncer and learned how to use it to optimize replicated setups as much as possible. In this chapter, we will take a look at a tool called pgpool. The idea behind pgpool is to bundle connection pooling with some additional functionality to improve replication, load balancing, and so on. It has steadily been developed over the years and can be downloaded freely from the www.pgpool.net website.

Installing pgpool

Just as we have seen for PostgreSQL, PgBouncer and most other tools covered in this book, we can either install pgpool from source or just use a binary. Again, we will describe how the code can be compiled from source.

To install pgpool, we have to download it first from the following path:

http://www.pgpool.net/download.php?f=pgpool-II-3.4.2.tar.gz.

Once this has been done, we can extract the tarball:

```
$ tar xvfz pgpool-II-3.4.2.tar.gz
```

The installation procedure is just like we have seen already. The first thing we have to call is configure along with some parameters. In our case, the main parameter is --with-pgsql, which tells the build process where to find our PostgreSQL installation.

```
$ ./configure --with-pgsql=/usr/local/pgsql/
```

Of course, there are some additional settings:

- --with-openssl builds pgpool with OpenSSL support thus allowing encrypted connections

- `--enable-table-lock` and `--enable-sequence-lock` are needed for compatibility with very old versions of pgpool
- `--with-memached` enabled `memcache` support to make sure the query cache has enough memory to do its job efficiently

Now, we can compile and install the software easily as follows:

```
make

make install
```

Installing additional modules

What you have just seen is a basic pgpool installation. However, to make things work really nicely, it can be beneficial to install additional modules such as `pgpool-regclass` and `insert_lock`. Installing `pgpool-regclass` is important to handle DDL replication. The `insert_lock` parameter is important to handle distributed writes. It is highly recommended to install this module because otherwise handling DDLs won't work. Up to now, we have not seen a practical setup where using this module did not make sense.

Let us install `pgpool-regclass` first as follows:

```
cd sql/pgpool-regclass/

make

make install
```

To enable the module, we have to deploy the `pgpool-regclass.sql` file. The module must be present in all databases we are going to use. The easiest way to achieve that is to simply load the SQL file into `template1`. Whenever a new database is created, `template1` will be cloned; so all new databases will automatically have this module.

It is also possible to use the following command:

```
CREATE EXTENSION pgpool_regclass;
```

The same applies to `insert_lock.sql`, which can be found in the `sql` directory of the pgpool source code. The easiest solution is to load this into `template1` directly as follows:

```
psql -f insert_lock.sql template1
```

Finally, there is the `pgpool_recovery` module. It is needed if you are planning to use online recovery in pgpool. Here is how installation works:

```
cd pgpool-II-x.x.x/sql/pgpool-recovery
```

First `cd` into the pgpool recovery directory. The sources can be compiled:

```
make
make install
```

Once the module has been installed, a simple `postgresql.conf` parameter has to be added as follows:

```
pgpool.pg_ctl = '/usr/local/pgsql/bin/pg_ctl'
```

A simple `pg_ctl reload` command will enable the setting.

Understanding the features of pgpool

The following features are provided by pgpool:

- Connection pooling
- Statement-level replication
- Load balancing
- Limiting connections
- In-memory caching

> When deciding which features to use, it is important to keep in mind that not all functionality is available at the same time. The following website contains an overview of what can go together and what cannot: `http://www.pgpool.net/docs/latest/pgpool-en.html#config`.

One core feature of pgpool is the ability to do connection pooling. The idea is pretty much the same as the one we outlined in the previous chapter. We want to reduce the impact of forking connections each and every time a webpage is opened. Instead, we want to keep connections open and reuse them whenever a new request comes along. Those concepts have already been discussed for PgBouncer in the previous chapter.

In addition to pooling, pgpool provides basic replication infrastructure made explicitly to increase a system's reliability. The thing here is that pgpool uses a statement-level approach to replicate data, which has some natural restrictions users have to keep in mind (more of that can be found later in this chapter).

One feature often requested along with replication is load balancing, and pgpool offers exactly that. You can define a set of servers and use the pooler to dispatch requests to the desired database nodes. It is also capable of sending a query to the node with the lowest load.

To boost performance, pgpool offers a query cache. The goal of this mechanism is to reduce the number of queries that actually make it to the real database servers—as many queries as possible should be served by the cache. We will take a closer look at this topic in this chapter.

Older versions of pgpool had a feature called "Parallel query." The idea was to parallelize a query to make sure that it scales out better. However, this feature has fortunately been removed. It caused a lot of maintenance work and created some false expectations on the user side as far as how things work.

Understanding the pgpool architecture

Once we have installed pgpool, it is time to discuss the software architecture. From a user's point of view, pgpool looks just like a normal database server, and you can connect to it like to any other server as shown in the following image:

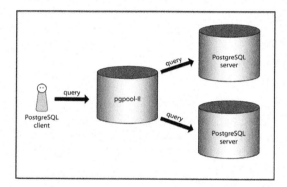

The pgpool tool will dispatch requests according to your needs.

Once you have understood the overall architecture as it is from a user's point of view, we can dig into a more detailed description:

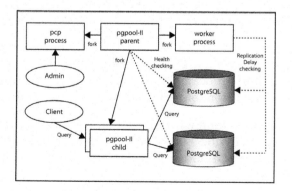

When pgpool is started, we fire up the pgpool parent process. This process will fork and create the so-called child processes. These processes will be in charge of serving requests to end users and handle all the interaction with our database nodes. Each child process will handle a couple of pool connections. This strategy will reduce the number of authentication requests to PostgreSQL dramatically.

In addition to that we have the PCP infrastructure needed to handle configuration and management. We will discuss this infrastructure a little later in this chapter.

Finally, we need a bunch of PostgreSQL database nodes as backend storage. End users will never connect to those nodes directly but always go through pgpool.

Setting up replication and load balancing

To set up pgpool, we can simply take an existing sample file containing a typical configuration, copy it to our configuration directory, and modify it:

```
$ cp /usr/local/etc/pgpool.conf.sample /usr/local/etc/pgpool.conf
```

It is a lot easier to just adapt this config file than to write things from scratch. In the following listing, you will see a sample config that you can use for a simple two-node setup:

```
listen_addresses = '*'
port = 9999
socket_dir = '/tmp'
pcp_port = 9898
pcp_socket_dir = '/tmp'

backend_hostname0 = 'localhost'
backend_port0 = 5432
backend_weight0 = 1
backend_data_directory0 = '/home/hs/db'
backend_flag0 = 'ALLOW_TO_FAILOVER'

backend_hostname1 = 'localhost'
backend_port1 = 5433
backend_weight1 = 1
backend_data_directory1 = '/home/hs/db2'
backend_flag1 = 'ALLOW_TO_FAILOVER'

enable_pool_hba = off
pool_passwd = 'pool_passwd'
authentication_timeout = 60
ssl = off
```

```
num_init_children = 32
max_pool = 4
child_life_time = 300
child_max_connections = 0
connection_life_time = 0
client_idle_limit = 0

connection_cache = on
reset_query_list = 'ABORT; DISCARD ALL'

replication_mode = on
replicate_select = off
insert_lock = on
load_balance_mode = on
ignore_leading_white_space = on
white_function_list = ''
black_function_list = 'nextval,setval'
```

Let us now discuss these settings in detail and see what each setting means:

- `pid_file_name`: Just like most software components, pgpool will write a PID file. We can explicitly define the position of this file. Usually, PID files will reside somewhere under `/var/`.

- `listen_addresses`: This setting is the exact counterpart of PostgreSQL's own `listen_addresses` setting. The idea here is to have a setting defining which IPs to listen on.

- `port`: This will define the TCP port on which the system will listen.

- `socket_dir`: There is no hard requirement to use TCP. UNIX sockets will be perfectly fine as well. The `socket_dir` parameter will define the location where these UNIX sockets will reside.

- `pcp_port`: This is the TCP port on which the administration interface will listen.

- `pcp_socket_dir`: This is the UNIX sockets directory the administration interface will use.

- `backend_hostname0`: This is the hostname of the first database in our setup.

- `backend_port0`: This is the TCP port of this system.

- `backend_weight0`: In pgpool, we can assign weights to individual nodes. A higher weight will automatically make sure that more requests will be sent there.

- `backend_data_directory0`: This is the PGDATA directory belonging to this instance.

- `backend_flag`: This setting tells pgpool if a node is allowed to failover or not. The following two settings are allowed:
  - ALLOW_TO_FAILOVER
  - DISALLOW_TO_FAILOVER

- `enable_pool_hba`: If this is set to `true`, pgpool will use `pool_hba.conf` for authentication. Here, pgpool follows the same concept as PostgreSQL.

- `pool_passwd`: This is the password file for pgpool.

- `authentication_timeout`: This defines the timeout for pool authentication.

- `ssl`: If this has been set to true, SSL will be enabled for client and backend connections. The `ssl_key` and `ssl_cert` parameters must be set as well to make this work.

- `num_init_children`: When pgpool is started, a number of connections will be preforked to make sure that response times stay low. This setting will define the number of initial children. The default value is 32.

- `max_pool`: This setting defines the maximum size of the pool per child. Please be aware that the number of connections from pgpool processes to the backends may reach *num_init_children * max_pool*. This parameter can only be set at the start server.

- `child_life_time`: This defines the number of seconds a child is allowed to be idle before it is terminated.

- `child_max_connections`: After this number of connections to the very same child, it will be terminated. In other words, a process will handle so many connections before it is recycled.

- `connection_life_time`: This tells you how long a connection may live before it is recycled.

- `client_idle_limit`: We need to disconnect a client if it has been idle for this amount of time.

- `connection_cache`: If this is set to `true`, connections to the (storage) backend will be cached.

- `reset_query_list`: This defines a list of commands, which has to be executed when a client exits a session. It is used to clean up a connection.

- `replication_mode`: This turns replication explicitly on. The default value is false.

- `replicate_select`: This indicates whether we can replicate SELECT statements or not.

- `insert_lock`: When replicating tables with sequences (data type `serial`), pgpool has to make sure that those numbers will stay in sync.

- `load_balance_mode`: Shall pgpool split the load to all hosts in the system? The default setting is false.

- `ignore_leading_white_space`: Shall leading whitespaces of a query be ignored or not?

- `white_function_list`: When pgpool runs a stored procedure, pgpool will have no idea what it actually does. The `SELECT func()` call can be a read or a write — there is no way to see from outside what will actually happen. The `white_function_list` parameter will allow you to teach pgpool which functions can be safely load balanced. If a function writes data, it must not be load balanced — otherwise, data will be out of sync on those servers. Being out of sync must be avoided at any cost.

- `black_function_list`: This is the opposite of the `white_function_list` parameter. It will tell pgpool which functions must be replicated to make sure that things stay in sync.

Keep in mind that there is an important relation between `max_pool` and a child process of pgpool. A single child process can handle up to the `max_pool` connections.

Password authentication

Once you have come up with a working config for pgpool, we can move ahead and configure authentication. In our case, we want to add one user called `hs`. The password of `hs` should simply be `hs`. The `pool_passwd` variable will be in charge of storing passwords. The format of the file is simple; it will hold the name of the user, a colon, and the MD5-encrypted password.

To encrypt a password, we can use the `pg_md5` script:

```
$ pg_md5 hs
789406d01073ca1782d86293dcfc0764
```

Then, we can add all of this to the config file storing users and passwords. In the case of pgpool, this file is called `pcp.conf`:

```
# USERID:MD5PASSWD
hs:789406d01073ca1782d86293dcfc0764
```

Firing up pgpool and testing the setup

Now that we have all components in place, we can start pgpool:

```
$ pgpool -f /usr/local/etc/pgpool.conf
```

If there is no error, we should see a handful of processes waiting for some work from those clients out there:

```
$ ps ax | grep pool
30927 pts/4      S+        0:00 pgpool -n
30928 pts/4      S+        0:00 pgpool: wait for connection request
30929 pts/4      S+        0:00 pgpool: wait for connection request
30930 pts/4      S+        0:00 pgpool: wait for connection request
30931 pts/4      S+        0:00 pgpool: wait for connection request
30932 pts/4      S+        0:00 pgpool: wait for connection request
```

As you can clearly see, pgpool will show up as a handful of processes in the process table.

Attaching hosts

Basically, we could already connect to pgpool and fire queries; but, this would instantly lead to disaster and inconsistency. Before we can move on to some real action, we should check the status of those nodes participating in the cluster. To do so, we can use a tool called pcp_node_info:

```
$ pcp_node_info 5 localhost 9898 hs hs 0
localhost 5432 3 0.500000
$ pcp_node_info 5 localhost 9898 hs hs 1
localhost 5433 2 0.500000
```

The format of this call to pcp_node_info is a little complicated and not too easy to read if you happen to see it for the first time.

Note that the weights are 0.5 here. In the configuration, we have given both backends a weight of 1. The pgpool tool has automatically adjusted the weight so that they add up to 1.

Here is the syntax of pcp_node_info:

```
pcp_node_info - display a pgpool-II node's information


Usage: pcp_node_info [-d] timeout hostname port# username password nodeID
  -d, --debug    : enable debug message (optional)
timeout          : connection timeout value in seconds.
command exits on timeout
```

```
hostname       : pgpool-II hostname
port#          : PCP port number
username       : username for PCP authentication
password       : password for PCP authentication
nodeID         : ID of a node to get information for


Usage: pcp_node_info [options]
  Options available are:
  -h, --help     : print this help
  -v, --verbose  : display one line per information
with a header
```

The first parameter is the timeout parameter. It will define the maximum time for the request. Then, we specify the host and the port of the PCP infrastructure. Finally, we pass a username and a password as well as the number of the host we want to have information about. The system will respond with a hostname, a port, a status, and the weight of the node. In our example, we have to focus our attention on the status column. It can return four different values:

- 0: This state is only used during the initialization. PCP will never display it.
- 1: Node is up. No connections yet.
- 2: Node is up. Connections are pooled.
- 3: Node is down.

In our example, we can see that node number 1 is basically returning status 3 — it is down. This is clearly a problem because if we were to execute a write now, it would not end up in both nodes but just in one of them.

To fix the problem, we can call pcp_attach_node and enable the node:

```
$ pcp_attach_node 5 localhost 9898 hs hs 0
$ pcp_node_info 5 localhost 9898 hs hs 0
localhost 5432 1 0.500000
```

Once we have added the node, we can check its status again. It will be up and running.

To test our setup, we can check out psql and display a list of all the databases in the system:

```
$ psql -l -p 9999
                    List of databases
```

```
   Name    | Owner | Encoding   |   Collate    | Ctype ...
-----------+-------+------------+--------------+-- ...
postgres   | hs    | SQL_ASCII  | en_US.UTF-8  | C ...
template0  | hs    | SQL_ASCII  | en_US.UTF-8  | C ...
template1  | hs    | SQL_ASCII  | en_US.UTF-8  | C ...
(3 rows)
```

The answer is as expected. We can see an empty database instance.

Checking the replication

If all nodes are up and running, we can already run our first operations on the cluster. In our example, we will simply connect to pgpool and create a new database. The `createdb` tool is a command-line tool that serves as abstraction for the CREATE DATABASE command, which can be replicated by pgpool nicely. In our example, we simply create a database called xy to see if replication works:

```
$ createdb xy -p 9999
```

To see if the command has been replicated as expected, we suggest connecting to both databases and seeing if the new database is present or not. In our example, everything has been working as expected:

```
$ psql xy -p 5433 -c "SELECT 1 AS x"
x
---
 1
(1 row)
```

Doing this basic check is highly recommended to make sure that nothing has been forgotten and everything has been configured properly.

One more thing, which can be highly beneficial when it comes to checking a running setup, is the `pcp_pool_status` parameter. It will extract information about the current setup and show information about configuration parameters currently in use.

The syntax of this command is basically the same as for all the `pcp_*` commands we have seen so far:

```
$ pcp_pool_status 5 localhost 9898 hs hs
name : listen_addresses
value: localhost
```

```
desc : host name(s) or IP address(es) to listen to

name : port
value: 9999
desc : pgpool accepting port number
```

...

In addition to this, we suggest performing the usual checks such as checking for open ports and properly running processes. These checks should reveal if anything of importance has been forgotten during the configuration.

Running pgpool with streaming replication

The pgpool tool can also be used with streaming instead of statement-level replication. It is perfectly fine to use PostgreSQL onboard replication and use pgpool just for load balancing and connection pooling.

In fact, it can even be beneficial to do so because you don't have to worry about side effects of functions or potential other issues. The PostgreSQL transaction log is always right, and it can be considered to be the ultimate law.

The pgpool statement-level replication was a good feature to replicate data before streaming replication was introduced into the core of PostgreSQL.

In addition to this, it can be beneficial to have just one master. The reason for this is simple. If you have just one master, it is hard to face inconsistencies. Also, the pgpool tool will create full replicas, so data has to be replicated anyway. There is absolutely no win if data must end up on both the servers anyway—writing to two nodes will not make things scale any better in this case.

How can you run pgpool without replication? The process is basically quite simple, as follows:

1. Set up PostgreSQL streaming replication (synchronous or asynchronous).
2. Change `replication_mode` in the pool config to `off`.
3. Set `master_slave` to `on`.
4. Set `master_slave_sub_mode` to stream.
5. Start `pgpool` as described earlier in this chapter.

In a basic setup, pgpool will assume that node number 0 will be the master. So, you have to make sure that your two nodes are listed in the config in the right order.

For a basic setup, these small changes to the config file are perfectly fine.

Optimizing the pgpool configuration for master/slave mode

The pgpool tool offers a handful of parameters to tweak the configuration to your needs. One of the most important things we have to take into consideration is that PostgreSQL supports both synchronous and asynchronous replication. Why is this relevant? Well, let us assume a simple scenario. Somebody wants to register on a website:

1. A write request comes in. pgpool will dispatch you to node 0 because we are facing a write.
2. The user clicks on the **Save** button.
3. The user will reach the next page; a read request will be issued

   ° If we end up on node 0, we will be fine—the data is expected to be there.

   ° If we end up on node 1, we might not see the data at this point if we are replicating asynchronously. Theoretically, there can also be a small window if you are using synchronous replication in this case.

This can lead to strange behavior on the client's side. A typical case of strange behavior would be: A user creates a profile. In this case, a row is written. At the very next moment, the user wants to visit his or her profile and checks the data. If he or she happens to read from a replica, the data might not be there already. If you are writing a web application, you must keep this in the back of your mind.

To get around this issue, you have following two choices:

* Replicate synchronously, which is a lot more expensive
* Set the `delay_threshold` parameter in the pooler config

The `delay_threshold` variable defines the maximum lag, a slave is allowed to have to still receive reads. The setting is defined in bytes of changes inside the XLOG. So, if you set this to `1024`, a slave is only allowed to be 1 KB of XLOG behind the master. Otherwise, it will not receive read requests.

Of course, unless this has been set to zero, it is pretty hard to make it totally impossible that a slave can ever return data that is too old; however, a reasonable setting can make it very unlikely. In many practical applications, this may be sufficient.

How does pgpool know how far a slave is behind? The answer is that this can be configured easily:

- `sr_check_period`: This variable defines how often the system should check those XLOG positions to figure out if the delay is too high or not. The unit used here is seconds.

- `sr_check_user`: The name of the user to connect to the primary via streaming to check for the current position in XLOG.

- `sr_check_password`: It stores password for the current user.

> If you really want to make sure that load balancing will always provide you with up-to-date data, it is necessary to replicate synchronously, which can be expensive.

Dealing with failovers and High Availability

Some obvious issues, which can be addressed with pgpool, are of High Availability and failover. In general, there are various approaches available to handle those topics with or without pgpool.

Using PostgreSQL streaming and Linux HA

The easiest approach to High Availability with pgpool is to use PostgreSQL onboard tools along with Linux HA. In this case, in our world, the best approach is to run pgpool without statement-level replication and use PostgreSQL streaming replication to sync the data.

The pgpool tool can be configured to do load balancing and automatically send write requests to the first and read requests to the second node.

What happens in case of failover? Let us assume that the master will crash. In this case, Linux HA would trigger the failover and move the service IP of the master to the slave. The slave can then be promoted to be the new master by Linux HA (if this is desired). The pgpool tool would then simply face a broken database connection and start over and reconnect.

Of course, we can also use Londiste or some other technology such as Slony to replicate data. However, for the typical case, streaming replication is just fine.

 Slony and SkyTools are perfect tools if you want to upgrade all nodes inside your pgpool setup with a more recent version of PostgreSQL. You can build Slony or Londiste replicas and then just suspend operations briefly (to stay in sync) and switch your IP to the host running the new version.

Practical experience has shown that using PostgreSQL onboard and operating system-level tools is a good way to handle failovers easily and, more important, reliably.

pgpool mechanisms for High Availability and failover

In addition to streaming replication and Linux HA, you can also use mechanisms provided by pgpool to handle failovers. This section will use those means provided by pgpool.

The first thing you have to do is to add the failover command to your pool configuration. Here is an example:

```
failover_command = '/usr/local/bin/pgpool_failover_streaming.sh %d %H
```

Whenever pgpool detects a node failure, it will execute the script we defined in the pool configuration and react according to our specifications. Ideally, this failover script will write a trigger file; this trigger file can then be seen by the slave system and turn it into a master.

The `recovery.conf` file on the slave might look like this:

```
standby_mode = 'on'
primary_conninfo = 'host=master_host user=postgres'
trigger_file = '/tmp/trigger_file0'
```

The `trigger_file` is checked for every 5 seconds. Once the failover occurs, pgpool can treat the second server as the new master.

The logical next step after a failover is to bring a new server back into the system. The easiest and most robust way of doing that is to:

1. Set up streaming replication
2. Wait until the server is back in sync

3. Briefly interrupt writes

4. Use `pcp_attach_node` to add the new node

5. Resume writes

Overall, this will only need a few seconds of service interruption.

 Theoretically, service interruptions are not necessary in the pgpool world; however, to make sure that there is not the slightest way of causing inconsistency, it might be worth turning off writes for some seconds. In the vast majority of cases out there, this will be tolerable.

Summary

The pgpool tool is one that has been widely adopted for replication and failover. It offers a vast variety of features including load balancing, connection pooling, and replication. The pgpool tool will replicate data on the statement level and integrate itself with PostgreSQL onboard tools such as streaming replication.

In the next chapter, we will dive into Slony and learn about logical replication. We will discuss the software architecture and see how Slony can be used to replicate data within a large server farm.

10
Configuring Slony

Slony is one of the most widespread replication solutions in the field of PostgreSQL. It is not only one of the oldest replication implementations, it is also one that has the most extensive support by external tools, such as pgAdmin3. For many years, Slony was the only viable solution available for the replication of data in PostgreSQL. Fortunately, the situation has changed and a handful of new technologies have emerged.

In this chapter, we will take a deep look at Slony, and you will learn how to integrate Slony into your replication setup. You will also find out which problems you can solve using Slony. A wide variety of use cases and examples will be covered.

The following topics will be covered in this chapter:

- Installing Slony
- The Slony system architecture
- Replicating tables
- Deploying DDLs
- Handling failovers
- Common pitfalls

Installing Slony

To install Slony, first download the most recent tarball from `http://slony.info`. As always, we will perform a source installation so that we are able to perform replication.

For the purpose of this chapter, we have used the version of Slony available at `http://main.slony.info/downloads/2.2/source/slony1-2.2.4.tar.bz2`.

Once we have downloaded the package, we can extract it by running the following command:

```
tar xvfj slony1-2.2.4.tar.bz2
```

The tarball will inflate, and we can move forward to compile the code. To build the code, we must tell Slony where to look for pg_config. The purpose of pg_config is to provide the add-on module with all of the information about the build process of PostgreSQL itself. In this way, we can ensure that PostgreSQL and Slony are compiled in the same way. The pg_config file is quite common and is widely used by many tools built on PostgreSQL. In our demo setup, PostgreSQL resides in /usr/local/pgsql, so we can safely assume that PostgreSQL will reside in the bin directory of the installation:

```
./configure --with-pgconfigdir=/usr/local/pgsql/bin
make


sudo make install
```

Once we have executed configure, we can compile the code by calling make. Then we can switch to root (if PostgreSQL has been installed as root) and install the binaries on their final destination. The process is again similar to that for other external tools built on PostgreSQL.

Understanding how Slony works

Before we start replicating our first database, we have to dive into Slony's architecture. It is important to understand how it works, otherwise it will be next to impossible to utilize this software in a useful and reasonable way.

In contrast to transaction log streaming, Slony uses logical replication. This means that it does not use internal binary data (such as the XLOG) but a logical representation of the data (in the case of Slony, it is text). Using textual data instead of the built-in transaction log has some advantages, but also some downsides, which will be discussed in detail in this chapter.

 Don't mix up the logical representation of data with PostgreSQL 9.4's replication slots. Slony is not based on the PostgreSQL transaction log.

Dealing with logical replication

First of all, we have to discuss what logical replication really means. The backbone of every Slony setup is the so-called **changelog** triggers. This means that whenever Slony has to replicate the contents of a table, it will create a trigger. This trigger will then store all changes made to the table in a log. A process called `slon` will then inspect this changelog and replicate those changes to the consumes. Let's take a look at the basic algorithm:

```
INSERT INTO table (name, tstamp) VALUES ('hans', now());

trigger fires
```

The data `'hans', '2015-02-26 13:26:02'` as well as some bookkeeping information will be stored in the log table, and then `COMMIT`.

After some time, the following will happen:

1.   The `slon` daemon will come along and read all changes since the last commit

2.   All changes will be replayed on the slaves

3.   Once this is done the log can be deleted

The following diagram shows the overall architecture of Slony:

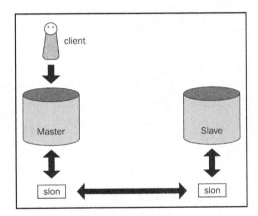

Keep in mind that the transport protocol is pure text. The main advantage here is that there is no need to run the same version of PostgreSQL on every node in the cluster, because Slony will abstract the version number. We cannot achieve this with transaction log shipping because, in the case of XLOG-based replication, all nodes in the cluster must use the same major version of PostgreSQL. The downside to Slony is that data replicated to a slave has to go through an expensive parsing step. In addition to that, polling `sl_log_*` and firing triggers is expensive. Therefore, Slony certainly cannot be considered a high-performance replication solution.

The change log is written for certain tables. This also means that we don't have to replicate all of those tables at the same time. It is possible to replicate just a subset of those tables on a node.

Because Slony is fairly independent of the PostgreSQL version, it can be used effectively for upgrade purposes. Of course, this is not a one-line process, but it is definitely a feasible option.

The slon daemon

As we have already stated, the `slon` daemon will be in charge of picking up the changes made to a specific table or set of tables, and transporting those changes to the desired destinations. The following diagram shows the basic architecture of Slony:

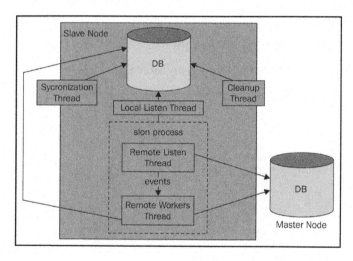

To make this work, we have to run exactly one `slon` daemon per database in our cluster.

 Note that we are talking about one `slon` daemon per database, not per instance. This is important to take into account when doing the actual setup.

As each database will have its own `slon` daemon, these processes will communicate with each other to exchange and dispatch data. Individual `slon` daemons can also function as relays and simply pass data. This is important if you want to replicate data from database A to database C through database B. The idea here is similar to what is achievable using streaming replication and cascading replicas.

An important thing about Slony is that there is no need to replicate an entire instance or an entire database. Replication is always related to a table or a group of tables. For each table (or for each group of tables), one database will serve as the master, while as many databases as desired will serve as slaves for that particular set of tables.

It might very well be the case that one database node is the master of tables A and B and another database is the master of tables C and D. In other words, Slony allows the replication of data back and forth. Which data has to flow, from where, and to where will be managed by the `slon` daemon.

The `slon` daemon itself consists of various threads serving different purposes, such as cleanup, listening for events, and applying changes to a server. In addition to these, it will perform synchronization-related tasks.

To interface with the `slon` daemon, you can use the command-line tool called `slonik`. It will be able to interpret scripts and talk to Slony directly.

Replicating your first database

After this little introduction, we can move forward and replicate our first database. To do so, we can create two databases in a database instance. We want to simply replicate between these two databases.

 It makes no difference if you replicate within an instance or between two instances — it works exactly the same way.

Creating the two databases should be an easy task once your instance is up and running:

```
hs@hs-VirtualBox:~$ createdb db1
hs@hs-VirtualBox:~$ createdb db2
```

Now we can create a table that should be replicated from database db1 to database db2:

```
db1=# CREATE TABLE t_test (id serial, name text,
PRIMARY KEY (id));
NOTICE:  CREATE TABLE will create implicit sequence "t_test_id_seq" for
serial column "t_test.id"
NOTICE:  CREATE TABLE / PRIMARY KEY will create implicit index "t_test_
pkey" for table "t_test"
CREATE TABLE
```

Create this table in both the databases in an identical manner, because the table structure won't be replicated automatically.

Replicating data structures and adding new tables to the system are not possible out of the box.

Once this has been done, we can write a slonik script to tell the cluster about our two nodes. The slonik interface is a command-line interface that we use to talk to Slony directly. You can also work with it interactively, but this is far from comfortable. In fact, it is really hard, and in the past we have rarely seen people do this in production environments.

A script used to register these nodes would look as follows:

```
#!/bin/sh

MASTERDB=db1
SLAVEDB=db2
HOST1=localhost
HOST2=localhost
DBUSER=hs

slonik<<_EOF_
cluster name = first_cluster;

    # define nodes (this is needed by pretty much
    # all slonik scripts)
node 1 admin conninfo = 'dbname=$MASTERDB host=$HOST1
user=$DBUSER';
node 2 admin conninfo = 'dbname=$SLAVEDB host=$HOST2
user=$DBUSER';

    # init cluster
```

```
init cluster ( id=1, comment = 'Master Node');

    # group tables into sets
create set (id=1, origin=1, comment='Our tables');
set add table (set id=1, origin=1, id=1,
  fully qualified name = 'public.t_test',
comment='sample table');

store node (id=2, comment = 'Slave node',
event node=1);
store path (server = 1, client = 2, conninfo='dbname=$MASTERDB
host=$HOST1 user=$DBUSER');
store path (server = 2, client = 1, conninfo='dbname=$SLAVEDB
host=$HOST2 user=$DBUSER');
_EOF_
```

First of all, we define a handful of environment variables. This is not necessary but can be quite handy to make sure that nothing is forgotten if there is a change. Then our slonik script starts.

The first thing we have to do is define a cluster name. This is important: with Slony, a cluster is more of a virtual thing, and it is not necessarily related to physical hardware. We will find out what this means later on, when talking about failovers. The cluster name is also used to prefix schema names in Slony.

In the next step, we have to define the nodes of this cluster. The idea here is that each node will have a number associated with a connection string. Once this has been done, we can call init cluster. During this step, Slony will deploy all of the infrastructure to perform replication. We don't have to install anything manually here.

Now that the cluster has been initialized, we can organize our tables into replication sets, which are really just a set of tables. In Slony, we will always work with replication sets. Tables are grouped into sets and replicated together. This layer of abstraction allows us to quickly move groups of tables around. In many cases, this is a lot easier than just moving individual tables one by one.

Finally, we have to define paths. What is a path? A path is basically the connection string for moving from A to B. The main question here is: why are paths needed at all? We have already defined nodes earlier, so why define paths? The answer is that the route from A to B is not necessarily the same as the route from B to A. This is especially important if one of these servers is in some DMZ while the other one is not. In other words, by defining paths, you can easily replicate between different private networks and cross firewalls while performing some NAT, if necessary.

As the script is a simple shell script, we can easily execute it:

```
hs@hs-VirtualBox:~/slony$ sh slony_first.sh
```

Slony has done some work in the background. By looking at our test table, we can see what has happened:

```
db1=# \d t_test
                      Table "public.t_test"
 Column |  Type   |                    Modifiers
--------+---------+--------------------------------------------------
 id     | integer | not null default nextval('t_test_id_seq'::regclass)
 name   | text    |
Indexes:
    "t_test_pkey" PRIMARY KEY, btree (id)
Triggers:
    _first_cluster_logtrigger AFTER INSERT OR DELETE
OR UPDATE ON t_test
FOR EACH ROW EXECUTE PROCEDURE _first_cluster.logtrigger('_first_
cluster', '1', 'k')
    _first_cluster_truncatetrigger BEFORE TRUNCATE ON t_test FOR EACH
STATEMENT EXECUTE PROCEDURE _first_cluster.log_truncate('1')
Disabled triggers:
    _first_cluster_denyaccess BEFORE INSERT OR DELETE OR UPDATE ON t_
test FOR EACH ROW EXECUTE PROCEDURE _first_cluster.denyaccess('_first_
cluster')
    _first_cluster_truncatedeny BEFORE TRUNCATE ON t_test FOR EACH
STATEMENT EXECUTE PROCEDURE _first_cluster.deny_truncate()
```

A handful of triggers have been deployed automatically to keep track of these changes. Each event is covered by a trigger.

Now that this table is under Slony's control, we can start replicating it. To do so, we have to come up with a `slonik` script again:

```
#!/bin/sh

MASTERDB=db1
SLAVEDB=db2
HOST1=localhost
HOST2=localhost
```

```
DBUSER=hs

slonik<<_EOF_
cluster name = first_cluster;

node 1 admin conninfo = 'dbname=$MASTERDB host=$HOST1 user=$DBUSER';
node 2 admin conninfo = 'dbname=$SLAVEDB host=$HOST2 user=$DBUSER';

subscribe set ( id = 1, provider = 1, receiver = 2, forward = no);
_EOF_
```

After stating the cluster name and listing the nodes, we can call `subscribe set`. The point here is that in our example, set number 1 is replicated from node 1 to node 2 (receiver). The `forward` keyword is important to mention here. This keyword indicates whether or not the new subscriber should store the log information during replication to make it possible for future nodes to be candidates for the provider. Any node that is intended to be a candidate for failover must have `forward = yes`. In addition to that, this keyword is essential to perform cascaded replication (meaning A replicates to B and B replicates to C).

If you execute this script, Slony will truncate the table on the slave and reload all of the data to make sure that things are in sync. In many cases, you may already know that you are in sync, and you would want to avoid copying gigabytes of data over and over again. To achieve this, we can add `OMIT COPY = yes`. This will tell Slony that we are sufficiently confident that the data is already in sync. This feature has been supported since Slony 2.0.

After defining what we want to replicate, we can fire up those two `slon` daemons in our favorite Unix shell:

```
$ slon first_cluster 'host=localhost dbname=db1'
$ slon first_cluster 'host=localhost dbname=db2'
```

This can also be done before we define this replication route, so the order is not of primary concern here.

Now we can move forward and check whether the replication is working nicely:

```
db1=# INSERT INTO t_test (name) VALUES ('anna');
INSERT 0 1
db1=# SELECT * FROM t_test;
id | name
----+------
  1 | anna
```

```
(1 row)

db1=# \q
hs@hs-VirtualBox:~/slony$ psql db2
psql (9.4.1)
Type "help" for help.

db2=# SELECT * FROM t_test;
id | name
---+------
(0 rows)

db2=# SELECT * FROM t_test;
id | name
--- +------
 1 |  anna
(1 row)
```

We add a row to the master, quickly disconnect, and query to check whether the data is already there. If you happen to be quick enough, you will see that the data comes with a small delay. In our example, we managed to get an empty table just to demonstrate what asynchronous replication really means.

> Let's assume you are running a book shop. Your application connects to server A to create a new user. Then the user is redirected to a new page, which queries some information about the new user—be prepared for the possibility that the data is not there yet on server B. This is a common mistake in many web applications dealing with load balancing. The same kind of delay happens with asynchronous streaming replication.

Deploying DDLs

Replicating just one table is clearly not enough for a productive application. Also, there is usually no way to ensure that the data structure never changes. At some point, it is simply necessary to deploy changes of the data structures (so-called **DDLs**).

The problem now is that Slony relies heavily on triggers. A trigger can fire when a row in a table changes. This works for all tables, but it does not work for system tables. So, if you deploy a new table or happen to change a column, there is no way for Slony to detect that. Therefore, you have to run a script to deploy changes inside the cluster to make it work.

> PostgreSQL 9.3 and beyond have some basic functionality to trigger DDLs, but that is not enough for Slony. However, future versions of PostgreSQL might very well be capable of handling triggers inside DDLs. The same applies to PostgreSQL 9.4 replication slots. Let's see whether those features will be supported in the long run, and how.

We need a `slonik` script for that:

```
#!/bin/sh

MASTERDB=db1
SLAVEDB=db2
HOST1=localhost
HOST2=localhost
DBUSER=hs

slonik<<_EOF_
cluster name = first_cluster;

node 1 admin conninfo = 'dbname=$MASTERDB host=$HOST1 user=$DBUSER';
node 2 admin conninfo = 'dbname=$SLAVEDB host=$HOST2 user=$DBUSER';

execute script (
  filename = '/tmp/deploy_ddl.sql',
  event node = 1
);
_EOF_
```

The key to our success is `execute script`. We simply pass an SQL file to the call and tell it to consult node 1. The content of the SQL file can be quite simple—it should simply list the DDLs we want to execute:

```
CREATE TABLE t_second (id int4, name text);
```

Running the file can be done just as before:

```
hs@hs-VirtualBox:~/slony$ ./slony_ddl.sh
```

The table will be deployed on both the nodes. The following listing shows that the table has also made it to the second node, which proves that things have been working as expected:

```
db2=# \d t_second
    Table "public.t_second"
 Column | Type    | Modifiers
--------+---------+-----------
 id     | integer |
 name   | text    |
```

Of course, you can also create new tables without using Slony, but this is not recommended. Administrators should be aware that all DDLs should go through Slony. The SQL deployment process has to reflect that, which is a major problem with Slony. For example, adding columns to a table without Slony being aware of it will definitely end up a disaster.

Adding tables to replication and managing problems

Once we have added this table to the system, we can add it to the replication setup. However, doing so is a little complex. First of all, we have to create a new table set and merge it with the one we already have. Burcado and Londiste are a bit more convenient here and DDLs are easier. So, for a brief moment, we will have two table sets involved. The script goes like this:

```
#!/bin/sh

MASTERDB=db1
SLAVEDB=db2
HOST1=localhost
HOST2=localhost
DBUSER=hs

slonik<<_EOF_
cluster name = first_cluster;

node 1 admin conninfo = 'dbname=$MASTERDB host=$HOST1 user=$DBUSER';
node 2 admin conninfo = 'dbname=$SLAVEDB host=$HOST2 user=$DBUSER';

create set (id=2, origin=1,
```

```
comment='a second replication set');
set add table (set id=2, origin=1, id=5,
fully qualified name = 'public.t_second',
  comment='second table');
subscribe set(id=1, provider=1,receiver=2);
merge set(id=1, add id=2,origin=1);
_EOF_
```

The key to our success is the merge call at the end of the script. It will make sure that the new tables become integrated into the existing table set. To make sure that nothing goes wrong, it makes sense to check out the Slony metadata tables (sl_table) and see which IDs are actually available.

When the script is executed, we will face an expected problem, as follows:

```
hs@hs-VirtualBox:~/slony$ sh slony_add_to_set.sh

<stdin>:7: PGRES_FATAL_ERROR select "_first_cluster".determineIdxnameU
nique('public.t_second', NULL); - ERROR:  Slony-I: table "public"."t_
second" has no primary key
```

We have created the table without a primary key. This is highly important—there is no way for Slony to replicate a table without a primary key. So we have to add this primary key. Basically, we have two choices of how to do this. The desired way here is definitely to use execute script, just as we have shown before. If your system is idling, you can also do it the quick and dirty way:

```
db1=# ALTER TABLE t_second ADD PRIMARY KEY (id);

NOTICE:  ALTER TABLE / ADD PRIMARY KEY will create implicit index "t_
second_pkey" for table "t_second"

ALTER TABLE

db1=# \q

hs@hs-VirtualBox:~/slony$ psql db2

psql (9.4.1)

Type "help" for help.


db2=# ALTER TABLE t_second ADD PRIMARY KEY (id);

NOTICE:  ALTER TABLE / ADD PRIMARY KEY will create implicit index "t_
second_pkey" for table "t_second"

ALTER TABLE
```

However, this is not recommended—it is definitely more desirable to use the Slony interface to make changes like these. Remember that DDLs are not replicated on Slony. Therefore, any manual DDL is risky.

Once we have fixed the data structure, we can execute the `slonik` script again and see what happens:

```
hs@hs-VirtualBox:~/slony$ sh slony_add_to_set.sh
<stdin>:6: PGRES_FATAL_ERROR lock table "_first_cluster".sl_event_lock,
"_first_cluster".sl_config_lock;select "_first_cluster".storeSet(2, 'a
second replication set'); - ERROR:  duplicate key value violates unique
constraint "sl_set-pkey"
DETAIL:  Key (set_id)=(2) already exists.
CONTEXT:  SQL statement "insert into "_first_cluster".sl_set
       (set_id, set_origin, set_comment) values
       (p_set_id, v_local_node_id, p_set_comment)"
PL/pgSQL function _first_cluster.storeset(integer,text) line 7 at SQL
statement
```

What you see is a typical problem that you will face with Slony. If something goes wrong, it can be really, really hard to get things back in order. This is a scenario you should definitely be prepared for.

> If you are working with Slony on a production system, always create yourself a perfectly working library with scripts to perform different tasks. It will greatly reduce your risk if you don't have to come up with fixes on the fly and during normal operations. Also, always make sure that you have got enough scripts around to handle most of the common issues, such as the one we have just outlined. Compiling those scripts is hard, but thinking of all potential cases and providing ready-to-use shell scripts to talk to Slony is definitely worth the effort. Remember that ad hoc scripting is dangerous in Slony; there are too many things that can go wrong which might be hard to fix later on.

So, to fix the problem, we can simply drop the table set again and start from scratch:

```
#!/bin/sh

MASTERDB=db1
SLAVEDB=db2
HOST1=localhost
HOST2=localhost
DBUSER=hs

slonik<<_EOF_
```

```
cluster name = first_cluster;

node 1 admin conninfo = 'dbname=$MASTERDB host=$HOST1
user=$DBUSER';
node 2 admin conninfo = 'dbname=$SLAVEDB host=$HOST2
user=$DBUSER';

drop set (id=2, origin=1);
_EOF_
```

To kill a table set, we can run `drop set`. It will help you get back to where you started. The script will execute cleanly:

```
hs@hs-VirtualBox:~/slony$ sh slony_drop_set.sh
```

Now we can restart again and add the table:

```
#!/bin/sh

MASTERDB=db1
SLAVEDB=db2
HOST1=localhost
HOST2=localhost
DBUSER=hs

slonik<<_EOF_
cluster name = first_cluster;

node 1 admin conninfo = 'dbname=$MASTERDB host=$HOST1
user=$DBUSER';
node 2 admin conninfo = 'dbname=$SLAVEDB host=$HOST2
user=$DBUSER';
create set (id=2, origin=1, comment='a second replication set');
set add table (set id=2, origin=1, id=5, fully qualified name =
'public.t_second', comment='second table');
subscribe set(id=1, provider=1,receiver=2);
subscribe set(id=2, provider=1,receiver=2);
merge set(id=1, add id=2,origin=1);
_EOF_
```

We can now cleanly execute the script, and everything will be replicated as expected:

```
hs@hs-VirtualBox:~/slony$ sh slony_add_to_set_v2.sh
<stdin>:11 subscription in progress before mergeSet. waiting
<stdin>:11 subscription in progress before mergeSet. waiting
```

As we have already stated in this chapter, we have intentionally made a small mistake, and you have seen how tricky it can be to get things straight even if it is just a small mistake. One of the reasons for this is that a script is basically not a transaction on the server side. So, if a script fails somewhere in the middle, it will just stop working. It will not undo the changes made so far. This can cause some issues, and these are outlined in the rest of this section.

So, once you have made a change, you should always take a look and check if everything is working nicely. One simple way to do this is to connect to the db2 database and do this:

```
db2=# BEGIN;

BEGIN

db2=# DELETE FROM t_second;

ERROR:  Slony-I: Table t_second is replicated and cannot be modified on a
subscriber node - role=0

db2=# ROLLBACK;

ROLLBACK
```

You can start a transaction and try to delete a row. It is supposed to fail. If it does not, you can safely roll back and try to fix your problem. As you are using a transaction that never commits, nothing can go wrong.

Performing failovers

Once you have learned how to replicate tables and add them to sets, it is time to learn about failover. Basically, we can distinguish between two types of failovers:

- Planned failovers
- Unplanned failovers and crashes

In this section, you will learn about both scenarios.

Planned failovers

Having planned failovers might be more of a luxury scenario. In some cases, you will not be so lucky and you will have to rely on automatic failovers or face unplanned outages.

Basically, a planned failover can be seen as moving a set of tables to some other node. Once that node is in charge of those tables, you can handle things accordingly.

In our example, we want to move all tables from node 1 to node 2. In addition to this, we want to drop the first node. Here is the code required:

```
#!/bin/sh

MASTERDB=db1
SLAVEDB=db2
HOST1=localhost
HOST2=localhost
DBUSER=hs

slonik<<_EOF_
cluster name = first_cluster;

node 1 admin conninfo = 'dbname=$MASTERDB host=$HOST1 user=$DBUSER';
node 2 admin conninfo = 'dbname=$SLAVEDB host=$HOST2 user=$DBUSER';

lock set (id = 1, origin = 1);
move set (id = 1, old origin = 1, new origin = 2);
wait for event (origin = 1, confirmed = 2, wait on=1);

drop node (id = 1, event node = 2);
_EOF_
```

After our standard introduction, we can call move set. The catch here is this: we have to create a lock to make this work. The reason is that we have to protect ourselves from changes made to the system when failover is performed. You must not forget this lock, otherwise you might find yourself in a truly bad situation. Just as in all of our previous examples, nodes and sets are represented using their numbers.

Once we have moved the set to the new location, we have to wait for the event to be completed, and then we can drop the node (if desired).

If the script is 100 percent correct, it can be executed cleanly:

```
hs@hs-VirtualBox:~/slony$ ./slony_move_set.sh
debug: waiting for 1,5000016417 on 2
```

Once we have failed over to the second node, we can delete data. Slony has removed the triggers that prevent this operation:

```
db2=# DELETE FROM t_second;
DELETE 1
```

The same has happened to the table on the first node. There are no more triggers, but the table itself is still in place:

```
db1=# \d t_second
    Table "public.t_second"
 Column |  Type   | Modifiers
--------+---------+-----------
 id     | integer | not null
 name   | text    |
Indexes:
    "t_second_pkey" PRIMARY KEY, btree (id)
```

You can now take the node offline and use it for other purposes.

 Using a planned failover is also the recommended strategy you should apply when upgrading a database to a new version of PostgreSQL with little downtime. Just replicate an entire database to an instance running the new version and perform a controlled failover. The actual downtime of this kind of upgrading will be minimal, and it is therefore possible to do it with a large amount of data.

Unplanned failovers

In the event of an unplanned failover, you may not be so lucky. An unplanned failover could be a power outage, a hardware failure, or some site failure. Whatever it is, there is no need to be afraid. You can still bring the cluster back to a reasonable state easily.

To do so, Slony provides the `failover` command:

```
failover (id = 1, backup node = 2);
drop node (id = 1, event node = 2);
```

This is all that you need to execute on one of the remaining nodes in order to perform a failover from one node to the other and remove the node from the cluster. It is a safe and reliable procedure.

Summary

Slony is a widespread tool used to replicate PostgreSQL databases at a logical level. In contrast to transaction log shipping, it can be used to replicate instances between various versions of PostgreSQL, and there is no need to replicate an entire instance. It allows us to flexibly replicate individual objects.

In the next chapter, we will focus our attention on SkyTools, a viable alternative to Slony. We will cover installation, generic queues, and replication.

11
Using SkyTools

Having introduced Slony, we will take a look at another popular replication tool. SkyTools is a software package originally developed by Skype, and it serves a variety of purposes. It is not a single program but a collection of tools and services that you can use to enhance your replication setup. It offers solutions for generic queues, a simplified replication setup, data transport jobs, as well as a programming framework suitable for database applications (especially transport jobs). Covering all aspects of SkyTools is not possible here. However, in this chapter, the most important features, concepts, and tools are covered to show you an easy way to enter this vast world of tools and ideas and benefit as much as possible.

In this chapter, we will discuss the following topics related to SkyTools:

- Building generic queues
- Using londiste for replication
- Handling XLOG and walmgr

As with all the chapters of this book, the most recent version of SkyTools will be used.

Installing SkyTools

SkyTools is an open source package, and can be downloaded freely from pgfoundry.org. For the purpose of this chapter, we have used version 3.2 which can be found at http://pgfoundry.org/frs/download.php/3622/skytools-3.2.tar.gz.

To install the software, we first need to extract the `.tar` file and run `configure`. The important thing here is that we have to tell `configure` where to find `pg_config`. This is important in order to ensure that SkyTools knows how to compile the code and where to look for libraries.

 The `configure` command will successfully execute if all the dependencies are met. If you are going to build from Git, you will need `git`, `autoconf`, `automake`, `asciidoc`, `xmlto`, and `libtool`. In addition to these, you will always need `rsync`, `psycopg2`, and Python (including the development libraries).

Once this has been executed successfully, we can run `make` and `make install` (which might have to be run as `root` if PostgreSQL has been installed as the `root` user):

```
./configure \
--with-pgconfig=/usr/local/pgsql/bin/pg_config
make
sudo make install
```

Once the code has been compiled, the system is ready for action.

Dissecting SkyTools

SkyTools is not just a single script but a collection of various tools serving different purposes. Once we have installed SkyTools, it makes sense to inspect these components in more detail:

- `pgq`: A generic queuing interface used to flexibly dispatch and distribute data
- `londiste`: An easy-to-use tool used to replicate individual tables and entire databases on a logical level
- `walmgr`: A toolkit used to manage transaction logging

In this chapter, we will discuss `pgq` and `londiste` in detail.

Managing pgq queues

One of the core components of SkyTools is `pgq`. It provides a generic queuing interface, which allows you to deliver messages from a provider to an arbitrary number of consumers.

The question is: what is the point of a queue in general? A queue has some very nice features. First of all, it will guarantee the delivery of a message. In addition to that, it will make sure that the order in which the messages are put into it is preserved. This is highly important in the case of replication because we must make sure that the messages will not overtake each other.

The idea behind a queue is to be able to send anything from an entity producing the data to any other host participating in the system. This is suitable for replication and for a lot more. You can use pgq as an infrastructure to flexibly dispatch information. Practical examples for this can be shopping cart purchases, bank transfers, or user messages. In this sense, replicating an entire table is more or less a special case. A queue is really a generic framework used to move data around.

In general, a queue knows two operations:

- **Enqueue**: Putting a message into the queue
- **Dequeue**: Fetching a message from the queue (this is also called "consuming" a message)

Those two operations form the backbone of every queue-based application.

 What we define as a queue in SkyTools is the same as what you would call "topic" in JMS terminology.

In contrast to other queuing systems, pgq guarantees that a message will be delivered, because queues are handled directly in a transactional way in PostgreSQL.

Running pgq

To use pgq inside a database, you have to install it as a normal PostgreSQL extension. If the installation process has worked properly, you can simply run the following instruction:

```
test=# CREATE EXTENSION pgq;
CREATE EXTENSION
```

Now that all modules have been loaded into the database, we create a simple queue.

Creating queues and adding data

For the purpose of this example, we create a queue named DemoQueue:

```
test=# SELECT pgq.create_queue('DemoQueue');
create_queue
--------------
            1
(1 row)
```

If the queue has been created successfully, a number will be returned. Internally, the queue is just an entry inside some pgq bookkeeping table:

```
test=# \x
Expanded display is on.
test=# TABLE pgq.queue;
-[ RECORD 1 ]------------+-----------------------------
queue_id                 | 1
queue_name               | DemoQueue
queue_ntables            | 3
queue_cur_table          | 0
queue_rotation_period    | 02:00:00
queue_switch_step1       | 1892
queue_switch_step2       | 1892
queue_switch_time        | 2015-02-24 12:06:42.656252+01
queue_external_ticker    | f
queue_disable_insert     | f
queue_ticker_paused      | f
queue_ticker_max_count   | 500
queue_ticker_max_lag     | 00:00:03
queue_ticker_idle_period | 00:01:00
queue_per_tx_limit       |
queue_data_pfx           | pgq.event_1
queue_event_seq          | pgq.event_1_id_seq
queue_tick_seq           | pgq.event_1_tick_seq
```

TABLE is equivalent to SELECT * FROM.... It can be used as an abbreviation.

The bookkeeping table outlines some essential information about our queue internals. In this specific example, it will tell us how many internal tables pgq will use to handle our queue, which table is active at the moment, how often it is switched, and so on. Practically this information is not relevant to ordinary users — it is merely an internal thing.

Once the queue has been created, we can add data to the queue. The function used to do this has three parameters. The first parameter is the name of the queue. The second and third parameters are data values to enqueue. In many cases, it makes a lot of sense to use two values here. The first value can nicely represent a key, while the second value can be seen as the payload of this message. Here is an example:

```
test=# BEGIN;
BEGIN
test=# SELECT pgq.insert_event('DemoQueue',
  'some_key_1', 'some_data_1');
insert_event
-------------
           1
(1 row)


test=# SELECT pgq.insert_event('DemoQueue',
  'some_key_2', 'some_data_2');
insert_event
-------------
           2
(1 row)


test=# COMMIT;
COMMIT
```

Adding consumers

In our case, we have added two rows featuring some sample data. Now we can register two consumers, which are supposed to get those messages in the proper order:

```
test=# BEGIN;
BEGIN
test=# SELECT pgq.register_consumer('DemoQueue',
  'Consume_1');
register_consumer
-------------------
                1
(1 row)


test=# SELECT pgq.register_consumer('DemoQueue',
  'Consume_2');
register_consumer
-------------------
                1
(1 row)


test=# COMMIT;
COMMIT
```

Two consumers have been created. A message will be marked as processed as soon as both the consumers have fetched it and marked it as done.

Configuring the ticker

Before we can actually see how the messages can be consumed, we have to briefly discuss the way pgq works. How does the consumer know which rows are there to consume? Managing a queue is not simple. Just imagine two concurrent transactions adding rows. A transaction can be replicated only if all the dependent transactions are replicated. Here is an example of the replication:

Connection 1	Connection 2
INSERT ... VALUES (1)	BEGIN;
INSERT ... VALUES (2)	BEGIN;
INSERT ... VALUES (3)	COMMIT;
INSERT ... VALUES (4)	COMMIT;

Remember that if we manage queues, we have to make sure that the total order is maintained so that we could give only row number 3 to the consumer if the transaction writing row number 4 had been committed. If we gave row number 3 to the consumer before the second transaction in connection 1 had finished, row number 3 would have effectively overtaken row number 2. This must not happen.

In the case of pgq, a so-called ticker process will take care of those little details.

The ticker (pgqd) process will handle the queue for us and decide what can be consumed. To make this process work, we create two directories. One will hold log files and the other will store the pid files created by the ticker process:

```
hs@hs-VirtualBox:~$ mkdir log
hs@hs-VirtualBox:~$ mkdir pid
```

Once we have created those directories, we have to come up with a configuration file for the ticker:

```
[pgqd]
logfile = ~/log/pgqd.log
pidfile = ~/pid/pgqd.pid

## optional parameters ##
# libpq connect string without dbname=
base_connstr = host=localhost

# startup db to query other databases
initial_database = postgres

# limit ticker to specific databases
database_list = test

# log into syslog
syslog = 0
syslog_ident = pgqd

## optional timeouts ##
# how often to check for new databases
check_period = 60

# how often to flush retry queue
retry_period = 30

# how often to do maintenance
```

```
    maint_period = 120

    # how often to run ticker
    ticker_period = 1
```

As we have already mentioned, the ticker is in charge of those queues. To make sure that this works nicely, we have to point the ticker to the PostgreSQL instance. Keep in mind that the connect string will be autocompleted (some information is already known by the infrastructure, and it is used for auto completion). Ideally, you will be using the `database_list` directive here to make sure that only those databases that are really needed will be taken.

As far as logging is concerned, you have two options here. You can either directly log to `syslog` or send the log to a log file. In our example, we have decided not to use `syslog` (`syslog` has been set to `0` in our configuration file). Finally, there are some parameters used to configure how often queue maintenance should be performed, and so on.

The ticker process can easily be started:

```
hs@hs-VirtualBox:~/skytools$ pgqd ticker.ini
2015-02-24 12:11:52.190 25566 LOG Starting pgqd 3.2
2015-02-24 12:11:52.194 25566 LOG test: pgq version ok: 3.2
2015-02-24 12:12:22.192 25566 LOG {ticks: 30, maint: 1, retry: 0}
2015-02-24 12:12:52.193 25566 LOG {ticks: 30, maint: 0, retry: 0}
```

The important thing here is that the ticker can also be started directly as a daemon. The `-d` command-line option will automatically send the process to the background and decouple it from the active terminal.

Consuming messages

Just adding messages to the queue might not be what we want. At some point, we would also want to consume this data. To do so, we can call `pgq.next_batch`. The system will return a number identifying the batch:

```
test=# BEGIN;
BEGIN
test=# SELECT pgq.next_batch('DemoQueue', 'Consume_1');
next_batch
-----------
         1
(1 row)
```

Once we have got the ID of the batch, we can fetch the data:

```
test=# \x
Expanded display is on.
test=# SELECT * FROM pgq.get_batch_events(1);
-[ RECORD 1 ]---------------------------
ev_id     | 1
ev_time   | 2015-02-24 12:15:39.854199+02
ev_txid   | 489695
ev_retry  |
ev_type   | some_key_1
ev_data   | some_data_1
ev_extra1 |
ev_extra2 |
ev_extra3 |
ev_extra4 |
-[ RECORD 2 ]---------------------------
ev_id     | 2
ev_time   | 2015-01-24 12:15:39.854199+02
ev_txid   | 489695
ev_retry  |
ev_type   | some_key_2
ev_data   | some_data_2
ev_extra1 |
ev_extra2 |
ev_extra3 |
ev_extra4 |


test=# COMMIT;
COMMIT
```

In our case, the batch consists of two messages. It is important to know that messages that have been enqueued in separate transactions or by many different connections might still end up in the same pack for the consumer. This behavior is totally intended. The correct order will be preserved.

Once a batch has been processed by the consumer, it can be marked as done:

```
test=# SELECT pgq.finish_batch(1);
finish_batch
--------------
           1
(1 row)
```

This means that the data has left the queue. Logically, pgq.get_batch_events will return an error for this batch ID if you try to dequeue it again:

```
test=# SELECT * FROM pgq.get_batch_events(1);
ERROR:   batch not found
CONTEXT:   PL/pgSQL function pgq.get_batch_events(bigint) line 16 at
assignment
```

 The message is gone only for this consumer. Other consumers will still be able to consume it once.

Keep in mind that PostgreSQL is perfectly capable of handling large amounts of data. An application might not be so lucky, so caution is advised. The pgq.get_batch_events command fetches all of the data at once, which can easily cause out-of-memory failures on the client side.

The solution to this problem is a function called get_batch_cursor. It allows users to consume data more slowly and in a more organized way. Here is the specification of the pgq.get_batch_cursor function, which comes in two flavors:

```
test=# \x
Expanded display is on.
test=# \df pgq.get_batch_cursor
List of functions
-[ RECORD 1 ]----------------------------------------------------
--------------------------
Schema              | pgq
Name                | get_batch_cursor
Result data type    | SETOF record
Argument data types | i_batch_id bigint, i_cursor_name text, i_quick_
limit integer, i_extra_where text,
       OUT ev_id bigint, OUT ev_time timestamp with time zone,
       OUT ev_txid bigint, OUT ev_retry integer, OUT ev_type text,
```

```
        OUT ev_data text, OUT ev_extra1 text, OUT ev_extra2 text,
        OUT ev_extra3 text, OUT ev_extra4 text
Type                    | normal
-[ RECORD 2 ]------------------------------------------------------------
-------------------
Schema                  | pgq
Name                    | get_batch_cursor
Result data type        | SETOF record
Argument data types | i_batch_id bigint, i_cursor_name text,
 i_quick_limit integer, OUT ev_id bigint,
        OUT ev_time timestamp with time zone, OUT ev_txid bigint,
        OUT ev_retry integer, OUT ev_type text, OUT ev_data text,
        OUT ev_extra1 text, OUT ev_extra2 text, OUT ev_extra3 text,
        OUT ev_extra4 text
Type                    | normal
```

Using the cursor here allows us to dequeue arbitrary amounts of data from a queue without any problems and without memory-related issues.

Dropping queues

If a queue is no longer needed, it can be dropped. However, you cannot simply call pgq.drop_queue. Dropping the queue is possible only if all consumers are unregistered. Otherwise, the system will error out:

```
test=# SELECT pgq.drop_queue('DemoQueue');
ERROR:  cannot drop queue, consumers still attached
CONTEXT:  PL/pgSQL function pgq.drop_queue(text) line 10 at RETURN
```

To unregister the consumer, we can do the following:

```
test=# SELECT pgq.unregister_consumer('DemoQueue',
  'Consume_1');
unregister_consumer
--------------------
                  1
(1 row)


test=# SELECT pgq.unregister_consumer('DemoQueue',
  'Consume_2');
```

```
unregister_consumer
--------------------
                  1
(1 row)
```

Now we can safely drop the queue:

```
test=# SELECT pgq.drop_queue('DemoQueue');
drop_queue
------------
          1
(1 row)
```

Using pgq for large projects

The pgq queue has been proven to be especially useful if you have to model a flow of messages that has to be transactional. The beauty of pgq is that you can put everything into a queue. You can also decide freely on the type of messages and their format (as long as you are using text).

It is important to see that pgq is not just something that is purely related to replication. It has a much wider range and offers a solid technology base for countless applications.

Using Londiste to replicate data

The pgq queue is the backbone of a replication tool called Londiste. The idea of Londiste is to have a mechanism that is more simplistic and easier to use than, say, Slony. If you use Slony in a large installation, it is very easy for a problem on one side of the cluster to cause some issues at some other point. This was especially true many years ago when Slony was still fairly new.

The main advantage of Londiste over Slony is that in the case of Londiste replication, there will be one process per "route." So, if you replicate from A to B, this channel will be managed by one Londiste process. If you replicate from B to A or A to C, these will be separate processes, and they will be totally independent of each other. All channels from A to somewhere might share a queue on the consumer, but the transport processes themselves will not interact. There is some beauty in this approach because if one component fails, it is unlikely to cause additional problems. This is not the case if all the processes interact, as they do in the case of Slony. In my opinion this is one of the key advantages of Londiste over Slony.

Replicating our first table

After this theoretical introduction, we can move ahead and replicate our first table. To do so, we create two databases inside the same instance (it makes no difference whether those databases are in the same instance or far apart):

```
hs@hs-VirtualBox:~$ createdb node1
hs@hs-VirtualBox:~$ createdb node2
```

Now run the following in both the databases:

```
node1=# CREATE TABLE t_test (id int4, name text,
t timestamp DEFAULT now(),
PRIMARY KEY (id));
NOTICE:  CREATE TABLE / PRIMARY KEY will create implicit index
"t_test_pkey" for table "t_test"
CREATE TABLE
```

In *Chapter 10*, *Configuring Slony*, we saw that DDLs are not replicated. The same rules apply to Londiste because both the systems are facing the same limitations on the PostgreSQL side.

Before we dig into the details, let's sum up the next steps to replicate our tables:

1. Write an `init` file and initialize the master.
2. Start Londiste on the master.
3. Write a slave configuration and initialize the slave.
4. Start Londiste on the slave.
5. Write a `ticker` config and start the ticker process.
6. Add desired tables to replication.

Let's get started with the first part of the process. We have to create an `init` file that is supposed to control the master:

```
[londiste3]
job_name = first_table
db = dbname=node1
queue_name = replication_queue
logfile = /var/log/londiste.log
pidfile = /var/pid/londiste.pid
```

The important part here is that every job must have a name. This makes sense so that we can distinguish between the processes easily. Then we have to define a connecting string to the master database as well as the name of the replication queue involved. Finally, we can configure a PID and a log file.

 Every job (running a Londiste process) must have a name. This is required, as Slony has a single process above a cluster (and so the cluster name is enough), but Londiste has one process per route.

To install important things and initialize the master node, we can call Londiste:

```
hs@hs-VirtualBox:~/skytools$ londiste3 londiste3.ini create-root node1
dbname=node1
2015-02-25 13:37:24,902 4236 WARNING No host= in public connect string,
bad idea
2015-02-25 13:37:25,118 4236 INFO plpgsql is installed
2015-02-25 13:37:25,119 4236 INFO Installing pgq
2015-02-25 13:37:25,119 4236 INFO   Reading from /usr/local/share/
skytools3/pgq.sql
2015-02-25 13:37:25,327 4236 INFO pgq.get_batch_cursor is installed
2015-02-25 13:37:25,328 4236 INFO Installing pgq_ext
2015-02-25 13:37:25,328 4236 INFO   Reading from /usr/local/share/
skytools3/pgq_ext.sql
2015-02-25 13:37:25,400 4236 INFO Installing pgq_node
2015-02-25 13:37:25,400 4236 INFO   Reading from /usr/local/share/
skytools3/pgq_node.sql
2015-02-25 13:37:25,471 4236 INFO Installing londiste
2015-02-25 13:37:25,471 4236 INFO   Reading from /usr/local/share/
skytools3/londiste.sql
2015-02-25 13:37:25,579 4236 INFO londiste.global_add_table is installed
2015-02-25 13:37:25,670 4236 INFO Initializing node
2015-02-25 13:37:25,674 4236 INFO Location registered
2015-02-25 13:37:25,755 4236 INFO Node "node1" initialized for queue
"replication_queue" with type "root"
2015-02-25 13:37:25,761 3999 INFO Done
```

In SkyTools, there is a very simple rule: the first parameter passed to the script is always the INI file containing the desired configuration. Then comes an instruction, as well as some parameters. The call will install all of the necessary infrastructure and return Done.

Once this has been completed, we can fire up a worker process:

```
hs@hs-VirtualBox:~/skytools$ londiste3 londiste3.ini worker
2015-02-25 13:41:31,761 4069 INFO {standby: 1}
2015-02-25 13:41:42,801 4069 INFO {standby: 1}
```

After firing up the worker on the master, we can take a look at the slave configuration:

```
[londiste3]
job_name = first_table_slave
db = dbname=node2
queue_name = replication_queue
logfile = /var/log/londiste_slave.log
pidfile = /var/pid/londiste_slave.pid
```

The main difference here is that we use a different connect string and a different name for the job. If the master and slave are two separate machines, the rest can stay the same.

Once we have compiled the configuration, we can create the leaf node:

```
hs@hs-VirtualBox:~/skytools$ londiste3 slave.ini create-leaf node2
dbname=node2 --provider=dbname=node1
2015-02-25 13:51:27,090 4246 WARNING No host= in public connect string,
bad idea
2015-02-25 13:51:27,117 4246 INFO plpgsql is installed
2015-02-25 13:51:27,118 4246 INFO pgq is installed
2015-02-25 13:51:27,122 4246 INFO pgq.get_batch_cursor is installed
2015-02-25 13:51:27,122 4246 INFO pgq_ext is installed
2015-02-25 13:51:27,123 4246 INFO pgq_node is installed
2015-02-25 13:51:27,124 4246 INFO londiste is installed
2015-02-25 13:51:27,126 4246 INFO londiste.global_add_table is installed
2015-02-25 13:51:27,205 4246 INFO Initializing node
2015-02-25 13:51:27,291 4246 INFO Location registered
2015-02-25 13:51:27,308 4246 INFO Location registered
2015-02-25 13:51:27,317 4246 INFO Subscriber registered: node2
2015-02-25 13:51:27,321 4246 INFO Location registered
2015-02-25 13:51:27,324 4246 INFO Location registered
2015-02-25 13:51:27,334 4246 INFO Node "node2" initialized for queue
"replication_queue" with type "leaf"
2015-02-25 13:51:27,345 4246 INFO Done
```

The key here is to tell the slave where to find the master (provider). Once the system knows where to find all of the data, we can fire up the worker here as well:

```
hs@hs-VirtualBox:~/skytools$ londiste3 slave.ini worker
2015-02-25 13:55:10,764 4301 INFO Consumer uptodate = 1
```

This should not cause any issues and work nicely if the previous command has succeeded. Now that we have everything in place, we can start with the final component of the setup—the ticker process:

```
[pgqd]

logfile = /home/hs/log/pgqd.log
pidfile = /home/hs/pid/pgqd.pid
```

The `ticker` config is pretty simple—all it takes is three simple lines. These lines are enough to fire up the ticker process. All of the relevant information is nicely stored in the `.ini` file and can, therefore, be used by SkyTools:

```
hs@hs-VirtualBox:~/skytools$ pgqd pgqd.ini
2015-02-25 14:01:12.181 4683 LOG Starting pgqd 3.2
2015-02-25 14:01:12.188 4683 LOG auto-detecting dbs ...
2015-02-25 14:01:12.310 4683 LOG test: pgq version ok: 3.2
2015-02-25 14:01:12.531 4683 LOG node1: pgq version ok: 3.2
2015-02-25 14:01:12.596 4683 LOG node2: pgq version ok: 3.2
2015-02-25 14:01:42.189 4683 LOG {ticks: 90, maint: 3, retry: 0}
2015-02-25 14:02:12.190 4683 LOG {ticks: 90, maint: 0, retry: 0}
```

If the ticker has started successfully, it means that we have the entire infrastructure in place. So far, we have configured all the processes needed for replication, but we have not yet told the system what to replicate.

The command for Londiste will offer us a set of commands to define exactly that. In our example, we simply want to add all tables and replicate them:

```
hs@hs-VirtualBox:~/skytools$ londiste3 londiste3.ini add-table --all
2015-02-25 14:02:39,367 4760 INFO Table added: public.t_test
```

Just like Slony, Londiste will install a trigger on the source (not on the slave as Slony does), which keeps track of all the changes. Those changes will be written to a `pgq` queue and dispatched by the processes we have just set up:

```
node1=# \d t_test
            Table "public.t_test"
```

```
Column |            Type            |    Modifiers
--------+---------------------------+---------------
id      | integer                   | not null
name    | text                      |
t       | timestamp without time zone | default now()
```

Indexes:
    "t_test_pkey" PRIMARY KEY, btree (id)
Triggers:
    _londiste_replication_queue AFTER INSERT OR DELETE OR UPDATE ON t_
test FOR EACH ROW EXECUTE PROCEDURE pgq.logutriga('replication_queue')
    _londiste_replication_queue_truncate AFTER TRUNCATE ON t_test FOR
EACH STATEMENT EXECUTE PROCEDURE pgq.sqltriga('replication_queue')

SkyTools and Londiste in particular offer a rich set of additional features to make your life easy. However, documenting all of those features would unfortunately exceed the scope of this book. If you want to learn more, we recommend taking a detailed look at the doc directory inside the SkyTools source code. You will find a couple of interesting documents.

A word about walmgr

The walmgr tool is supposed to simplify file-based transaction log shipping. Back in the old days (before version 9.0), it was pretty common to use walmgr to simplify base backups. With the introduction of streaming replication, the situation seems to have changed a little.

Setting up streaming has become so easy that add-ons are not as important anymore as they used to be. Of course, this is our subjective observation, which might not be what you may have observed in the recent past.

To make sure that the scope of this book does not explode, we have decided not to include any details about walmgr in this chapter. For further information, we invite you to review the documentation directory inside the walmgr source code. It contains some easy-to-use examples as well as some background information about the replication technique.

Summary

In this chapter, we discussed SkyTools, a tool package provided and developed by Skype. It provides you with generic queues (pgq) as well as a replicator called Londiste. In addition to these, SkyTools provides walmgr, which can be used to handle WAL files.

The next chapter will focus on Postgres-XC, a solution capable of scaling reads as well as writes. It provides users with a consistent view of data and automatically dispatches queries inside the cluster.

12

Working with Postgres-XC

In this chapter, we have to focus our attention on a write-scalable, multimaster, synchronous, symmetric, and transparent replication solution for PostgreSQL, called **PostgreSQL eXtensible Cluster (Postgres-XC)**. The goal of this project is to provide the end user with a transparent replication solution, which allows higher levels of loads by horizontally scaling to multiple servers.

In an array of servers running Postgres-XC, you can connect to any node inside the cluster. The system will make sure that you get exactly the same view of the data on every node. This is really important, as it solves a handful of problems on the client side. There is no need to add logic to applications that write to just one node. You can balance your load easily. Data is always instantly visible on all nodes after a transaction commits. Postgres-XC is wonderfully transparent, and application changes are not required for scaling out.

The most important thing to keep in mind when considering Postgres-XC is that it is not an add-on to PostgreSQL; it is a code fork. Some years ago, the code was forked because adding massive functionality, as Postgres-XC does, is not easy in the main code base of PostgreSQL. Postgres-XC does not use Vanilla PostgreSQL version numbers, and the code base usually lags behind the official PostgreSQL source tree.

Note that there is also a second project out there, called Postgres-XL. It shares many similarities with Postgres-XC, but it is not the same thing and represents one more code fork developed by a different group of people.

This chapter will provide you with information about Postgres-XC. We will cover the following topics in this chapter:

- The Postgres-XC architecture
- Installing Postgres-XC
- Configuring a cluster

- Optimizing storage
- Performance management
- Adding and dropping nodes

Understanding the Postgres-XC architecture

Before we dive head-on into Postgres-XC installation and ultimately into configuration, we need to take a deep look at the basic system architecture of this marvelous piece of software, as shown here:

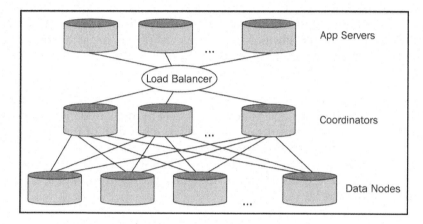

In general, a Postgres-XC system consists of the following essential components:

- Data nodes
- A **Global Transaction Manager (GTM)**
- A coordinator
- A GTM proxy

Let's take a look at the purpose of each of those components.

Data nodes

A data node is the actual storage backbone of the system. It will hold all or a fraction of the data inside the cluster. It is connected to the Postgres-XC infrastructure and will handle the local SQL execution.

GTM

The GTM provides the cluster with a consistent view of the data. A consistent view is necessary because otherwise, it would be impossible to load-balance in an environment that is totally transparent to the application.

A consistent view is provided through a cluster-wide snapshot. In addition to this, the GTM will create **Global Transaction IDs (GXIDs)**. These GXIDs are essential because transactions must be coordinated cluster-wide. Users expect a consistent view of the data; the GXID provides exactly that.

Beside this core functionality, the GTM also handles global values for sequences and global transaction IDs.

Coordinators

Coordinators are a piece of software that serve as entry points for our applications. An application will connect to one of the available Coordinators. It will be in charge of the SQL parsing, analysis, creation of the global execution plan, and global SQL execution.

GTM proxy

The GTM proxy can be used to improve performance. Given the Postgres-XC architecture, each transaction has to issue a request to the GTM. In many cases, this can lead to latency, and subsequently performance issues. The GTM proxy will step in, collect requests to the GTM in the form of blocks of requests, and send them together.

One advantage here is that connections can be cached to avoid a great deal of overhead caused by their opening and closing all the time.

 Do you remember our introduction about the speed of light? This is where it all comes together. Sending requests back and forth might cause latency issues, and therefore, the overhead must be reduced as much as possible to make sure that performance stays high.

Installing Postgres-XC

Postgres-XC can be downloaded from `http://sourceforge.net/projects/postgres-xc/files/Version_1.2/`. For this book, we have used version 1.2.1 of Postgres-XC, which is based on PostgreSQL 9.3.2.

To compile the code, we have to extract the code using the following command:

```
tar xvfz pgxc-v1.2.1.tar.gz
```

Then we can compile the code just like standard PostgreSQL using the following commands:

```
cd postgres-xc-1.2.1
./configure --prefix=/usr/local/postgres-xc
make
make install
```

Once this has been executed, we can move ahead and configure the cluster.

Configuring a simple cluster

In this chapter, we want to set up a cluster consisting of three data nodes. A Coordinator and a GTM will be in charge of the cluster. For each component, we have to create a directory:

```
[hs@localhost data]$ ls -l
total 0
drwxrwxr-x 2 hs hs 6 Feb 26 01:16 gtm
drwxrwxr-x 2 hs hs 6 Feb 26 01:16 node1
drwxrwxr-x 2 hs hs 6 Feb 26 01:16 node2
drwxrwxr-x 2 hs hs 6 Feb 26 01:16 node3
drwxrwxr-x 2 hs hs 6 Feb 26 01:16 node4
```

Keep in mind that, to make life simple, we will set up the entire cluster on a single server. In production, you would logically use different nodes for different components. It is not very common to use many XC nodes on the same box to speed things up.

Creating the GTM

In the first step, we have to initialize the directory that handles the GTM. To do so, we can simply call `initgtm`:

```
[hs@localhost data]$ initgtm -Z gtm /data/gtm/
The files belonging to this GTM system will be owned by user "hs".
```

This user must also own the server process.

```
fixing permissions on existing directory /data/gtm ... ok
creating configuration files ... ok.


Success. You can now start the GTM server using:

    gtm -D /data/gtm
or
    gtm_ctl -Z gtm -D /data/gtm -l logfile start
```

Don't expect anything great and magical from initgtm. It merely creates some basic configuration needed for handling the GTM. It does not create a large database infrastructure there.

However, it already gives us a clue on how to start the GTM, which will be done later on in the process.

Then we have to initialize those four database nodes that we want to run. To do so, we have to run initdb, just as for any Vanilla PostgreSQL database instance. However, in the case of Postgres-XC, we have to tell initdb what name the node will have. In our case, we will create the first node called node1 in the node1 directory. Each node will need a dedicated name. This is done as follows:

```
[hs@localhost data]$ initdb -D /data/node1/ --nodename=node1
The files belonging to this database system will be owned by user "hs".
… *snip* ...
Success.
 You can now start the database server of the Postgres-XC coordinator
using:
    postgres --coordinator -D /data/node1/
or
    pg_ctl start -D /data/node1/ -Z coordinator -l logfile
 You can now start the database server of the Postgres-XC datanode using:
    postgres --datanode -D /data/node1/
or
    pg_ctl start -D /data/node1/ -Z datanode -l logfile
```

We can call `initdb` for all the four instances that we will run. To make sure that those instances can coexist in the very same test box, we have to change the port for each of those boxes. In our example, we will simply use the following ports: 5432, 5433, 5434, and 5435.

To change the port, just edit the port setting in the `postgresql.conf` file of each instance. Also, make sure that each instance has a different `socket_directory` directory, otherwise you cannot start more than one instance.

Now that all the instances have been initialized, we can start the GTM. This works as follows:

```
[hs@localhost ~]$ gtm_ctl -D /data/gtm/ -Z gtm start
server starting
```

To see whether it works, we can check for the process, like this:

```
[hs@localhost ~]$ ps ax | grep gtm
32152 pts/1    S      0:00 /usr/local/postgres-xc/bin/gtm -D /data/gtm
```

You can also use `pgrep` instead of a normal `grep`. Then we can start all of those nodes one after the other.

In our case, we will use one of those four nodes as the Coordinator. The Coordinator will be using port 5432. To start it, we can call `pg_ctl` and tell the system to use this node as a Coordinator:

```
pg_ctl -D /data/node1/ -Z coordinator start
```

The remaining nodes will simply act as data nodes. We can easily define the role of a node on startup:

```
pg_ctl -D /data/node2/ -Z datanode start
pg_ctl -D /data/node3/ -Z datanode start
pg_ctl -D /data/node4/ -Z datanode start
```

Once this has been done, we can check whether those nodes are up and running.

We simply connect to a data node to list those databases in the system:

```
[hs@localhost ~]$ psql -h localhost -l -p 5434
                        List of databases
```

```
    Name     | Owner | Encoding  |   Collate   | Ctype
-------------+-------+-----------+-------------+-------
 postgres    | hs    | SQL_ASCII | en_GB.UTF-8 | C
 template0   | hs    | SQL_ASCII | en_GB.UTF-8 | C
 template1   | hs    | SQL_ASCII | en_GB.UTF-8 | C
(3 rows)
```

We are almost done now, but before we can get started, we have to familiarize those nodes with each other. Otherwise, we will not be able to run queries or commands inside the cluster. If the nodes don't know each other, an error will show up:

```
[hs@localhost ~]$ createdb test -h localhost -p 5432
createdb: database creation failed: ERROR:  No Datanode defined in
cluster
HINT:  You need to define at least 1 Datanode with CREATE NODE.
```

To tell the systems about the locations of the nodes, we connect to the Coordinator and run the following instructions:

```
[hs@localhost ~]$ psql postgres -h localhost -p 5432
psql (PGXC , based on PG 9.3.2)
Type "help" for help.


postgres=# CREATE NODE node2 WITH (TYPE = datanode, HOST = localhost,
PORT = 5433);
CREATE NODE
postgres=# CREATE NODE node3 WITH (TYPE = datanode, HOST = localhost,
PORT = 5434);
CREATE NODE
postgres=# CREATE NODE node4 WITH (TYPE = datanode, HOST = localhost,
PORT = 5435);
CREATE NODE
```

Once those nodes are familiar with each other, we can connect to the Coordinator and execute whatever we want. In our example, we will simply create a database:

```
[hs@localhost ~]$ psql postgres -p 5432 -h localhost
psql (PGXC , based on PG 9.3.2)
Type "help" for help.


postgres=# CREATE DATABASE test;
CREATE DATABASE
```

To know whether commands have been replicated successfully, we can connect to a data node and check whether the database is actually present. The code is shown as follows:

```
[hs@localhost ~]$ psql -l -p 5433 -h localhost
                          List of databases
     Name    |  Owner |  Encoding  |   Collate    | Ctype
-------------+--------+------------+--------------+-------
 postgres    | hs     | SQL_ASCII  | en_GB.UTF-8  | C
 template0   | hs     | SQL_ASCII  | en_GB.UTF-8  | C
 template1   | hs     | SQL_ASCII  | en_GB.UTF-8  | C
 test        | hs     | SQL_ASCII  | en_GB.UTF-8  | C
(4 rows)
```

> Keep in mind that you always have to connect to a Coordinator to make sure that commands are replicated nicely. Connecting to a data node should only be done to verify that everything is up and running as it should be. Never execute SQL on a data node. Always use the Coordinator to do that.
>
> You can run SQL on a data node directly, but it will not be replicated. Be careful! Directly running SQL there is dangerous, and therefore should not be encouraged to avoid running out of sync, producing inconsistencies, and the like.

Optimizing for performance

Postgres-XC is not just a fancy version of PostgreSQL but rather a truly distributed system. This means that you cannot just store data and expect things to be fast and efficient out of the box. If you want to optimize for speed, it can be highly beneficial to understand how data is stored behind the scenes and how queries are executed.

Sure, you can just load data and things will work, but if performance is really an issue, you should try to think of how you can use your data. Keep in mind there is no point in using a distributed database system if your database system is not heavily loaded. So, if you are a user of Postgres-XC, we expect your load and your requirements to be high.

Dispatching the tables

One of the most important questions is: where to store data? Postgres-XC cannot know what you are planning to do with your data and what kind of access pattern you are planning to run. To make sure that users get some control over where to store data, CREATE TABLE offers some syntax extensions:

```
[ DISTRIBUTE BY { REPLICATION | ROUNDROBIN | { [HASH | MODULO ]
( column_name ) } } ]
[ TO { GROUP groupname | NODE ( nodename [, ... ] ) } ]
```

The DISTRIBUTE BY clause allows you to specify where to store a table. If you want to tell Postgres-XC that a table has to be on every node in the cluster, we recommend using REPLICATION. This is especially useful if you are creating a small lookup table or a table that is frequently used in many queries.

If the goal is to scale out, it is recommended to split a table into a list of nodes. But why would anybody want to split the table? The reason is actually quite simple. If you give full replicas of a table to all the data nodes, it actually means that you will have one write per node. Clearly, this is not more scalable than a single node because each node has to take all of the load. For large tables facing heavy writes, it can therefore be beneficial to split the table into various nodes. Postgres-XC offers various ways to do this.

The ROUNDROBIN command will just spread the data more or less randomly, HASH will dispatch data based on a hash key, and MODULO will simply evenly distribute data, given a key.

To make management of tables a little easier, Postgres-XC allows you to group nodes into so-called node groups. This can come in pretty handy if a table is not supposed to reside on all the nodes inside the cluster but, say, only half of them.

To group the nodes, you can call CREATE NODE GROUP:

```
test=# \h CREATE NODE GROUP
Command:     CREATE NODE GROUP
Description: create a group of cluster nodes
Syntax:
CREATE NODE GROUP groupname
WITH nodename [, ... ]
```

Keep in mind that a node group is static; you cannot add nodes to it later on. So if you start organizing your cluster, you have to think beforehand which areas your cluster will have.

In addition to that, it is pretty hard to reorganize the data once it has been dispatched. If a table is spread to, say, four nodes, you cannot easily add a fifth node to handle the table. First of all, adding a fifth node will require a rebalance. Secondly, most of those features are still under construction and not yet fully available for end users. At this point, Postgres-XC has no satisfactory means of growing large clusters and shrinking them.

Optimizing joins

Dispatching your data cleverly is essential if you want to join it. Let's assume a simple scenario consisting of three tables:

- t_person: This table consists of a list of people in our system
- t_person_payment: This table consists of all the payments a person has made
- t_postal_code: This table consists of a list of the postal codes in your area

Let's assume that we have to join this data frequently. In this scenario, it is highly recommended to partition t_person and t_person_payment by the same join key. Doing that will allow Postgres-XC to join and merge a lot of stuff locally on the data nodes, instead of having to ship data around within the cluster. Of course, we can also create full replicas of the t_person table if this table is read so often that it makes sense to do so.

The t_postal_code table is a typical example of a table that might be replicated to all the nodes. We can expect postal codes to be pretty static. In real life, postal codes basically rarely change (at least not 1,000 postal codes per second or so). The table will also be really small, and it will be needed by many other joins as well. A full replica makes perfect sense here.

When coming up with proper partitioning logic, we just want to remind you of a simple rule: Try to perform calculations locally; that is, try to avoid moving data around at any cost.

Optimizing for warehousing

If your goal is to use Postgres-XC to perform business intelligence and data warehousing, you have to make sure that your scan speed will stay high. This can be achieved by using as much hardware as possible at the same time. Scaling out your fact tables to many hosts will make perfect sense here.

We also recommend fully replicating fairly small lookup tables so that as much work as possible can be performed on those data nodes. What does *small* mean in this context? Let's imagine that you are storing information about millions of people around the world. You might want to split data across many nodes. However, it will clearly not make sense if you split the list of potential countries on different nodes. The number of countries on this planet is limited, so it is simply more viable to have a copy of this data on all the nodes.

Creating a GTM proxy

Requesting transaction IDs from the GTM is a fairly expensive process. If you are running a large Postgres-XC setup that is supposed to handle an **Online Transaction Processing** (**OLTP**) workload, the GTM can actually cause a bottleneck. The more the Global Transaction IDs we need, the more important the performance of the GTM.

To work around this issue, we can introduce a GTM proxy. The idea is that transaction IDs will be requested in larger blocks. The core idea is that we want to avoid network traffic and, especially, latency. The concept is pretty similar to how grouping commits in PostgreSQL works.

How can a simple GTM proxy be set up? First of all, we have to create a directory where the config is supposed to exist. Then we can make the following call:

```
initgtm -D /path_to_gtm_proxy/ -Z gtm_proxy
```

This will create a config sample, which we can adapt easily. After defining a node name, we should set gtm_host and gtm_port to point to the active GTM. Then we can tweak the number of worker threads to a reasonable value to make sure that we can handle more load. Usually, we configure the GTM proxy in such a way that the number of worker threads match the number of nodes in the system. This has been proven to be a robust configuration.

Finally, we can start the proxy infrastructure:

```
gtm_ctl -D /path_to_gtm_proxy/ -Z gtm_proxy start
```

The GTM proxy is now available to our system.

Creating tables and issuing queries

After this introduction to Postgres-XC and its underlying ideas, it is time to create our first table and see how the cluster will behave. The next example shows a simple table. It will be distributed using the hash key of the id column:

```
test=# CREATE TABLE t_test (id int4)
DISTRIBUTE BY HASH (id);
CREATE TABLE
test=# INSERT INTO t_test
SELECT * FROM generate_series(1, 1000);
INSERT 0 1000
```

Once the table has been created, we can add data to it. After completion, we can check whether the data has been written correctly to the cluster:

```
test=# SELECT count(*) FROM t_test;
count
-------
  1000
(1 row)
```

Not surprisingly, we have 1,000 rows in our table.

The interesting thing here is to see how the data is returned by the database engine. Let's take a look at the execution plan of our query:

```
test=# explain (VERBOSE TRUE, ANALYZE TRUE,
NODES true, NUM_NODES true)
SELECT count(*) FROM t_test;
QUERY PLAN
-------------------------------------------------------
 Aggregate  (cost=2.50..2.51 rows=1 width=0)
(actual time=5.967..5.970 rows=1 loops=1)
   Output: pg_catalog.count(*)
   -> Materialize  (cost=0.00..0.00 rows=0 width=0)
        (actual time=5.840..5.940 rows=3 loops=1)
        Output: (count(*))
        ->Data Node Scan (primary node count=0,
```

```
node count=3) on
            "__REMOTE_GROUP_QUERY__"
(cost=0.00..0.00 rows=1000 width=0)
            (actual time=5.833..5.915 rows=3 loops=1)
                Output: count(*)
                Node/s: node2, node3, node4
                Remote query: SELECT count(*)   FROM
(SELECT id FROM ONLY t_test
WHERE true) group_1
 Total runtime: 6.033 ms
(9 rows)
```

PostgreSQL will perform a so-called data node scan. This means that PostgreSQL will collect data from all the relevant nodes in the cluster. If you look closely, you can see which query will be pushed down to those nodes inside the cluster. The important thing here is that the count is already shipped to the remote node. All the counts coming back from our nodes will then be rounded into a single count. This kind of plan is much more complex than a simple local query, but it can be very beneficial as the amount of data grows. This is because each node will perform only a subset of the operation. The fact that each node performs only a subset of operations is especially useful when many things are running in parallel.

The Postgres-XC optimizer can push down operations to the data nodes in many cases, which is good for performance. However, you should still keep an eye on your execution plans to make sure they are reasonable.

Adding nodes

Postgres-XC allows you to add new servers to the setup at any point in the process. All you have to do is set up a node as we have seen before and call CREATE NODE on the controller. The system will then be able to use this node.

However, there is one important point about this: if you have partitioned a table before adding a new node, this partitioned table will stay in its place. Some people may expect that Postgres-XC magically rebalances this data to new nodes. User intervention is necessary for rebalancing. It is your task to move new data there and make good use of the server.

It is necessary for Postgres-XC to behave in this way because adding a new node would lead to unexpected behavior otherwise.

Rebalancing data

Since Postgres-XC 1.2, there has been a new feature in Postgres-XC. It allows you to add a server to the infrastructure during normal operations. While adding the node itself is easy, rebalancing data is not so easy.

Basically, the following command is available:

```
ALTER TABLE ... ADD NODE ( nodename [, ... ] );
```

However, there is a catch—Postgres-XC will lock up the table, move stuff to the coordinates, and redispatch data from there. While this is no problem for small tables, it is a serious issue for large tables, because it will take a while until data is nicely resharded and dispatched again.

In addition to this, it can be a capacity issue in the Coordinator part of the infrastructure. If a multi-TB table is resharded, the storage on the Coordinator might not be large enough. The main issue is as follows: the more important sharding is, the more critical resharding really is.

If you decide to use Postgres-XC, it is important to think ahead and start with enough shards to make things work flawlessly. Otherwise, unexpected downtimes might occur. For analytical processes, this might be okay, but it is definitely not okay for large-scale OLTP operations. The main question now is, "How can we figure out how many nodes are needed?" This is not as easy as it might sound. In many cases, testing empirically is the best method to avoid oversizing or undersizing.

Handling failovers and dropping nodes

In this section, we will take a look at how failovers can be handled. We will also see how nodes can be added to and removed from a Postgres-XC setup in a safe and reliable way.

Handling node failovers

If you execute a query in Postgres-XC, it might be dispatched to many different nodes inside the cluster. For example, performing a sequential scan on a highly partitioned table will involve many different nodes. The question now is: what happens if one or some of those data nodes are down?

The answer is pretty simple—Postgres-XC will not be able to perform the requests by making use of failed nodes. This can result in a problem for both reads and writes. A query trying to fetch from a failed node will return an error indicating that no connection is available. At this point, Postgres-XC is not yet very fault tolerant. Hopefully, this will change in the future.

For you as a user, this means that if you are running Postgres-XC, you have to come up with a proper failover and **High Availability (HA)** strategy for your system. We recommend creating replicas of all the nodes to make sure that the controller can always reach an alternative node if the primary data node fails. Linux HA is a good option to make nodes fail-safe and achieve fast failovers.

At the moment, it is not possible to rely solely on Postgres-XC to create an HA strategy.

From Postgres-XC 1.2 onwards, nodes can be added and removed during production. However, keep in mind that resharding might be necessary before this, which is still a major issue.

Replacing the nodes

Once in a while, it might be that you want to drop a node. To do so, you can simply call DROP NODE from your psql shell:

```
test=# \h DROP NODE
Command:     DROP NODE
Description: drop a cluster node
Syntax:
DROP NODE nodename
```

If you want to perform this kind of operation, you have to make sure that you are a superuser. Normal users are not allowed to remove a node from the cluster.

Whenever you drop a node, make sure that there is no more data on it that might be usable by you. Removing a node is simply a change inside Postgres-XC's metadata, so the operation will be quick and the relevant data will be removed from your view of the data. Postgres-XC will not prevent you from shooting yourself in the foot.

One issue is how to actually figure out the location of the data. Postgres-XC has a set of system tables that allow you to retrieve information about nodes, data distribution, and so on. The following example shows how a table can be created and how we can figure out where it is:

```
test=# CREATE TABLE t_location (id int4)
  DISTRIBUTE BY REPLICATION;
CREATE TABLE
test=# SELECT node_name, pcrelid, relname
  FROM   pgxc_class AS a, pgxc_node AS b,
pg_class AS c
WHERE   a.pcrelid = c.oid
```

```
      AND b.oid = ANY (a.nodeoids);
node_name | pcrelid |   relname

----------+---------+-----------

node2     |   16406 | t_location

node3     |   16406 | t_location

node4     |   16406 | t_location

(3 rows)
```

In our case, the table has been replicated to all the nodes.

There is one tricky thing you have to keep in mind when dropping nodes: if you drop a name and recreate it with the same name and connection parameters, it will not be the same. When a new node is created, it will get a new object ID. In PostgreSQL, the name is not as important as the ID of an object. This means that even if you drop a node accidentally and recreate it using the same name, you will still face problems. Of course, you can always magically work around it by tweaking the system tables, but this is not what you should do.

Therefore, we highly recommend being very cautious when dropping nodes from a production system. It is never really recommended to do this.

Running a GTM standby

A data node is not the only thing that can cause downtime in the event of a failure. The GTM should also be made fail-safe to make sure that nothing can go wrong in the event of a disaster. If the transaction manager is missing, there is no useful way of using your Postgres-XC cluster.

To make sure that the GTM cannot be a single point of failure, you can use a GTM standby. Configuring a GTM standby is not hard to do. All you have to do is create a GTM config on a spare node and set a handful of parameters in gtm.conf:

```
startup = STANDBY
active_host = 'somehost.somedomain.com'
active_port = '6666'
synchronous_backup = off
```

First of all, we have to set the startup parameter to STANDBY. This will tell the GTM to behave as a slave. Then we have to tell the standby where to find the main productive GTM. We do so by adding a hostname and a port.

Finally, we can decide whether the GTM should be replicated synchronously or asynchronously.

To start the standby, we can use `gtm_ctl` again. This time, we use the `-Z gtm_standby` variable to mark the node as standby.

Summary

In this chapter, we dealt with Postgres-XC, a distributed version of PostgreSQL that is capable of horizontal partitioning and query distribution. The goal of the Postgres-XC project is to have a database solution capable of scaling out writes transparently. It offers a consistent view of the data and various options for distributing data inside the cluster.

It is important to know that Postgres-XC is not just a simple add-on of PostgreSQL, but a fully compliant code fork.

The next chapter will cover PL/Proxy, a tool used to shard PostgreSQL database systems. You will learn how to distribute data to various nodes and shard it to handle large setups.

13
Scaling with PL/Proxy

Adding a slave here and there is really a nice scalability strategy, which is basically enough for most modern applications. Many applications will run perfectly well with just one server; you might want to add a replica to add some security to the setup, but in many cases, this is pretty much what people need.

If your application grows larger, you can, in many cases, just add slaves and scale out reading. This too is not a big deal and can be done quite easily. If you want to add even more slaves, you might have to cascade your replication infrastructure, but for 98 percent of all applications, this is going to be enough.

In those rare, leftover 2 percent of cases, PL/Proxy can come to the rescue. The idea of PL/Proxy is to be able to scale out writes. Remember that transaction-log-based replication can scale out only reads; there is no way to scale out writes.

 If you want to scale out writes, turn to PL/Proxy. However, before this is done, consider fixing your database system by adding missing indexes and other entries. Work through the output of `pg_stat_statements` and see what can be done to avoid adding dozens of servers for no reason. This strategy has proven to be effective many times before.

Understanding the basic concepts

As we have mentioned before, the idea behind PL/Proxy is to scale out writes as well as reads. Once the writes are scaled out, reading can easily be scaled with the techniques we have already outlined in this book before. It is really necessary to point out that writes are the key issue here because reads are more easily scaled using plain old replicas.

The question now is: how can you ever scale out writes? To do so, we have to follow an old Roman principle, which has been widely applied in warfare: "Divide et impera" (in English: "Divide and conquer"). Once you manage to split a problem into many small problems, you are always on the winning side.

Applying this principle to the database work means that we have to split writes and spread them to many different servers. The main aim here is to split up data wisely.

As an example, we simply assume that we want to split user data. Let's assume further that each user has a username to identify themselves.

How can we split data now? At this point, many people would suggest splitting data alphabetically somehow. Say, everything from A to M goes to server 1, and the rest to server 2. This is actually a pretty bad idea because we can never assume that data is evenly distributed. Some names are simply more likely than others, so if you split by letters, you will never end up with roughly the same amount of data in each partition (which is highly desirable). However, we definitely want to make sure that each server has roughly the same amount of data, and find a way to extend the cluster to more boxes easily. Anyway, we will talk about useful partitioning functions later on.

Dealing with the bigger picture

Before we take a look at a real setup and how to partition data, we have to discuss the bigger picture. Technically, PL/Proxy is a stored procedure language, and it consists of just a handful of commands. The only purpose of this language is to dispatch requests to servers inside the cluster.

Let's take a look at the following diagram:

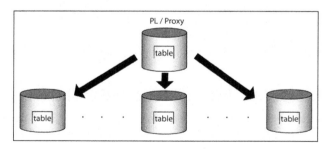

We take PL/Proxy and install it on a server that will act as the proxy for our system. Whenever we run a query, we ask the proxy to provide us with the data. The proxy will consult its rules and figure out which server the query has to be redirected to. Basically, PL/Proxy is a way of sharding a database instance.

The way of asking the proxy for data is by calling a stored procedure. You have to go through a procedure call in standard PostgreSQL.

So, if you issue a query, PL/Proxy will try to hide a lot of complexity from you and just provide you with the data, no matter where it comes from.

Partitioning the data

As we have just seen, PL/Proxy is basically a way of distributing data across various database nodes. The core question now is: how can we split and partition data in a clever and sensible way? In this book, we have already explained that an alphabetical split might not be the very best of all ideas because data won't be distributed evenly.

Of course, there are many ways to split the data. In this section, we will take a look at a simple, yet useful, way. This way can be applied to many different scenarios. Let's assume for this example that we want to split data and store it in an array of 16 servers. This is a good number because 16 is a power of 2. In computer science, powers of 2 are usually good numbers, and the same applies to PL/Proxy.

The key to evenly dividing your data depends on first turning your text value into an integer:

```
test=# SELECT 'www.postgresql-support.de';

?column?

---------------------------

 www.postgresql-support.de

(1 row)


test=# SELECT hashtext('www.postgresql-support.de');

hashtext

------------

 -1865729388

(1 row)
```

We can use a PostgreSQL built-in function (not related to PL/Proxy) to hash texts. It will give us an evenly distributed integral number. So, if we hash 1 million rows, we will see evenly distributed hash keys. This is important because we can split data into similar chunks.

Now we can take this integer value and keep just the lower 4 binary bits. This will allow us to address 16 servers:

```
test=# SELECT hashtext('www.postgresql-support.de')::bit(4);
hashtext
----------
 0100
(1 row)

test=# SELECT hashtext('www.postgresql-support.de')::bit(4)::int4;
hashtext
----------
        4
(1 row)
```

The final four bits are `0100`, which are converted back to an integer. This means that this row is supposed to reside on the fifth node (if we start counting from 0).

Using hash keys is by far the simplest way of splitting data. It has some nice advantages, as in, if you want to increase the size of your cluster, you can easily add just one bit without having to rebalance the data inside the cluster.

Of course, you can always come up with more complicated and sophisticated rules to distribute the data.

Setting up PL/Proxy

After this brief theoretical introduction, we can move forward and run some simple PL/Proxy setups. To do so, we simply install PL/Proxy and see how it can be utilized.

Installing PL/Proxy is an easy task. First of all, we have to download the source code from `http://pgfoundry.org/frs/?group_id=1000207`. Of course, you can also install binary packages if prebuilt packages are available for your operating system. However, in this section, we will simply perform an installation from source and see how things work on a very basic level:

1. The first step in the installation process is to unpack the TAR archive. This can easily be done using the following command:

   ```
   tar xvfz plproxy-2.5.tar.gz
   ```

2. Once the TAR archive has been unpacked, we can enter the newly created directory and start the compilation process by simply calling `make && make install`.

Make sure that your PATH variable points to the PostgreSQL binary directory. Depending on your current setup, it might also be necessary to run your installation procedure as root.

3. If you want to make sure that your installation is really fine, you can also run make installcheck. It runs some simple tests to make sure that your system is operating correctly.

A basic example

To get you started, we want to set up PL/Proxy in such a way that we can fetch random numbers from all the four partitions. This is the most basic example. It will show all the basic concepts of PL/Proxy.

To enable PL/Proxy, we have to load the extension into the database first:

```
test=# CREATE EXTENSION plproxy;
CREATE EXTENSION
```

This will install all of the relevant code and infrastructure you need to make PL/Proxy work. Then we want to create four databases, which will carry the data we want to partition:

```
test=# CREATE DATABASE p0;
CREATE DATABASE
test=# CREATE DATABASE p1;
CREATE DATABASE
test=# CREATE DATABASE p2;
CREATE DATABASE
test=# CREATE DATABASE p3;
CREATE DATABASE
```

Once we have created these databases, we can run CREATE SERVER. The question is: what is SERVER? Well, in this context, you can see SERVER as some kind of remote data source providing you with the data you need. SERVER is always based on a module (in our case, PL/Proxy) and may carry a handful of options. In the case of PL/Proxy, these options are just a list of partitions. There can be some additional parameters as well, but the list of nodes is by far the most important thing here:

```
CREATE SERVER samplecluster FOREIGN DATA WRAPPER plproxy
  OPTIONS (   partition_0 'dbname=p0 host=localhost',
```

```
partition_1 'dbname=p1 host=localhost',
partition_2 'dbname=p2 host=localhost',
partition_3 'dbname=p3 host=localhost');
```

Once we have created the server, we can move ahead and create ourselves a nice user mapping. The purpose of a user mapping is to tell the system which user we are going to be on the remote data source. It might very well be the case that we are user A on the proxy, but user B on the underlying database servers. If you are using a foreign data wrapper to connect to, say, Oracle, this will be essential. In the case of PL/Proxy, it is quite often the case that users on the partitions and the proxy are simply the same.

So, we can create a mapping as follows:

```
CREATE USER MAPPING FOR hs SERVER samplecluster;
```

If we are working as a superuser on the system, this will be enough. If we are not a superuser, we have to grant permission to the user who is supposed to use our virtual server. We have to grant the USAGE permission to get this done:

```
GRANT USAGE ON FOREIGN SERVER samplecluster TO hs;
```

To see whether our server has been created successfully, we can check out the pg_foreign_server system table. It holds all of the relevant information about our virtual server. Whenever you want to figure out which partitions are present, you can simply consult the system table and inspect srvoptions:

```
test=# \x
Expanded display is on.
test=# SELECT * FROM pg_foreign_server;
-[ RECORD 1 ]
srvname     | samplecluster
srvowner    | 10
srvfdw      | 16744
srvtype     |
srvversion  |
srvacl      | {hs=U/hs}
srvoptions  | {"partition_0=dbname=p0 host=localhost","partition_1=dbname
=p1 host=localhost","partition_2=dbname=p2 host=localhost","partition_3=d
bname=p3 host=localhost"}
```

As we have mentioned before, PL/Proxy is primarily a stored procedure language. We have to run a stored procedure to fetch data from our cluster. In our example, we want to run a simple SELECT statement on all the nodes of samplecluster:

```
CREATE OR REPLACE FUNCTION get_random() RETURNS setof text AS $$
    CLUSTER 'samplecluster';
    RUN ON ALL;
    SELECT random();
$$ LANGUAGE plproxy;
```

The procedure is just like an ordinary stored procedure. The only special thing here is that it has been written in PL/Proxy. The CLUSTER keyword will tell the system which cluster to take. In many cases, it can be useful to have more than just one cluster (maybe if different datasets are present on different sets of servers).

Then we have to define where to run the code. We can run on ANY (any server), ALL (on all servers), or a specific server. In our example, we have decided to run on all servers.

The most important thing here is that when the procedure is called, we will get one row per node because we have used RUN ON ALL. In the case of RUN ON ANY, we would have got only one row because the query would have been executed on any node inside the cluster:

```
test=# SELECT * FROM get_random();
get_random
-------------------
 0.879995643626899
 0.442110917530954
 0.215869579929858
 0.642985367681831
(4 rows)
```

Partitioned reads and writes

After the previous example, we want to focus on using PL/Proxy to partition the reads. Remember that the purpose of PL/Proxy is to spread the load that we want to scale out to more than just one database system.

To demonstrate how this works, we have to distribute user data to our four databases. In the first step, we have to create a simple table on all four databases inside the cluster:

```
p0=# CREATE TABLE t_user (
  username  text,
  password  text,
  PRIMARY KEY (username)
);
NOTICE:  CREATE TABLE / PRIMARY KEY will create implicit index "t_user_
pkey" for table "t_user"
CREATE TABLE
```

Once we have created the data structure, we can come up with a procedure to actually dispatch data into this cluster. A simple PL/Proxy procedure will do the job:

```
CREATE OR REPLACE FUNCTION create_user(name text,
pass text) RETURNS void AS $$
        CLUSTER 'samplecluster';
        RUN ON hashtext($1);
$$ LANGUAGE plproxy;
```

The point here is that PL/Proxy will inspect the first input parameter and run a procedure called `create_user` on the desired node. `RUN ON hashtext($1)` will be our partitioning function. So, the goal here is to find the right node and execute the same procedure there. The important part is that on the desired node, the `create_user` procedure won't be written in PL/Proxy but simply in SQL, PL/pgSQL, or any other language. The only purpose of the PL/Proxy function is to find the right node to execute the underlying procedure.

The procedure on each of the nodes that actually puts the data into the table is pretty simple:

```
CREATE OR REPLACE FUNCTION create_user(name text,
pass text)
    RETURNS void AS $$
        INSERT INTO t_user VALUES ($1, $2);
$$ LANGUAGE sql;
```

It is simply an INSERT statement wrapped in a stored procedure that can do the actual work on those nodes.

Once we have deployed this procedure on all the four nodes, we can give it a try:

```
SELECT create_user('hans', 'paul');
```

The PL/Proxy procedure in the `test` database will hash the input value and figure out that the data has to be on `p3`, which is the fourth node:

```
p3=# SELECT * FROM t_user;
username | password
----------+----------
hans      | paul
(1 row)
```

The following SQL statement will reveal why the fourth node is correct:

```
test=# SELECT hashtext('hans')::int4::bit(2)::int4;
hashtext
----------
        3
(1 row)
```

Keep in mind that we will start counting at 0, so the fourth node is actually number 3.

> Keep in mind that the partitioning function can be any deterministic routine. However, we strongly advise you to keep it as simple as possible. Also, keep in mind that the way the `hashtext` function in PostgreSQL works is not guaranteed to stay the same forever. It might be worth writing your own hashing function to do the job.

In our example, we executed a procedure on the proxy and relied on the fact that a procedure with the same name will be executed on the slave. But what if you want to call a procedure on a proxy that is supposed to execute some other procedure in the desired node? For mapping a proxy procedure to some other procedure, there is a command called `TARGET`.

To map `create_user` to `create_new_user`, just add the following line to your PL/Proxy function:

```
CREATE OR REPLACE FUNCTION create_user(name text,
pass text) RETURNS void AS $$
        CLUSTER 'samplecluster';
  TARGET create_new_user;
        RUN ON hashtext($1);
$$ LANGUAGE plproxy;
```

Extending and handling clusters in a clever way

Setting up your cluster is not the only task you will have to do. If things are up and running, you might have to tweak them here and there.

Adding and moving partitions

Once a cluster has been up and running, you might figure out that your cluster is too small and is not able to handle the load generated by your client applications. In this case, it might be necessary to add hardware to the setup. The question is: how can this be done in the most intelligent way?

The best thing you can do is to create more partitions than needed straightaway. So, if you consider getting started with four nodes or so, you have to create 16 partitions straightaway and run four partitions per server. Extending your cluster will be pretty easy in this case using following:

- Replicating all the productive nodes
- Reconfiguring PL/Proxy to move the partitions
- Dropping unnecessary partitions from the old nodes

To replicate those existing nodes, you can simply use the technologies outlined in this book, such as streaming replication, londiste, or Slony.

 Streaming replication is usually the simplest way to extend a cluster.

The main point here is: how can you tell PL/Proxy that a partition has moved from one server to some other server?

```
ALTER SERVER samplecluster
    OPTIONS (SET partition_0
'dbname=p4 host=localhost');
```

In this case, we have moved the first partition from p0 to p4. Of course, the partition can also reside on some other host; PL/Proxy will not care which server it has to go to to fetch the data. You just have to make sure that the target database has all the tables in place and that PL/Proxy can reach this database.

Adding partitions is not difficult on the PL/Proxy side either. Just as before, you can simply use ALTER SERVER to modify your partition list, as follows:

```
ALTER SERVER samplecluster
    OPTIONS (
        ADD partition_4 'dbname=p5 host=localhost',
        ADD partition_5 'dbname=p6 host=localhost',
        ADD partition_6 'dbname=p7 host=localhost',
        ADD partition_7 'dbname=p8 host=localhost');
```

As we have already mentioned, adding these partitions is simple; however, doing this in practice is really hard. The problem is this: how should you handle your old data, which is already in the database? Moving data around inside your cluster is not something trivial at all, and it can result in high system usage during system rebalancing. In addition to this, it can be pretty error-prone to move data around during production.

Basically, there are just two ways out:

- You can make your partitioning function cleverer and make it treat the new data differently from the old data. However, this can be error-prone and will add a lot of complexity and legacy to your system.

- A cleverer way is if you increase the size of your cluster, we strongly recommend doubling the size of the cluster straightaway. The beauty of this is that you need just one more bit in your hash key; if you move from four to, say, five nodes, there is usually no way to grow the cluster without having to move a large amount of data around. You would want to avoid rebalancing data at any cost.

Increasing the availability

PL/Proxy is a highly scalable infrastructure used to handle arrays of servers. But what happens if a server fails? The more the boxes you have in your system, the more likely it will be that one of them fails.

To protect yourself against these kinds of issues, you can always turn to streaming replication and Linux HA. An architecture of PL/Proxy might look as follows:

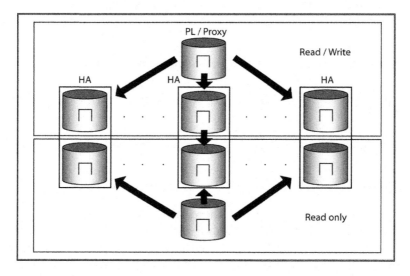

Each node can have its own replica, and therefore, we can fail over each node separately. The good thing about this infrastructure is that you can scale out your reads, while improving availability at the same time.

The machines in the read-only area of the cluster will provide your system with some extra performance.

Managing foreign keys

If you are dealing with a lot of data (terabytes or more), using integrity constraints might not be the best idea of all. The reason for this is that checking the foreign keys on every write on the database is fairly expensive and might not be worth the overhead. So, it might be better to take precautions within your application to prevent the wrong data from reaching the database in the first place. Keep in mind that this is not only about inserting but also about updates and deletes.

One important thing about PL/Proxy is that you cannot simply use foreign keys out of the box. Let's assume you have got two tables that are in a *1:n* relationship. If you want to partition the right side of the equation, you will also have to partition the other side. Otherwise, the data you want to reference will simply end up in some other database. An alternative would simply be to fully replicate the referenced tables.

In general, it has been proven to be fairly beneficial to just avoid foreign key implementations because you need a fair amount of trickery to get foreign keys right. A workaround would be to use functions inside the *CHECK* constraints, checking the child tables for the corresponding value.

Upgrading the PL/Proxy nodes

From time to time, it might be necessary to update or upgrade PostgreSQL and PL/Proxy. Upgrading PL/Proxy is the simpler part of the problem. The reason for this is that PL/Proxy is usually installed as a PostgreSQL extension. CREATE EXTENSION offers all of the functionality required to upgrade the infrastructure on the servers running PL/Proxy:

```
test=# \h CREATE EXTENSION
Command: CREATE EXTENSION
Description: install an extension
Syntax:
CREATE EXTENSION [ IF NOT EXISTS ] extension_name
[ WITH ] [ SCHEMA schema_name ]
[ VERSION version ]
[ FROM old_version ]
```

What you have to do is run CREATE EXTENSION with a target version and define the version you want to upgrade from. All the rest will happen behind the scenes automatically.

If you want to upgrade a database partition from one PostgreSQL version to the next major release (minor releases will only need a simple restart of the node), it will be a bit more complicated. When running PL/Proxy, it is safe to assume that the amount of data in your system is so large that performing a simple dump/reload is out of the question, because you would simply face far too much downtime.

To get around this problem, it is usually necessary to come up with an upgrade policy based on replication. You can use Slony or londiste to create yourself a logical replica of the old server on some new server, and then just tell PL/Proxy to connect to the new version when the replica has fully caught up. The advantage of using Slony or londiste here is that both solutions can replicate between different versions of PostgreSQL nicely.

Just as we have seen before, you can move a partition to a new server by calling ALTER SERVER. In this way, you can replicate and upgrade one server after the other and gradually move to a more recent PostgreSQL version in a risk-free and downtime-free manner.

Summary

In this chapter, we discussed an important topic—PL/Proxy. The idea behind PL/Proxy is to have a scalable solution to shard PostgreSQL databases. It has been widely adopted by many companies around the globe and it allows you to scale writes as well as reads.

14
Scaling with BDR

In this chapter, you will be introduced to a brand new technology called BDR. **Bidirectional Replication (BDR)**, is definitely one of the rising stars in the world of PostgreSQL. A lot of new stuff will be seen in this area in the very near future, and people can expect a thriving project.

This chapter will be about these topics:

- Understanding the BDR replication concepts
- Installing BDR
- Setting up a simple cluster
- Modifying the cluster and failover
- Understanding BDR's performance

Before digging into all the technical details, it is important to understand the fundamental technical aspects of BDR.

Understanding BDR replication concepts

Back in the old days, way before 9.0 was introduced, people had to use Slony to replicate data. The core problem with solutions such as Slony is that there is a need for a changelog trigger, which actually writes data twice. Trigger-based solutions are hard to administer, are not able to handle DDLs, and are in general a bit tricky to operate.

BDR has been invented to put an end to trigger-based solutions and turn PostgreSQL into a more robust, more scalable, and easier way to administer solutions. Trigger-based replication is really a thing of the past, and should not be seen in a modern infrastructure anymore. You can safely bet on BDR—it is a long-term, safe solution.

Understanding eventual consistency

In the early parts of this book, the CAP theory was discussed. It is a vital ingredient, which should always be kept in mind when a new database technology is evaluated. In the case of BDR, the system is *eventually consistent*. What does this mean? Wikipedia (http://en.wikipedia.org/wiki/Eventual_consistency) offers the following definition:

> *Eventual consistency is a consistency model used in distributed computing to achieve high availability that informally guarantees that, if no new updates are made to a given data item, eventually all accesses to that item will return the last updated value.*

This definition is actually so good and simple that it makes sense to include it here. The idea of eventual consistency is that data is not immediately the same on all nodes, but after some time, it actually will be (if nothing happens).

Eventual consistency also implies that data will be replicated asynchronously by default, and therefore, not all the nodes see the same data all the time. You have to expect to see slightly different data, depending on the host you are connected to.

 BDR does support synchronous replication as well. However, it is not as safe as a classical two-phase commit transaction.

Handling conflicts

Given the consistency model, an important topic pops up: what about conflicts? In general, all systems using the *eventually consistent* model need some sort of conflict resolution. The same applies to BDR.

The beauty of BDR is that conflict management is pretty flexible. By default, BDR offers an unambiguous conflict resolution algorithm, which defines that the last update always wins.

However, there is more; in BDR, it is possible to write conflict resolution algorithms on your own. A server-side stored procedure can be used to define exactly what has to be done when a conflict happens. This mechanism gives users maximum flexibility and helps achieve more complicated goals.

One more advantage of BDR is that conflicting changes can be logged in a table. In other words, if a conflict happens, it is still possible to reverse engineer what was really going on in the system. Data is not silently forgotten but preserved for later investigation.

When talking about conflicts, the use case of BDR has to be kept in mind; BDR has been designed as a (geographically) distributed database system, which allows you to handle a lot of data. From a consistency point of view, there is one thing that really has to be kept in mind: how likely is it that a guy in New York and a guy in Rome change the very same row at the very same time on their nodes? If this kind of conflict is the standard case, BDR is really not the right solution. However, if a conflict almost never happens (which is most likely the case in 99 percent of all applications), BDR is really the way to go. Remember that a conflict can happen only if the same row is changed by many people at the same time, or if a primary key is violated. It does not happen if two people touch two rows that are completely independent of each other. *Eventually consistent* is therefore a reasonable choice for some use cases.

Distributing sequences

Sequences are a potential source of conflicts. Imagine hundreds of users adding data to the very same table at the very same time. Any auto-increment column will instantly turn out to be a real source of conflicts, as instances tend to assign the same or similar numbers all over again.

Therefore, BDR offers support for distributed sequences. Each node is assigned not just as single value but a range of values, which can then be used until the next block of values is assigned. The availability of distributed sequences greatly reduces the number of potential conflicts and helps your system run way more smoothly than otherwise possible.

Handling DDLs

Data structures are by no means constant. Once in a while, it can happen that structures have to be changed. Maybe a table has to be added, or a column has to be dropped, and so on.

BDR can handle this nicely. Most DDLs are just replicated, as they are just sent to all nodes and executed. However, there are also commands that are forbidden. Here are two of the more prominent ones:

```
ALTER TABLE ... ALTER COLUMN ... USING();
ALTER TABLE ... ADD COLUMN ... DEFAULT;
```

Keep in mind that conflicts will be very likely anyway under concurrency, so not having those commands is not too much of an issue. In most cases, the limitations are not critical. However, they have to be kept in mind.

In many cases, there is a workaround for those commands, such as setting explicit values, and other ways.

Use cases for BDR

There are both good and bad use cases for BDR. Of course, this rule applies for every piece of software. However, a database system is somewhat different, and careful thinking is necessary before making a decision.

Good use cases for BDR

In general, BDR works best if a certain set of data is only modified in one node. This greatly reduces the likelihood of conflicts and helps you enjoy a smooth process.

What does modifying in one node actually mean? Let's suppose there are three locations: Vienna, Berlin, and London. Somebody working in Vienna is more likely to modify Austrian data than a German working in Berlin. The German operator is usually modifying data of German clients rather than data of Austrians or Britons. The Austrian operator is most likely going to change Austrian data. Every operator in every country should see all the data of the company. However, it is way more likely that data is changed where it is created. From a business point of view, it is basically impossible that two folks located in different countries change the same data at the same time—conflicts are not likely.

In addition to this, it is very beneficial if the workload consists mostly of writes rather than UPDATE or DELETE operations. Insertion is less likely to cause conflicts and is, therefore, a good workload for BDR.

Bad use cases for BDR

However, there are also some workloads that are not so beneficial to BDR in general. If consistency is your primary goal and is really the key to your application, then BDR is certainly not the right thing to use. Due to the asynchronous nature of the product, conflicts and consistency can nullify each other.

One more bad scenario for BDR is that if all the nodes need to see exactly the same data at the very same time, BDR has a hard time.

BDR can write data quite efficiently. However, it is not able to scale writes infinitely because at this point, all the writes still end up on every server. Remember that scaling writes can only happen by actually splitting the data. So, if you are looking for a solution that can scale out writes better, PL/Proxy might be a better choice.

Logical decoding does the trick

The key concept behind BDR is logical decoding. As already mentioned in this book, logical decoding has been invented to dissect the transaction log stream and to turn binary logs back into a more readable format such as SQL. The advantage of a logical stream over a binary one is that replication can happen across version boundaries more easily.

Another important advantage is that there is no need to synchronize the physical XLOG position. As already shown in previous chapters of this book, XLOG addresses are highly critical and must not be changed to make things work. Therefore, XLOG-based replication is always single-master and multiple-slave replication. There is simply no way to unify two binary XLOG streams into one stream of changes. Logical decoding solves the problem in an elegant way because the entire problem of XLOG synchronization is left out. By replicating real, physical changes in the form of SQL, a lot of flexibility is gained and new options for future improvements are provided.

The entire XLOG decoding thing basically goes on behind the scenes; end users don't notice it.

Installing BDR

Installing BDR is easy. The software is available as a source package, and it can be deployed directly as a binary package. Of course, it is also possible to install the code from source. However, it is likely that this procedure might change, as more and more changes are moved into the core of PostgreSQL. Therefore, I have decided to skip the source installation.

Installing binary packages

In previous chapters, you learned how to install BDR on Linux using precompiled binary packages of the software. The Linux distribution chosen to show how the installation works is CentOS 7 (to find information about other packages, check out `http://bdr-project.org/docs/stable/installation.html`).

The installation process itself is easy. First, `repo` can be installed:

```
yum install http://packages.2ndquadrant.com/postgresql-bdr94-2ndquadrant/
yum-repo-rpms/postgresql-bdr94-2ndquadrant-redhat-1.0-2.noarch.rpm
```

In the next step, BDR can be deployed:

```
yum install postgresql-bdr94-bdr
```

Once BDR has been installed on all the nodes, the system is ready for action.

 Keep in mind that BDR is still at a fairly early state of development, so the subsequent processes might change over time.

Setting up a simple cluster

Once the installation has been done, it is time to get started and actually set up a simple cluster. In this scenario, a cluster consisting of three nodes will be created.

Note that all the data nodes will be on the same physical box in order to make life easier for beginners.

Arranging storage

The first thing administrators have to do is create some space for PostgreSQL. In this simplistic example, just three directories are created:

```
[root@localhost ~]# mkdir /data
[root@localhost ~]# mkdir /data/node1 /data/node2 /data/node3
```

Make sure that these directories belong to postgres (if PostgreSQL is really running as postgres, which is usually a good idea):

```
[root@localhost ~]# cd /data/
[root@localhost data]# chown postgres.postgres node*
```

Once these directories have been created, everything needed for a successful setup is in place:

```
[root@localhost data]# ls -l
total 0
drwxr-xr-x 2 postgres postgres 6 Apr 11 05:51 node1
drwxr-xr-x 2 postgres postgres 6 Apr 11 05:51 node2
drwxr-xr-x 2 postgres postgres 6 Apr 11 05:51 node3
```

Creating database instances

After creating some space for our experiments, it makes sense to cross-check our system path. Make sure that the right version of PostgreSQL is in your path. Some users have reported problems during the setup process because accidentally, some operating-system-provided version of PostgreSQL was in the path. Therefore, it makes sense to simply check the path and set it accordingly, if needed:

```
export PATH=/usr/pgsql-9.4/bin:$PATH
```

Then the three database instances can be created. The initdb command can be used just as in the case of any ordinary instance:

```
[postgres@localhost ~]$ initdb -D /data/node1/ -A trust
[postgres@localhost ~]$ initdb -D /data/node2/ -A trust
[postgres@localhost ~]$ initdb -D /data/node3/ -A trust
```

To make the setup process more simplistic, trust will be used as the authentication method. User authentication is, of course, possible but it is not the core topic of this chapter, so it is better to simplify this part as much as possible.

Now that the three database instances have been created, it is possible to adjust postgresql.conf. The following parameters are needed:

```
shared_preload_libraries = 'bdr'
wal_level = 'logical'
track_commit_timestamp = on
max_connections = 100
max_wal_senders = 10
max_replication_slots = 10
max_worker_processes = 10
```

The first thing to do is to actually load the BDR module into PostgreSQL. It contains some important infrastructure for replication. In the next step, logical decoding has to be enabled. It will be the backbone of the entire infrastructure.

To make BDR work, it is necessary to turn track_commit_timestamp on. In standard PostgreSQL 9.4, this setting is not there. It comes with BDR and will most likely be present in future versions of PostgreSQL. Knowing the timestamp of the commit is essential to BDR's internal conflict resolution algorithm (last wins).

Then max_wal_senders has to be set along with replication slots. These settings are needed for streaming replication as well, and should not come as a big surprise.

Finally, there is `max_worker_processes`. BDR launches some custom worker processes in the background as soon as PostgreSQL is launched. Those worker processes are based on the standard background worker API, and are needed to handle data transport during replication. Making sure that enough processes are available is essential to replication.

Finally, some more conflict-related settings can be used:

```
# Handling conflicts
#bdr.default_apply_delay=2000    # milliseconds
#bdr.log_conflicts_to_table=on
```

Now that `postgresql.conf` has been configured, it is time to focus our attention on `pg_hba.conf`. In the most simplistic case, simple replication rules have to be created:

```
local    replication    postgres                       trust
host     replication    postgres    127.0.0.1/32        trust
host     replication    postgres    ::1/128             trust
```

Note that in a real, productive setup, a wise administrator would configure a special replication user and set a password, or use some other authentication method. For simplicity reasons, this process has been left out here.

Starting up the database works just as with vanilla PostgreSQL:

```
pg_ctl -D /data/node1/ start
pg_ctl -D /data/node2/ start
pg_ctl -D /data/node3/ start
```

For our tests, one database per instance is needed:

```
createdb test -p 5432
createdb test -p 5433
createdb test -p 5434
```

Loading modules and firing up the cluster

So far, so good! To make sure that BDR can do its job, it has to be loaded into the database. Two extensions are needed, namely `btree_gist` and `bdr`:

```
[postgres@localhost node1]$ psql test -p 5432

test=# CREATE EXTENSION btree_gist;

CREATE EXTENSION

test=# CREATE EXTENSION bdr;

CREATE EXTENSION
```

These extensions must be loaded into all three databases created before. It is not enough to load them into just one component. It is vital to load them into all databases.

Finally, our database nodes have to be put into a BDR group. So far, there are only three independent database instances, which happen to contain some modules. In the next step, these nodes will be connected to each other.

The first thing to do is to create a BDR group:

```
test=# SELECT bdr.bdr_group_create(
    local_node_name := 'node1',
    node_external_dsn := 'port=5432 dbname=test'
);
 bdr_group_create
------------------


(1 row)
```

Basically, two parameters are needed: the local name and a database connection to connect to the node from a remote host. To define `local_node_name`, it is easiest to just give the node a simple name.

To check whether the node is ready for BDR, call the following function. If the answer is as follows, it means that things are fine:

```
test=# SELECT bdr.bdr_node_join_wait_for_ready();
 bdr_node_join_wait_for_ready
------------------------------


(1 row)
```

Now it is time to add those other nodes to the replication system:

```
test=# SELECT bdr.bdr_group_join(
    local_node_name := 'node2',
    node_external_dsn := 'port=5433 dbname=test',
    join_using_dsn := 'port=5432 dbname=test'
);
 bdr_group_join
----------------


(1 row)
```

Again, a NULL value is a good sign. First, the second node is added to BDR. Then the third node can join as well:

```
test=# SELECT bdr.bdr_group_join(
    local_node_name := 'node3',
    node_external_dsn := 'port=5434 dbname=test',
    join_using_dsn := 'port=5432 dbname=test'
);
 bdr_group_join
----------------

(1 row)
```

Once all the nodes have been added, the administrator can check whether all of them are ready:

```
[postgres@localhost node2]$ psql test -p 5433
test=# SELECT bdr.bdr_node_join_wait_for_ready();
 bdr_node_join_wait_for_ready
------------------------------

(1 row)

[postgres@localhost node2]$ psql test -p 5434
test# SELECT bdr.bdr_node_join_wait_for_ready();
 bdr_node_join_wait_for_ready
------------------------------

(1 row)
```

If both queries return NULL, it means that the system is up and running nicely.

Checking your setup

After this simple process, BDR is up and running. In order to check whether everything is working as expected, it makes sense to check for replication-related processes:

```
[postgres@localhost ~]$ ps ax | grep bdr
31296 ?        Ss     0:00 postgres: bgworker: bdr supervisor
31396 ?        Ss     0:00 postgres: bgworker: bdr db: test
31533 ?        Ss     0:00 postgres: bgworker: bdr supervisor
```

```
31545 ?         Ss       0:00 postgres: bgworker: bdr supervisor
31553 ?         Ss       0:00 postgres: bgworker: bdr db: test
31593 ?         Ss       0:00 postgres: bgworker: bdr db: test
31610 ?         Ss       0:00 postgres: bgworker: bdr
(6136360420896274864,1,16385,)->bdr (6136360353631754624,1,
...
31616 ?         Ss       0:00 postgres: bgworker: bdr
(6136360353631754624,1,16385,)->bdr (6136360420896274864,1,
```

As you can see, each instance will have at least three BDR processes. If these processes are around, it is usually a good sign and replication should work as expected.

A simple test can reveal whether things are working or not:

```
test=# CREATE TABLE t_test (id int, t timestamp DEFAULT now() );
CREATE TABLE
```

After table creation, the structure should look like this:

```
test=# \d t_test
              Table "public.t_test"
 Column |             Type            |    Modifiers
--------+-----------------------------+---------------
 id     | integer                     |
 t      | timestamp without time zone | default now()
Triggers:
    truncate_trigger AFTER TRUNCATE ON t_test FOR EACH STATEMENT EXECUTE
PROCEDURE bdr.queue_truncate()
```

The table looks as expected. There is just one exception: a TRUNCATE trigger has been created automatically. Keep in mind that replication slots are able to stream INSERT, UPDATE, and DELETE statements. DDLs and TRUNCATE are now row-level information, so those statements are not in the stream. The trigger will be needed to catch TRUNCATE and replicate it as plain text. Do not attempt to alter or drop the trigger.

To test replication, a simple INSERT statement does the job:

```
test=# INSERT INTO t_test VALUES (1);
INSERT 0 1
test=# TABLE t_test;
 id |              t
----+----------------------------
  1 | 2015-04-11 08:48:46.637675
(1 row)
```

In this example, the value has been added to the instance listening to 5432. A quick check reveals that the data has been nicely replicated to the instance listening to 5433 and 5434:

```
[postgres@localhost ~]$ psql test -p 5434
test=# TABLE t_test;
 id |             t
----+---------------------------
  1 | 2015-04-11 08:48:46.637675
(1 row)
```

Handling conflicts

As already stated earlier in this chapter, conflicts are an important thing when working with BDR. Keep in mind that BDR has been designed as a distributed system, so it only makes sense to use it when conflicts are not very likely. However, it is important to understand what happens in the event of a conflict.

To show what happens, here is a simple table:

```
test=# CREATE TABLE t_counter (id int PRIMARY KEY);
CREATE TABLE
```

Then a single row is added:

```
test=# INSERT INTO t_counter VALUES (1);
INSERT 0 1
```

To run the test, a simple SQL query is needed. In this example, 10,000 UPDATE statements are used:

```
[postgres@localhost ~]$ head -n 3 /tmp/script.sql
UPDATE t_counter SET id = id + 1;
UPDATE t_counter SET id = id + 1;
UPDATE t_counter SET id = id + 1;
```

The nasty part now is that this script is executed three times, once on each node:

```
[postgres@localhost ~]$ cat run.sh
#!/bin/sh
psql test -p 5432 < /tmp/script.sql > /dev/null &
psql test -p 5433 < /tmp/script.sql > /dev/null &
psql test -p 5434 < /tmp/script.sql > /dev/null &
```

As the same row is hit again and again, the number of conflicts is expected to skyrocket.

 Note that this is not what BDR has been built for in the first place. It is just a demo meant to show what happens in the event of a conflict.

Once those three scripts have been completed, it is already possible to check out what has happened on the conflict side:

```
test=# \x
Expanded display is on.
test=# TABLE bdr.bdr_conflict_history LIMIT 1;
-[ RECORD 1 ]------------+----------------------------
conflict_id              | 1
local_node_sysid         | 6136360318181427544
local_conflict_xid       | 0
local_conflict_lsn       | 0/19AAE00
local_conflict_time      | 2015-04-11 09:01:23.367467+02
object_schema            | public
object_name              | t_counter
remote_node_sysid        | 6136360353631754624
remote_txid              | 1974
remote_commit_time       | 2015-04-11 09:01:21.364068+02
remote_commit_lsn        | 0/1986900
conflict_type            | update_delete
conflict_resolution      | skip_change
local_tuple              |
remote_tuple             | {"id":2}
local_tuple_xmin         |
local_tuple_origin_sysid |
error_message            |
error_sqlstate           |
error_querystring        |
error_cursorpos          |
error_detail             |
error_hint               |
error_context            |
```

```
error_columnname          |
error_typename            |
error_constraintname      |
error_filename            |
error_lineno              |
error_funcname            |
```

BDR provides a simple and fairly easy way to read the table that contains all the conflicts row after row. On top of the LSN, the transaction ID and some more information relevant to the conflict are shown. In this example, BDR has done a `skip_change` resolution. Remember that every change will hit the same row, as we are asynchronous multi-master, which is very nasty for BDR. In this example, `UPDATE` statements have indeed been skipped; this is vital to understand. BDR can skip changes in your cluster in the event of a conflict or concurrency.

Understanding sets

So far, the entire cluster has been used. Everybody was able to replicate data to everybody else. In many cases, this is not what is desired. BDR provides quite some flexibility in this area.

Unidirectional replication

BDR can perform not only bidirectional replication but also unidirectional replication. In some cases, this can be very handy. Consider a system that is just there to serve some reads. A simple unidirectional slave might be what you need.

BDR provides a simple function to register a node as a unidirectional slave:

```
bdr.bdr_subscribe(local_node_name,
    subscribe_to_dsn,
    node_local_dsn,
    apply_delay integer DEFAULT NULL,
    replication_sets text[] DEFAULT ARRAY['default'],
    synchronize bdr_sync_type DEFAULT 'full')
```

Of course, it is also possible to remove a node from unidirectional replication again:

```
bdr.bdr_unsubscribe(local_node_name)
```

The setup process is fairly simple and fits nicely into BDR's fundamental design principles.

Handling data tables

The beauty of BDR is that there is no need to replicate entire instances to a cluster. Replication can be very fine-grained, and administrators can decide what goes where. Two functions are available for handling table replication sets:

```
bdr.table_set_replication_sets(p_relation regclass, p_sets text[])
```

This sets the replication sets of a table. The previous assignment will be overwritten.

If you want to figure out which replication sets a table belongs to, the following function can be called:

```
bdr.table_get_replication_sets(relation regclass)    text[]
```

We expect to see more functionality in the area of partial replication as BDR progresses over time. It will allow you to flexibly dispatch data as needed.

Controlling replication

For maintenance reasons, it might be necessary to hold and resume replication from time to time. Just imagine a major software update. It might do something nasty to your data structure. You definitely don't want faulty stuff to be replicated to your entire system. Therefore, it can come in handy to stop replication briefly and restart it once things have proven to be fine.

Two functions are available for this job:

```
SELECT bdr.bdr_apply_pause()
```

To restart things again, the following procedure can be used:

```
SELECT bdr.bdr_apply_resume()
```

Connections to the remote node (or nodes) are retained, but no data is read from them. The effects of pausing `apply` are not persistent, so the replay will resume if PostgreSQL is restarted or the postmaster carries out crash recovery after a backend crash. Terminating individual backend using `pg_terminate_backend` will not cause a replay to resume, nor will reloading the postmaster, without a full restart. There is no option to pause a replay from only one peer node.

Summary

BDR is a rising star in the world of PostgreSQL replication. Currently, it is still under heavy development, and we can expect a lot more in the very near future (maybe even when you are holding this book in your hands).

BDR is asynchronous and multi-master, and allows people to run geographically distributed databases. It is important to note that BDR is especially useful when the odds of a replication conflict are low.

15
Working with Walbouncer

In the final chapter of this book, you will be guided through a tool released in 2014, called walbouncer. Most of the techniques covered in this book have explained how to replicate an entire database instance, how to shard, and more. In the final chapter, which is about walbouncer, it's all about filtering the stream of the transaction log to selectively replicate database objects from one server to a set of (not necessarily identical) slaves.

The following topics will be covered in this chapter:

- Basic concepts of walbouncer
- Installing walbouncer
- Selectively replicating databases, tables, and tablespaces

The walbouncer tool is available for PostgreSQL 9.4 or higher.

The concepts of walbouncer

The purpose of the PostgreSQL transaction log is to help a failed database instance recover itself in the event of a crash. It can also be used to replicate an entire database instance, as already discussed in our chapters about synchronous as well as asynchronous replication.

The trouble is that it is necessary to replicate entire database instances. In many real-world scenarios, this can be a problem. Let's assume there is a central server containing information about students studying in many universities. Each university should have a copy of its data. As of PostgreSQL 9.4, this was not possible using a single database instance because streaming replication is only capable of fully replicating an instance. Running many instances is clearly a lot more work and, maybe, not the desired methodology.

The idea behind walbouncer is to connect to the PostgreSQL transaction log and filter it. In this scenario, a slave will receive only a subset of the data, thus filtering out all of the data that may be critical from legal or a security point of view. In the case of our university example, each university would only have a replica of its own database, and therefore, there is no way to see data from other organizations. Hiding data is a huge step forward when it comes to securing systems. There might also be a use case for walbouncer for the purpose of sharding.

The following diagram shows how this works:

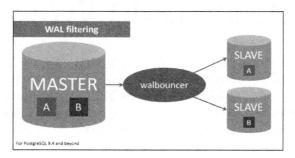

The walbouncer tool is a process sitting between the master and the slaves. It connects to the master, fetches the transaction log, and filters it before it is transmitted to the slaves. In this example, two slaves are available for consuming the transaction log just like regular slaves.

The walbouncer tool is ideal for geographically distributed database systems because it allows us to easily decide which data has to go where and which database is needed in which location. A basic block diagram is shown here:

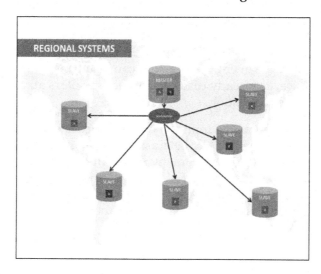

Filtering XLOG

The core question now is: how is it possible for walbouncer to filter the transaction log? Remember that transaction log positions are highly critical, and fiddling around with those transaction log positions is not trivial, dangerous, and in many cases, not feasible at all.

The solution to this problem lies deep in the core of PostgreSQL. The core knows how to handle dummy transaction log entries. To cut out all of the data that is not destined to reach a certain box, dummy XLOG is injected, replacing the original one. The slave can now safely consume the XLOG and ignore those dummy records. The beauty of this technique is in the fact that the master and slave can stay unchanged—no patching is needed. All of the work can be done exclusively by walbouncer, which simply acts as some sort of XLOG proxy.

The technique used has some consequences, as follows:

- Each slave will receive the same number of XLOG records, regardless of the amount of data that has actually changed in the target system

- Metadata (system tables) has to be replicated completely and must not be left out

- The target system will still see that a certain database is supposed to exist, but using it will simply fail

The last item especially deserves some attention. Remember that the system cannot analyze the semantics of a certain XLOG records; all it does is check whether it is needed or not. Therefore, metadata has to be copied as it is. When a slave system tries to read filtered data, it will receive a nasty error indicating that data files are missing. If a query cannot read a file from the disk, it will naturally indicate error and roll back. This behavior might be confusing for some people, but it is the only possible way to solve the underlying technical problem.

Installing walbouncer

The walbouncer tool can be downloaded freely from the Cybertec website (`http://www.cybertec.at/postgresql_produkte/walbouncer/`) and installed using the following steps:

1. For the purpose of this book, the following file has been used:

   ```
   wget http://cybertec.at/download/walbouncer-0.9.0.tar.bz2
   ```

2. The first thing to do is to extract the tarball, as follows:

   ```
   tar xvfj walbouncer-0.9.0.tar.bz2
   ```

3. Once the package has been extracted you can enter the directory. Before calling make, it is important to check for missing libraries. Make sure that support for YAML is around. On my CentOS test system, the following command does the job:

```
[root@localhost ~]# yum install libyaml-devel
```

4. The library will be installed by these lines:

```
---> Package libyaml-devel.x86_64 0:0.1.4-11.el7_0 will be
installed
--> Processing Dependency: libyaml = 0.1.4-11.el7_0 for package:
libyaml-devel-0.1.4-11.el7_0.x86_64
```

5. In the next step, just call make. The code compiles cleanly. Finally, only make install is left:

```
[root@localhost walbouncer-0.9.0]# make install
cp walbouncer /usr/local/pgsql/bin/walbouncer
```

The binary needed to run walbouncer will be copied to your PostgreSQL binary directory (in my case, this is /usr/local/pgsql/).

As you can see, deploying walbouncer is easy, and all it takes is a few commands.

Configuring walbouncer

Once the code has been deployed successfully, it is necessary to come up with a simple configuration to tell walbouncer what to do. To demonstrate how walbouncer works, a simple setup has been created here. In this example, two databases exist on the master. Only one of them should end up on the slave:

```
$ createdb a
$ createdb b
```

The goal is to replicate a to the slave and skip the rest.

Before getting started with a base backup, it makes sense to back up a walbouncer config. A basic configuration is really simple and easy to perform:

```
listen_port: 5433
master:
    host: localhost
    port: 5432
configurations:
    - slave1:
```

```
    filter:
        include_databases: [a]
```

The configuration consists of the following components:

- `listen_port`: This is needed. It defines which port walbouncer uses to listen from. Slaves can connect to this port and stream the transaction log directly from the bouncer.

- `master`: The next section will tell walbouncer where to find its master. In our case, the master is on the same host and listens on port 5432. Notice that there is no database listed. The system connects to the stream of XLOG, so no database information is needed there.

- `configurations`: This covers the slave configuration. It is possible to list more than one slave. For each slave, a couple of filters can be applied. In this case only the a database should be included; the rest is filtered out.

Creating a base backup

Once the config has been written, it's time to clone an initial database instance. The tricky thing here is that there is no such thing as pg_basebackup around, which does most of the work for you out of the box. The reason is that pg_basebackup has been designed to copy an entire database instance. In the case of walbouncer, the idea is to have only parts of the data on the target system. Therefore, users have to fall back to more basic means of creating backups. The method of choice is the traditional way to perform base backups.

However, before it is possible to get started, it is important to prepare the master for standard streaming replication. This includes:

- Adjusting postgresql.conf (wal_level, wal_keep_segments, max_wal_senders, and so on)
- Adjusting pg_hba.conf on the master
- Setting the data directory on the slave to chmod 700

All of these steps have already been described in *Chapter 4, Setting Up Asynchronous Replication*. As already mentioned, the tricky part is the initial base backup. Assuming that the a database has to be replicated, it is necessary to find its object ID:

```
test=# SELECT oid, datname FROM pg_database WHERE datname = 'a';
  oid  | datname
-------+---------
 24576 | a
(1 row)
```

In this example, the object ID is 24576. The general rule is as follows: all databases with OIDs larger than 16383 are databases created by users. These are the only databases that can be filtered in a useful way.

Now go to the data directory of the master and copy everything but the *base* directory to the directory where your slave resides. In this example, this little trick is applied: there are no filenames starting with a, so it is possible to safely copy everything starting with c and add the backup label to the copy process. Now the system will copy everything but the base directory:

```
cp -Rv [c-z]* backup_label ../slave/
```

Once everything has been copied to the slave, which happens to be on the same box in this example, the missing base directory can be created in the slave directory:

```
$ mkdir ../slave/base
```

In the next step, all the databases that are needed can be copied over. Currently, the situation on the sample master is as follows:

```
[hs@localhost base]$ ls -l
total 72
drwx------ 2 hs hs 8192 Feb 24 11:53 1
drwx------ 2 hs hs 8192 Feb 24 11:52 13051
drwx------ 2 hs hs 8192 Feb 25 11:49 13056
drwx------ 2 hs hs 8192 Feb 25 11:48 16384
drwx------ 2 hs hs 8192 Feb 25 10:32 24576
drwx------ 2 hs hs 8192 Feb 25 10:32 24577
```

All OIDs larger than 16383 are databases created by end users. In this scenario, there are three such databases.

Therefore, all system databases (template0, template1, and postgres) as well as the database required on the slave can be copied to the base directory:
```
cp -Rv 24576 1 13051 13056 ../../slave/base/
```

 Note that normally, the slave is on a remote system, so rsync or something similar should be used. In this example, everything is on the same node to make life easier for you.

The important thing is that in most setups, the base directory is by far the largest directory. Once the data has been secured, the backup can be stopped, as follows:

```
test=# SELECT pg_stop_backup();
NOTICE:  WAL archiving is not enabled; you must ensure that all required
WAL segments are copied through other means to complete the backup
 pg_stop_backup
----------------
 0/2000238
(1 row)
```

So far, everything is the same as during normal streaming replication—the only difference is that not all directories in the base directory are actually synchronized to the slave.

In the next step, a simple `recovery.conf` file can be created:

```
slave]$ cat recovery.conf
primary_conninfo = 'host=localhost port=5433'
standby_mode = on
```

The most important thing here is that the port of the slave has to be put into the config file. The slave won't see its master directly anymore, but will consume all of its XLOG through walbouncer.

Firing up walbouncer

Once the configuration has been completed, it is possible to fire up walbouncer. The syntax of walbouncer is pretty simple:

```
$ walbouncer --help
```

The walbouncer tool proxys PostgreSQL streaming replication connections and optionally does filtering

```
Options:
  -?, --help                Print this message
  -c, --config=FILE         Read configuration from this file.
  -h, --host=HOST           Connect to master on this host.
```

	Default localhost
-P, --masterport=PORT	Connect to master on this port.
	Default 5432
-p, --port=PORT	Run proxy on this port. Default 5433
-v, --verbose	Output additional debugging information

All of the relevant information is in the `config` file anyway, so a simple startup is ensured:

```
$ walbouncer -v -c config.ini
[2015-02-25 11:56:57] wbsocket.c INFO: Starting socket on port 5433
```

The `-v` option is not mandatory. All it does is to provide us with a bit more information about what is going on. Once the `starting socket` message shows up, it means that everything is working perfectly.

Finally, it's time to start the slave server. Go to the slave's data directory and fire it up, as follows:

```
slave]$ pg_ctl -D . -o "--port=5444" start
server starting
LOG:   database system was shut down in recovery at 2015-02-25 11:59:12
CET
LOG:   entering standby mode
LOG:   redo starts at 0/2000060
LOG:   record with zero length at 0/2000138
INFO:  WAL stream is being filtered
DETAIL:  Databases included: a
LOG:   started streaming WAL from primary at 0/2000000 on timeline 1
LOG:   consistent recovery state reached at 0/2000238
LOG:   database system is ready to accept read only connections
```

The `.` here means local directory (of course, putting the full path is also a good idea — definitely). Then comes one more trick: when syncing a slave over and over again for testing purposes on the same box, it can be a bit annoying to change the port over and over again. The `-o` option helps overwrite the `config` file settings in `postgresql.conf` so that the system can be started directly on some other port.

> If PostgreSQL is started on a separate server, it is of course useful to start the server through normal `init` procedures.

As soon as the slave comes to life, walbouncer will start issuing more logging information, telling us more about the streaming going on:

```
[2015-02-25 11:58:37] wbclientconn.c INFO: Received conn from
0100007F:54729
[2015-02-25 11:58:37] wbclientconn.c DEBUG1: Sending authentication
packet
[2015-02-25 11:58:37] wbsocket.c DEBUG1: Conn: Sending to client 9 bytes
of data
[2015-02-25 11:58:37] wbclientconn.c INFO: Start connecting to
host=localhost port=5432 user=hs dbname=replication replication=true
application_name=walbouncer
FATAL:  no pg_hba.conf entry for replication connection from host "::1",
user "hs"
```

Once those messages are displayed, the system is up and running and the transaction log is flowing from the master to the slave.

It is time to test the setup now:

```
$ psql -h localhost -p 5444 b
FATAL:  database "b" does not exist
DETAIL:  The database subdirectory "base/24577" is missing.
```

When a connection to a filtered database is established, PostgreSQL will error out and tell the user that the files needed to serve this request are not there. This is exactly the kind of behavior expected — the request should be rejected due to a lack of data.

When connecting to the database included in the database instance, everything works like a charm:

```
$ psql -h localhost -p 5444 a
psql (9.4.1)
Type "help" for help.


a=#
```

The next test checks whether the data is nicely replicated from the master to the slave. To perform the check, a table can be created on the master:

```
a=# CREATE TABLE a (aid int);
CREATE TABLE
```

As expected, the table will end up on the slave nicely:

```
a=# \d
        List of relations
 Schema | Name | Type  | Owner
--------+------+-------+-------
 public | a    | table | hs
(1 row)
```

The system is now ready for action and can be used safely.

Using additional configuration options

The walbouncer tool can do a lot more for users than has been outlined so far. A couple of additional configuration parameters are available.

The first example shows what can be done if more than one slave is around:

```
listen_port: 5433
master:
    host: localhost
    port: 5432
configurations:
    - slave1:
        match:
            application_name: slave1
        filter:
            include_tablespaces: [spc_slave1]
            exclude_databases: [test]
```

Inside the configuration block, there is the slave1 section. The slave1 configuration will be chosen if a slave connects itself using slave1 as application_name (as outlined in the application_name clause). If this configuration is chosen by the server (there can be many such slave sections), the filters listed in the next block are applied. Basically, each type of filter comes in two incarnations: include_ and exclude_. In this example, only the spc_slave1 tablespace is included. The final setting says that only test is excluded (all other databases are included if the tablespace filter matches them).

Of course, it is also possible to state this:

```
exclude_tablespaces: [spc_slave1]
include_databases: [test]
```

In this case, all the tablespaces but `spc_slave1` are included. Only system databases and the database `test` are replicated. Given those `include_` and `exclude_` settings, it is possible to flexibly configure what to replicate to which slave.

Keep in mind that `application_name` is also needed for synchronous replication. If the `application_name` argument passed by the walbouncer is the same as the one listed in `synchronous_standby_names`, synchronous replication is possible.

As you can see, `application_name` really serves two purposes here: it decides which `config` block to use, and tells the master which level of replication is required.

Adjusting filtering rules

One question that is often asked is whether it is possible to adjust filtering rules. Objects might be added later, or objects might be removed. In many cases, this is a very common scenario people ask for on a regular basis.

Changing the configuration of a walbouncer setup is not as simple as it might seem. The core problems are synchronizing the XLOG and making sure that all the dependent objects are in place. Let's go through the core challenges one by one.

Removing and filtering objects

Basically, removing objects is fairly simple. The first thing to do is to shut down the slave as well as walbouncer. Once this is done, those objects that are not needed anymore can be physically deleted from the filesystem of the slave. The crucial part here is finding those objects. Again, digging into the system tables is the method of choice here. The core system tables or views involved are as follows:

- `pg_class`: This table contains a list of objects (tables, indexes, and so on). It is important to fetch the object ID from this table.
- `pg_namespace`: This is used to fetch information about schemas.
- `pg_inherit`: Information about inheritance used in the table.

There is no general guideline on how to find all of those objects, because things depend highly on the types of filters applied.

The most simplistic way to come up with the proper SQL queries to find those objects (files) — which have to be deleted — is to use the -E option along with psql. If psql is started with -E, it shows the SQL code behind all of those backslash commands. The SQL code on the frontend can come in handy. Here is some example output:

```
test=# \q
hs@chantal:~$ psql test -E
psql (9.4.1)
Type "help" for help.

test=# \d
********* QUERY **********
SELECT n.nspname as "Schema",
  c.relname as "Name",
  CASE c.relkind WHEN 'r' THEN 'table' WHEN 'v' THEN 'view' WHEN 'm' THEN
'materialized view' WHEN 'i' THEN 'index' WHEN 'S' THEN 'sequence' WHEN
's' THEN 'special' WHEN 'f' THEN 'foreign table' END as "Type",
  pg_catalog.pg_get_userbyid(c.relowner) as "Owner"
FROM pg_catalog.pg_class c
     LEFT JOIN pg_catalog.pg_namespace n ON n.oid = c.relnamespace
WHERE c.relkind IN ('r','v','m','S','f','')
     AND n.nspname <> 'pg_catalog'
     AND n.nspname <> 'information_schema'
     AND n.nspname !~ '^pg_toast'
  AND pg_catalog.pg_table_is_visible(c.oid)
ORDER BY 1,2;
**************************


          List of relations
 Schema |         Name        | Type  | Owner
--------+---------------------+-------+-------
 ...
```

Once the files have been deleted from the base directory, walbouncer and the slave instance can be restarted. Keep in mind that walbouncer is a tool used to make normal streaming more powerful. Therefore, slaves are still read-only, and it is not possible to use commands such as DELETE and DROP. You really have to delete files from disk.

Adding objects to slaves

Adding objects is by far the most complicated task. Therefore, it is highly recommended to use a safer, simpler approach to the problem. The safest and most reliable approach is to completely resync an instance, which needs new objects.

Simply use the mechanism described earlier in this chapter to avoid all pitfalls.

Summary

In this chapter, the working of walbouncer, a tool used to filter transaction logs, was discussed. In addition to the installation process, all the configuration options and a basic setup were outlined.

You learned how to build geographically distributed setups.

Index

A

archive
archive_command, checking 118
checking 117
transaction log archive, monitoring 118
archive_command
%f 66
%p 66
asynchronous replication
versus synchronous replication 6
Atomicity, Consistency, Isolation,
and Durability (ACID) 30
availability
about 129, 130
measuring 128, 129

B

bandwidth 5
base backups
creating, traditional methods used 73
network bandwidth, observing 74
pg_basebackup, using 69
tablespace issues 74
taking 68, 69
base directory
about 23, 24
data files, increasing 24
I/O, performing in chunks 25
relation forks 25
BDR
about 255
binary packages, installing 259, 260
installing 259
URL 259

BDR group
creating 263
BDR replication
about 255
eventual consistency, defining 256
logical decoding 259
use cases 258
Bidirectional Replication. *See* **BDR**

C

Call Detail Records (CDRs) 48
CAP theorem
about 2
Availability 2
Consistency 2
defining 2, 3
Partition tolerance 2
cascaded replication
configuring 88, 89
changelog triggers 187
checkpoints
bulk loading 47
checkpoint_segments, defining 45
checkpoint_timeout, defining 45
configuring 45
data, writing 46
defining 45
I/O spikes 47, 48
stock market data, storing 46
tuning 44
checkpoint_timeout parameter 46
check_postgres
URL 123
cleanup
defining 97

X

Thank you for buying
PostgreSQL Replication
Second Edition

About Packt Publishing

Packt, pronounced 'packed', published its first book, *Mastering phpMyAdmin for Effective MySQL Management*, in April 2004, and subsequently continued to specialize in publishing highly focused books on specific technologies and solutions.

Our books and publications share the experiences of your fellow IT professionals in adapting and customizing today's systems, applications, and frameworks. Our solution-based books give you the knowledge and power to customize the software and technologies you're using to get the job done. Packt books are more specific and less general than the IT books you have seen in the past. Our unique business model allows us to bring you more focused information, giving you more of what you need to know, and less of what you don't.

Packt is a modern yet unique publishing company that focuses on producing quality, cutting-edge books for communities of developers, administrators, and newbies alike. For more information, please visit our website at www.packtpub.com.

About Packt Open Source

In 2010, Packt launched two new brands, Packt Open Source and Packt Enterprise, in order to continue its focus on specialization. This book is part of the Packt Open Source brand, home to books published on software built around open source licenses, and offering information to anybody from advanced developers to budding web designers. The Open Source brand also runs Packt's Open Source Royalty Scheme, by which Packt gives a royalty to each open source project about whose software a book is sold.

Writing for Packt

We welcome all inquiries from people who are interested in authoring. Book proposals should be sent to author@packtpub.com. If your book idea is still at an early stage and you would like to discuss it first before writing a formal book proposal, then please contact us; one of our commissioning editors will get in touch with you.

We're not just looking for published authors; if you have strong technical skills but no writing experience, our experienced editors can help you develop a writing career, or simply get some additional reward for your expertise.

PostgreSQL for Data Architects

ISBN: 978-1-78328-860-1   Paperback: 272 pages

Discover how to design, develop, and maintain your database application effectively with PostgreSQL

1. Understand how to utilize the most frequently used PostgreSQL ecosystem-related tools and technologies.

2. A hands-on guide focused primarily on providing a practical approach to learning about architecture and design considerations for database architects.

3. The book covers PostgreSQL from a data architect's perspective – covering topics from installation from source to designing tables using SQL Power Architect, as well as deciding replication and failover strategies.

PostgreSQL 9 High Availability Cookbook

ISBN: 978-1-84951-696-9   Paperback: 398 pages

Over 100 recipes to design and implement a highly available server with the advanced features of PostgreSQL

1. Create a PostgreSQL cluster that stays online even when disaster strikes.

2. Avoid costly downtime and data loss that can ruin your business.

3. Perform data replication and monitor your data with hands-on industry-driven recipes and detailed step-by-step explanations.

PostgreSQL Server Programming

ISBN: 978-1-84951-698-3   Paperback: 264 pages

Extend PostgreSQL and integrate the database layer into your development framework

1. Understand the extension framework of PostgreSQL, and leverage it in ways that you haven't even invented yet.

2. Write functions, create your own data types, all in your favourite programming language.

3. Step-by-step tutorial with plenty of tips and tricks to kick-start server programming.

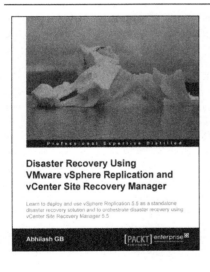

Disaster Recovery using VMware vSphere Replication and vCenter Site Recovery Manager

ISBN: 978-1-78217-644-2   Paperback: 162 pages

Learn to deploy and use vSphere Replication 5.5 as a standalone disaster recovery solution and to orchestrate disaster recovery using vCenter Site Recovery Manager 5.5

1. Learn how to deploy and use vSphere Replication as a standalone disaster recovery solution.

2. Configure SRM to leverage array-based or vSphere replication engine.

3. Use SRM to orchestrate the execution of recovery plans.

Please check **www.PacktPub.com** for information on our titles

CPSIA information can be obtained
at www.ICGtesting.com
Printed in the USA
LVOW02s2204130916

504490LV00023B/291/P